The Conceptual Foundations of Descriptive Cataloging

Library and Information Science

Consulting Editors: *Harold Borko and Elaine Svenonius*
Graduate School of Library and Information Science
University of California, Los Angeles

The Conceptual Foundations of Descriptive Cataloging

Edited by

Elaine Svenonius

Graduate School of Library and Information Science
University of California
Los Angeles, California

ACADEMIC PRESS, INC.
Harcourt Brace Jovanovich, Publishers
San Diego New York Berkeley Boston
London Sydney Tokyo Toronto

ACADEMIC PRESS, INC.
San Diego, California 92101

United Kingdom Edition published by
ACADEMIC PRESS LIMITED
24-28 Oval Road, London NW1 7DX

Library of Congress Cataloging-in-Publication Data

The Conceptual foundations of descriptive cataloging / [edited by]
   Elaine Svenonius.
      p.   cm. — (Library and information science)
   Papers delivered at a conference held at the University of
California, Los Angeles, on Feb. 14 and 15, 1987.
   Bibliography: p.
   Includes index.
   ISBN 0-12-678210-5   (alk. paper)
   1. Descriptive cataloging—Data processing—Congresses.
2. Machine-readable bibliographic data—Congresses.
3. Bibliography—Data bases—Congresses. 4. Catalogs, On-line-
-Congresses.   I. Svenonius, Elaine. II. Series.
Z694.A15C66   1989
025.3′2′0285—dc19   88-28819
                                                    CIP

PRINTED IN THE UNITED STATES OF AMERICA
89 90 91 92   9 8 7 6 5 4 3 2 1

This work is dedicated to UCLA's Cataloging Teachers

Seymour Lubetzky and Betty Baughman

Contents

List of Contributors

Numbers in parentheses indicate the pages on which the authors' contributions begin.

John Attig (135)
Bibliographic Services Department
Pennsylvania State University Libraries
University Park, Pennsylvania 16802

Michael Carpenter (73)
School of Library and Information Science
Louisiana State University
Baton Rouge, Louisiana 70803

Tom Delsey (51)
Acquisitions and Bibliographic Services Branch
National Library of Canada
Ottawa, Ontario
Canada K1A ON4

John Duke (117)
Bibliographic Services
James Branch Cabell Library
Virginia Commonwealth University
Richmond, Virginia 23220

Ronald Hagler (197)
School of Library, Archival and Information Studies
University of British Columbia
Vancouver, British Columbia
Canada V6T 1W5

Sara Shatford Layne (185)
Physical Sciences and Technology Libraries
University of California, Los Angeles
Los Angeles, California 90024

Edward T. O'Neill (167)
Office of Research
OCLC
Dublin, Ohio 43017-0702

Anne B. Piternick (29)
School of Library, Archival and Information Studies
University of British Columbia
Vancouver, British Columbia
Canada V6T 1W5

Helen F. Schmierer (101)
Systems Office
Regenstein Library
University of Chicago
Chicago, Illinois 60637

Tadayoshi Takawashi (65)
Library Science Course
Shizuoka Prefectural University Junior College
Hammatsu-shi, Shizuoka-ken
432 Japan

Barbara Tillett (149)
Cataloging Department
University of California, San Diego
La Jolla, California 92093

Ben Tucker (45)
Office for Descriptive Cataloging Policy
Library of Congress
Washington, D.C. 20540

Diane Visine-Goetz (167)
Office of Research
OCLC
Dublin, Ohio 43017-0702

Arnold S. Wajenberg (21)
University Library
University of Illinois, Urbana-Champaign
Urbana, Illinois 61801

Patrick Wilson (5)
School of Library and Information Studies
University of California
Berkeley, California 94720

Preface

The papers in this volume were delivered at the Conference on the Conceptual Foundations of Descriptive Cataloging held at the University of California, Los Angeles, on February 14 and 15, 1987. The two-day conference, sponsored by the Council on Library Resources, was convened for the purpose of stimulating visionary thinking about the future direction of descriptive cataloging. No immediate practical outcome of the conference was anticipated; rather, its objective was to sow ideas about the conceptual foundations of descriptive cataloging with the hope that they would grow and in time contribute to improving the design of bibliographic systems.

The present code of descriptive cataloging, the *Anglo-American Cataloging Rules* (AACR), is a prototypical set of rules for the design of a bibliographic database. The rules it contains have been refined and validated by over a hundred years experience in the cataloging of an extraordinary variety of bibliographic entities. A model set of rules, however, cannot remain static. AACR is currently being altered by two powerful forces: the political and economic drive toward cooperation and the technological drive toward automation. In the literature of library and information science, there is surprisingly little discussion of the impact of these forces on code development. Nor is there much discussion about what might constitute an optimal set of rules for organizing bibliographic information in a cooperative and online environment. It is almost as if a moratorium had been imposed on such discussions. One of the motives for mounting the Conference on the Conceptual Foundations of Descriptive Cataloging was to reopen discussion by providing a forum for open-minded debate about the future direction of cataloging.

The conference was predicated upon the assumption that, however AACR develops, by disjointed increments or by wholesale revision, it is imperative that the development be guided by theoretical considerations. The alternative to theoretical guidance is to let the code grow like Topsy, the effect of which would be to undo all the connections, order, and coherence built into it. The eventual result would be a code that does not meet the objectives set for it, a code that contains inconsistencies and redundancies, a code that is not rationalized with respect to costs, machine capabilities, and possibilities of cooperation; in short, a code without conceptual foundations.

In planning the Conference, the following topics were identified as productive of debatable issues related to the conceptual foundations of descriptive cataloging:

- Objectives of the catalog and the means to reach them
- Concept of Authorship: past and future
- Standardization and the proliferation of rule interpretations
- Access points and main entry
- Impact of technology on code design
- Bibliographic structure
- Integration

Except for the first, an attempt was made to find two authors for each topic. Those who were found are recognized scholars in the area of bibliographic control. Together they have written fourteen thoughtful papers about the concepts underlying code design. In them, they raise questions that should interest managers of code development, designers of bibliographic databases, and students of cataloging. They reaffirm bibliographic principles and verities of the past while offering a vision that understands possibilities and desiderata.

Acknowledgments

Acknowledgment is directed primarily to those who made the 1987 Conference on the Conceptual Foundations of Descriptive Cataloging possible and successful. First, thanks are due to the Council on Library Resources for providing financial support for the conference. Special thanks go to Dorothy J. Anderson, assistant dean of the Graduate School of Library and Information Science, at the University of California, Los Angeles, who served as organizing consultant, and Kathleen M. Scott, a dedicated, optimistic, and careful administrative assistant. Several members of the University Research Library at the University of California, Los Angeles, contributed help in one capacity or another, including Melissa Bernhardt, Allyson Carlyle, Jim Davis, Jain Fletcher, Pat Hall, Dorothy McGarry, Daniel Pugh, and Ron Watson. From the Library School, thanks are owed to Professor John Richardson and to students Peter Hadley, David Abels, and Dee Michel, the latter for the indexing of this volume. Two speakers at the conference whose contributions are not reflected in this volume deserve great thanks: Robert M. Hayes, who in a stirring welcome applauded the conference's purpose, and Seymour Lubetzky, who in a performance that was truly masterly, summarized the proceedings of the conference.

Elaine Svenonius

I

The Objectives
of the Catalog
and the Means
to Reach Them

The design of a tool for bibliographical control begins with a statement of objectives. The objectives for present-day catalogs were formulated over a century ago by Charles Ammi Cutter (Cutter, 1876, p. 10):

1. To enable a person to find a book of which either
   A.   the author
   B.   the title   is known
   C.   the subject

2. To show what the library has
   D.   by a given author
   E.   on a given subject
   F.   in a given kind of literature

3. To assist in the choice of a book
   G.   as to its edition (bibliographically)
   H.   as to its character (literary or topical)

Cutter's objectives remained unchallenged for more than 75 years, years which brought changes in the rules and mechanics of cataloging as well as in the technological, economic, and political infrastructure of cataloging. The first suggestion of revision came in 1953, with Seymour Lubetzky's rewording of the second objective (Lubetzky, 1953, p. 36): ". . . to reveal to the user of the catalog, under one form of the author's name, what works the library has by a given author and what editions or translations of a given work." A significant difference in the Lubetzky and Cutter formulations is that the former explicitly calls for collocating the various physical manifestations of a work, such as different editions and translations of it. That different editions of a work should be gathered and displayed in physical proximity is only implied in Cutter's third objective, an objective which, interestingly, is often overlooked in discussions of catalog objectives.

Only 30 years have elapsed since Lubetzky's reformulation of the objectives of the catalog, yet these three decades have probably witnessed more dramatic changes to the cataloging infrastructure than the preceding seven. Not only have catalogs been automated, but also an unprecedented amount of cooperative cataloging has led to the emergence of international standards, global catalogs, and linked systems. The question must be asked: Are the objectives that have guided catalog code construction in the past still relevant today? It is the most seminal of the questions to be considered in this volume on the conceptual foundations of descriptive cataloging and, appropriately, the one to be addressed first.

The title of the first chapter is "The Second Objective" and it is written by Patrick Wilson, Professor at the School of Library and Information Studies at Berkeley. Wilson begins by questioning the phrase "descriptive cataloging." Isn't it time, he asks, to reconceptualize the organizing activity that has been called by that name? He then postulates three desiderata which, if realized, could form the basis of a new paradigm for bibliographic organization: (1) to provide access in a local library catalog to virtual as well as actual copies of bibliographic items, (2) to take the second objective of the catalog, rather than the first, as primary, and (3) to recognize in bibliographical description changing textual states.

The technology of availability differs in the manual and online environments in that in the latter distance becomes inconsequential. Sitting at a terminal it is theoretically possible to actualize on demand the full text of a book stored anywhere in the world. The implication for libraries is that they should design their catalogs to organize not only the actual books they own, but also the virtual ones to which they provide access.

The prospect of a future in which catalog descriptions are global rather than local in their reference raises a very important question about the relative priority of the objectives of the catalog. Heretofore prominence has been given to the first objective in the sense that local cataloging took as its point of departure the physical item just acquired, the book or publication. But, Wilson asks, is this reasonable if from a user's view the work, rather than the publication, is the entity of primary bibliographic interest? Shouldn't the work be taken as the basic unit of cataloging? Shouldn't the second objective be taken seriously and given priority over the first?

Basic to a consideration of the objectives of the catalog is a definition of *work*. Wilson proposes a definition that differs significantly from Lubetzky's. In testing the bounds of his definition he considers how it can accommodate emerging products of electronic publishing, such as open-ended texts that continue to be altered and conglomerate texts with multiple and diffuse authorship. He considers as well what is meant by works that are derivative or dependent.

In his philosophical approach to the nature and purpose of bibliographic organization, Wilson contributes valuably to the literature on the conceptual foundations of—whatever we should be calling that activity that now goes by the name of *descriptive cataloging*.

The Second Objective

Patrick Wilson

Thirteen years away from the twenty-first century, in the middle of a hurricane of social and technological change, there is something at least faintly odd about a meeting to talk about the conceptual foundations of descriptive cataloguing. The catalog as we have known it for 100 years is surely dead or dying, and might not the same be said for descriptive cataloguing? We should not be reassured by the close resemblance of present online catalogs to the card catalogs they replace; that is worrisome rather than reassuring. Are we missing the opportunity to make fundamental changes in our old practices? Should we be talking about cataloguing at all? I want to propose a change in the way we think about the things there are to catalog; in the course of the discussion, it may become plausible that "descriptive cataloguing" is the wrong label to use for the organizing activity that is required.

Of all the varieties of technological change we have been encountering, one of the most impressive is the change in the technology of availability. We have learned that we can read at a distance: a store of information located at one place can be examined anywhere else, at least in principle. I sit in my office and look at files located far away—perhaps in Ceylon? I don't know and it doesn't matter to me (so long as someone else is paying). The thing about the printed book was that the storage medium, ink marks on paper, was also the display medium. Reading a book was a matter of looking directly at the information store; what I saw was the store itself. That is not true for every storage medium; the microfilm reader involves projection of an image *from* a piece of film *to* a screen, and I look at the screen, not at the film. But at least the storage medium, the film, was close, physically and optically, to the display medium, the screen. Now distance has become irrelevant, and the medium still further from being itself legible than the microform was. The information store can be inspected only by using an image-producing device. That device can now produce either an ephemeral display on a screen or a durable copy on paper: in either case, a copy, short lived or long lasting, in a form that can be read without the need for further equipment. More spectacularly even than that, the information store can be duplicated, the remote source of copies giving rise to a new nearby source of copies. And finally, the copies that can be produced from a source are no longer limited to simple reproductions of all or segments of the information store; they can be the result of intervening transformations of the information stored: the result of selection, combination, reorganization, reformatting, and more. So the copy that is produced need not correspond exactly to the information store from which it derives. We are a long way from the simple identity of storage and display represented by manuscript or printed book.

What these technological changes do to the traditional idea of a library collection is clear enough. When storage medium and display medium were the same, the only way to get the information in a store was to have in hand a copy of the store itself; availability of information required availability of a physical object that was simultaneously the carrier and the display of information. No longer; availability of a store of information at a place does not require the presence of an actual display but only a *virtual* display, that is, the possibility of producing a visual display, transitory or lasting. Availability at a place does not require the physical presence of a copy, but only the possibility of *producing* a copy, and the collection of actual and virtual copies now constitutes the available stock of information. Some visual displays are available due to the physical presence of a directly legible information store, for instance a copy of a printed book; some are available due to the physical presence of an information store that is not directly legible but that is the source from which visual displays can be produced on demand, for example a microform or a compact disk; and some are available due to the possibility of calling up a remote source and generating a visible display, or first duplicating (downloading) part of the source and then producing a visible display. For the user, in many circumstances and for many purposes, it will be a matter of indifference which of these three possibilities is the actuality; a virtual copy may be as good as an actual copy, if it can be actualized on demand. Mr. Lancaster has spoken of the disembodiment of the library (Lancaster, 1982, p. 108); we might as well say that the possibility of reembodiment or rematerialization at a place is what defines the collection available at that place.

If a catalog is a guide to the contents of a collection available at a place, then a catalog must include the virtual as well as the actual copies available at that place. Already we include in our catalogs information sources that are only potentially the sources of useable copies; unreadable microforms are included because they are sources of legible copies, or are listed as if they were already legible. As far as the user is concerned, listing a microform in a catalog is listing a virtual copy, and it is a short step from this to listing a virtual copy producible by calling up a remote source. As time goes on, the artificiality and inconsistency of listing some but not other virtual copies, all equally available, will become glaringly obvious. The bad conscience that finally drives librarians to worry about the immense microform collections held in their libraries but unrepresented in their catalogs will force realization that equally available virtual copies are equally in need of representation *as* available (Joachim, 1986).

But a remote source available to one is potentially available to all; and as the technology of information transmission marches on, increasingly the information held in *any* form by one library will be available to others in some form without physical transportation of physical objects. There is still a long way to go, but the direction is fairly clear: what one library has will be virtually present in any other library as well. The same collection will be virtually available to everyone, and the differences among local catalogs would be confined to differences in the form of availability. The distinction between local and union catalog fades into practical insignificance. If we are to think usefully about descriptive cataloguing, we must think of a future in which actual legible copies may constitute only a tiny fraction of the collection available at a particular place, and in which virtual copies are treated on a par with actual copies.

Thinking of that kind of future, it is time to take a fresh look at the question of the objectives of the catalog. In the well-known formulation of Mr. Lubetzky, there are two objectives: the first, to "enable the user . . . to determine readily whether or not the library has the book he wants;" the second, to reveal what works the library has by a given author and what editions or translations of a given work (Lubetzky, 1953, p. 36). That first objective is of course unacceptable as it stands; the book cannot claim its old priority, and a library's "having" an item has to be reinterpreted in view of the actual/virtual distinction. But let us put that aside, for there is a more pressing question about the second objective: namely, the question of why it should be assigned second place rather than first. In three working papers prepared for the 1961 International Conference on Cataloguing Principles, Lubetzky, Verona, and Leonard Jolley all agree that the object of interest, in the normal search of a catalog, is not a particular book or other publication, but rather the work represented by the book. In Verona's words, "the object of the reader's essential interest is not the publication but the work represented by it. There is no denying the fundamental truth of this statement, which appears to assign greater importance to works than to books in relation to the catalog" (Verona, 1963, p. 147). Jolley agreed that "it is quite obvious that the reader is normally interested primarily in a work rather than in a specific publication" (Jolley, 1963, p. 160). Given such agreement, one might wonder why anyone would then agree that the objective of showing what works were in a collection was the *second* rather than the first objective.[1] If the objectives were of equal importance, neither having priority over the other, it would not matter which was called first and which second. But it is clear that the first objective has had priority over the second, in at least two ways. First, in practice, the first objective has served as a screen or filter to determine which works, and which appearances of works, would be eligible for separate representation in the catalog. In practice, the only works considered under the second objective have been those that occupied the entire content of one or more physical volumes. There are exceptions, but not many. In general, our pursuit of the second objective has been restricted to showing relationships among books with different title-page titles that contained the same work; a work that happened not to be published as a separate book would not be represented in the catalog at all, nor would all appearances of a work be shown. Unless a work appears as a book, it simply doesn't count.

But there is nothing whatever in the *idea* of a work that requires works to be published between separate covers in books. A work that happens to be published in a journal, or in a book along with a number of other works by other people, is no less a work than if it had been published as a separate pamphlet; it does not suddenly become a work by being reprinted separately. There are old printed library catalogs in which the first objective did not serve as a screen, catalogs that do come close to showing what works of an author the library contained, listing not only books but also journal articles and book chapters as well.[2] They took the second objective more seriously than we have done recently; if we wish to take it seriously, we will have to make our catalogs into what we may call (borrowing from the Surgeon General) *index* catalogs, showing all the works represented in the collection, not just those that happen to have been published separately. Descriptive cataloguing has been confined to dealing with publishers' packages or containers first and foremost, and only secondarily with the works they contain. If we decided to take the second objective seriously, if we promoted it from second place to first place, if we threw over the dominance of the publishers' package and recognized the predominance of the work, we would basically change the nature of the catalog. If we combine this change of priority of objectives with the aim of showing virtual as well as actual copies, then not only do we move toward erasing the distinction between local and union catalogs, but also toward erasing that between catalogs and indexes, or catalogs and bibliographies. There would be no basic difference of principle left between a local catalog showing everything virtually available at a particular place, and a general bibliography of what there was in the bibliographic universe. Descriptive cataloguing would disappear as a separate specialty, merging with bibliographical description in general.

But there is another way in which the first objective has had practical priority over the second: that is in the very structure of the system of bibliographical records. The *unit* of record, the basic unit of cataloguing, has been the book or more generally the publisher's unit, not the work. What we describe in a basic unit record is a particular publisher's item; we may describe it *as* an appearance of a particular work, but still the basic fact is that we are describing a particular book or serial or other publication unit. There is an alternative, that could have been chosen and that would have been the natural choice if the second objective had been the first objective rather than second. If the work is the object of main interest, the unit described will be the work; the unit record would be a work record, not a book record. The content of such a record might take any number of particular forms, but there would inevitably be two parts: the first part would give information about the work itself, its proper name, its authorship, description of its content, historical or contextual information relating to its creation. The second part would give information on its various publication appearances, the actual or virtual copies of the work that exist. The first part would presumably include at least a standardized form of the author's name and a standardized name for the work itself. The second part would be open ended, a potentially growing location record telling us that the work appears *in* such and such a book, also *in* such and such a journal, and *in* such and such a microfiche collection, and so on. This sort of record structure is not novel; something like it can be found in old printed catalogs and many bibliographies, and recently has been proposed for certain cases of serials cataloguing (Graham, 1986). As far as I can see, there is no reason why a system cannot have both kinds of record: the conventional bibliographical record for particular publications, the work record for particular works. Both sorts of record might simply be derivatives of quite different underlying records, different ways of displaying information. But works and publications are entities of completely different types, and it is hardly surprising that their treatment should call for different sorts of record structures. The practical dominance of the first objective has, along with the limiting technology of the card catalog, prevented us from even considering the form of record appropriate to a bibliographical system in which the second objective had first priority. But now we can think of new and more appropriate ways of showing the works we have in a collection.

Now if works and publications are entities of entirely different types, and if we were going to think of our job as being that of showing what works there are in a collection, then it would be a good idea for us to get clear about what type of entity a work *is*. It's not obvious, and in fact I'm not sure there *is* a straightforward story that applies to all sorts of work. I won't even try to outline a general account, but will stick to what is arguably still the most important sort of work for us, the linguistically or symbolically expressed work, the work of discourse or organized data expressed in words and numerals. This is the copyright law category of "literary works"; works of this kind have the peculiarity that though they are, as is required for copyright, "fixed in a tangible medium of expression," they are only incidentally fixed in any particular tangible form (*Copyright Act of 1976, U.S. Code,* Title 17, Sec. 101). The real substance of the production of such a work is abstract, a string or ordered array of symbols. This string or ordered array of symbols is the text of the work; I claim that the text of a work *is* the work. Though abstract, the product, the work, can be displayed, and *completely* displayed; the writer is not joking or lying or mistaken when he says "Here it is, here's my latest work," and then gives you a copy of a string of words. That string of words *is* the work, and *any* copy of the string is a copy of the work. Asking to see the text of a work is not like asking to see a part of an object or an ingredient of a mixture; it is not as if the work produced by a writer had a verbal part and other, more spiritual, parts, so that getting the text would be getting only the grosser part and missing the good part. What you see is what there *is;* the work produced simply *is* that particular verbal construction. And if you haven't seen that verbal construction, you haven't seen the work.

This view of the nature of a "literary" work has consequences, some of which may be counterintuitive. The principal one is that a translation of a work is a different work; if you've read Plato or Marx in translation, you haven't read any work by Plato or Marx, but a different work by someone else, though directly derived from works of Plato or Marx. I find this a comfortable view, though others may not. Sophisticated people are likely to qualify their claims to be familiar with the works of Plato or Marx, as "in translation of course." This may reflect an awareness that whatever those strings of English words may be, they are not strings produced by Plato or Marx.

The identification of work with text may seem to imply that different complete texts must be texts of different works: that a revised edition of a work must be a different work, for instance. But this is not so. The text that we identify with a work need not be simple or fixed. We can recognize at least three major types of textual object. The first is the finished, stable object: the completed, or anyway abandoned, work. The second is the unfinished growing object, where parts already completed are stable and new parts are continually added. The third is the unfinished and changing object, where parts already produced are changed, new parts are added, and old parts are subtracted. The constantly updated and expanding database is an example of the third case, but it is useful to remember that the card catalog of old was also an example, changing from day to day as new cards were filed and alterations made on old cards. We tend to use the first type of textual object as our model, thinking primarily of finished stable texts. But we would do better to think of a finished text as the final one of a series of states of the work; there may be numerous drafts, sketches, and versions that were produced in the course of the work and for some reason preserved; the writer may have kept tinkering at the work for a long time, producing successive revisions and improved versions.[3] As long as an author keeps working on a particular verbal object, we can think of the situation as that of the constantly updated database: a particular text will represent today's state of the work, which may differ from tomorrow's state of the work. The *whole work* is the *whole sequence* of momentary states, that is, a sequence of texts; the text of the work is divisible into subtexts representing different momentary states of the construction. A particular edition, then, insofar as it represents a changed textual state, is literally a separate *part* of the whole sequence of texts that is the work. A work is a text, but a text that can be subdivided into successive textual *states,* any of which may happen to be published or made available. The momentary state of a database corresponds to a virtual copy, and we can think of the work that consists of the textual content of that database as a sequence of virtual-state copies. In this way the three different types of textual object—the finished, the growing, the changing—are all reduced to one basic type: the sequence of momentary textual states. Most states of most works are not preserved; for most works, only one state is preserved, the final state, or the official or approved state. For some works, *no* state at all may be preserved; one may have access to the current state, which may change from minute to minute, but no actual copies of any state may be made and preserved. This would be truly an evanescent object, which nevertheless can be treated as a ''literary'' work on a par with others, if we treat virtual copies on a par with actual ones.

We naturally think of cases where each momentary state consists of a single complete text, but things can get more complex than that. Ithiel Pool has written of a possible ''decline of canonical texts produced in uniform copies,'' suggesting that electronic publishing allows a return to something like the manuscript tradition, where each copy is unique. In a data network, he notes, "one person types out comments at a terminal and gives colleagues on the network access to the comments. As each person copies, modifies, edits, and expands the text, it changes from day to day. With each change, the text is stored somewhere in a different version" (Pool, 1983, p. 213). This certainly complicates the notion of a work; but that is all. What is being described is simply a changing database that happens to exist in several simultaneous states as well as in several successive states, and where no state is marked as the "official" or primary state. It is a simple matter, at least conceptually, to extend the idea of a text consisting of successive momentary states to the idea of a text consisting of many different simultaneous and successive states.

Given that a work can be a very complex textual object, there are bound to be cases in which it is hard to tell whether a text is to count as part of the text of a certain work, or as somehow related to, but not properly a part of, that work. There are works in the useful but neglected category of "dependent works," including things that appear as supplements, appendices, and so on, that may be considered as works in their own right but may *also* be recognized as integral parts of larger works. But there is also the huge category of *derivative* works, in the sense of the Copyright Law, works "based upon one or more preexisting works, such as a translation, . . . or any other form in which a work may be recast, transformed, or adapted" (*Copyright Act of 1976, U.S. Code*, Title 17, Sec. 101). Unlike dependent works, derivative works cannot be recognized as integral parts of the works from which they derive. Reading a paraphrase or a parody of Kant's *Critique of Pure Reason* is not reading part of the text of that Critique, hence not reading part of that work.

But while it is unavoidable that we recognize a category of derivative works, it is by no means easy to give a rule or procedure for recognizing instances of the category. The problem can be illustrated from our new technological situation. Now a copy of an electronically stored work need not be a replica of the text of the information store from which it is produced, but may be the result of various simple or complex transformations of that text. Suppose the result is to be something made publicly available and hence to appear in a catalog: is the result of transformation of a work to be treated as a new work, as a derivative work, or as just another copy of the original? The inclination may be to say that any manipulation beyond literal copying results in a new derivative work, but this inclination has absurd results if taken literally. As in copyright law, we have to apply a somewhat relaxed standard of identity of copies, accepting as copies of the same text copies that are not literally the same in every last detail. The slighter the transformation, the less plausible to claim that it has produced a new work. The greater the transformation, the more plausible. The information technology that makes an information source available at long distance also makes possible the production of derivative works involving anything from very slight to almost total transformation. There is a continuum; the difference between production of a trivial variant copy of a work and production of a new derivative work is one that finally can only be made arbitrarily. For pure cases of vagueness such as this, there are no nonarbitrary boundary lines to be found, which means that the notion of *the text* is not finally well defined at all, except by arbitrary decision.

Dependent works are, and derivative works are not, literally parts of the works on which they depend or from which they derive. These are only two of the many questions about parts and wholes. It is a basic fact about the works we are interested in that they can have parts that are works in their own right, and that they can themselves be parts of larger works. But which parts are really works in their own right, and which things that are really works in their own right are also parts of larger works—and parts of which works? Not every part of a work is a work, and not all works are parts of larger works. So what tells us which parts are works and which works are parts? An instant reflex would be to fall back on the criterion of literary warrant: a part that has been separately published, or two works that have been published together, *ipso facto* constitute works. This won't do; we won't allow that every fragment of a newly discovered work that happens to be published as a separate magazine article thereby becomes a work in its own right. Though there are works called *Hamlet* and *Macbeth,* there is no such work as *Hamlet-and-Macbeth,* no matter how often they happen to be published together in a single volume. The combination of literary warrant and an established individual title might avoid most such objections; but while this might give a reasonable practical rule, it will not pick out all the right things. As it may be only a matter of chance whether the parts of a larger work are themselves published separately and are treated as works in their own right, so it may be only a matter of chance whether the parts of a larger work are ever assembled into one publication unit and treated as a single work. Publication history is not enough to settle questions of what constitutes one work. The notion of a work lends itself as readily to application to distributed collective efforts and piecemeal publication as to one-person efforts and single publication. There are recent reports of a mathematical proof constructed not by a single person and published in a single article or monograph, but constructed by dozens of people and published in hundreds of articles in a score of journals (*Chronicle of Higher Education* 6 August 1986, p. 6). Whatever may happen in the future, the situation now would be: *the* proof consists of many related pieces of text by many authors; the pieces together constitute a single work, whose text is scattered among many publications. The fact that the text appears as a scatter of journal articles is no barrier at all to considering it as the text of a single work; it might sometime in the future appear as a single publication unit, but before it does so, would we not be justified in considering it a single work? And if the objective is to show what works there are in a collection, should not such a unit be exhibited?

But what an odd task it would be from a traditional cataloguer's point of view to try to show in a catalog all the works whose text was scattered. It is common for people to speak of scientific and scholarly work as constituting a group effort and publication as a group conversation, with a collective outcome or result. And just as a person may want to locate a copy, in any publication form, of a particular text, so one may want to locate the scattered textual appearances of a collective effort, a work that represents the joint production of a group. This is the sort of task that bibliography is meant to make possible; but interestingly enough, we think of this as the task of "subject bibliography," not of descriptive bibliography or descriptive cataloguing.[4] If we thought of this as a task for cataloguing, we would tremble at the idea of having to recognize all the different groups of people who might be considered to be engaged in a collective effort, the textual outcome of which constituted a work. How would we recognize the candidate groups? And how would we choose those whose scattered publications were to be represented *as* a single work? There is no mechanical procedure; there is hardly even a heuristic for doing this. Nor is it something that we could hope to do completely or finally. While we might reasonably hope to make a complete description of all the publication units contained in a collection, we cannot reasonably hope to make a complete description of all the works contained in the collection. There will be works in the collection that we will not represent *as* works. There will in addition be countless *fragments* of works that we will not represent—small or large parts of a work embedded in other works. There will be texts whose status is uncertain or disputed or changing: not quite recognized as a work in its own right, becoming recognized as such. And there will be texts arbitrarily declared to be, or not to be, works in their own right.

Now given that completeness is unattainable and in fact undefined, we might as well ask the inevitable question: how literally are we to take the objective of showing which works are in a collection? Granted that a journal article and an essay published as a chapter in a collection surely are works and surely are to be shown as being in the collection, what about the very small contributions constituted by, say, letters to the editor published in a journal, or brief introductions by editors of publications containing works by other people? Is every book review a work? Is every distinct news story in a newspaper? Surely a poem is a work; but are we to list as separate works every poem by every poet that is represented in a collection? Every song, every hymn? If we think of a single file that has to be searched as a whole, the idea seems mad. But if we think of a system of articulated subfiles, penetrable separately, it is not so obviously mad. Successful access systems have to allow us to screen out whole categories of material, and the more inclusive the system is, the more crucial that we be able to vary the size and texture of the screen. But given the possibility of screening out poems, hymns, book reviews, and so on, for a particular search, does any objection in principle to the inclusion of such small works remain? Would an access system that allowed us to locate appearances of individual poems actually be *worse* than one that did not? If the matter of size is to be a matter of principle, one will have to find reasons for thinking that there is a threshold of size below which works are better not shown. I don't think such reasons will be found. Realistically we cannot be confident of ever attaining a complete record of the works in a bibliographic universe, but this ideal can still serve as our goal. Acceptance of the second objective *is* acceptance of this goal.

We have alternatives. We can take the first objective as setting the limits of our ambitions: describe the separate publishers' pieces, then decorate the descriptions with some allusions to the works they represent. *Or,* we can take the second as setting the limits of our ambitions: describe as nearly as we can *all* the works at our disposal. We have been taking the first as the measure of our ambition; I say, this has been a terrible mistake, we should have taken the *second*. It is not too late to change. Taking the second objective, together with the principle that virtual copies are to be treated on a par with actual copies, and recognizing that the works we are concerned with may often be a rapidly changing sequence of momentary textual states, these three elements might be just the elements needed for a reconceptualization of the task of what *hitherto* has been called descriptive cataloguing, the basis for revised conceptual foundations for whatever replaces descriptive cataloguing.

Notes

1. For Domanovszky, the first objective takes precedence over the second theoretically but not practically; but his entire discussion is based on a notion of "elemental objects" that are selected by the first objective, and "practical dominance" means only that uniform author headings and uniform titles are used for books, not works (Domanovszky, 1975, p. 106).

2. An example of such a catalog is the printed *Catalogue of the Library of the Peabody Institute of the City of Baltimore* (Peabody Institute, 1883–1892).

II

The Concept of Authorship: Past and Future

Authorship has long been regarded as the primary identifying attribute of a work, at least in the Anglo-American tradition of cataloging. *Authorship,* thus, is a fundamental concept in cataloging theory and any consideration of the foundations of cataloging is obliged to address the problem of its definition. In 1936 Julia Pettee characterized the Anglo-American development of the authorship concept as a continual broadening, an attempt to stretch the concept to bring in "lambs outside the fold" (Pettee, 1936, p. 286). Among those brought into the fold were editors of collections and corporate bodies, a practice looked askance upon by some European cataloging theorists.

For most of the present century, the authorship concept has remained fairly stable, but in the last 15 years it has begun to fluctuate ambiguously, sometimes stretching still further and at other times shrinking. In 1974 shrinking occurred when editors of collections were no longer accorded authorship status. The concept shrank still further when with the publication of the second edition of the *Anglo-American Cataloging Rules* (AACR2) this status was denied to corporate bodies. At the same time, however, that editors and corporate bodies were driven from the fold, the concept was stretched to embrace spirits and some performers.

What do these changing views of authorship signify? Is there a weakening of the authorship principle—the principle that states that author entry is to be preferred over any other entry form whenever possible? Does the principle no longer serve a useful purpose as a determinant of main entry? Does entry under author conflict with user convenience, particularly now that our cataloging rules are designed for multimedia catalogs? Perhaps the most intriguing question suggested by the changing view of authorship is whether or not we now need a new definition of *author,* one that is appropriate for global catalogs functioning in a multimedia, international, online environment?

Two chapters in this volume address some of the many questions surrounding the concept of authorship. The first is by Arnold Wajenberg, Principal Cataloger at the University of Illinois Library at Urbana-Champaign, and is entitled "A Cataloger's View of Authorship." Wajenberg opens his chapter by examining various past definitions of *author.* He looks at conundrums that strain these definitions and introduces one that is new to discussions of authorship and poses a heretofore unimagined difficulty (see p. 23). He then boldly suggests that for a certain class of works the concept of authorship may not be important, *viz.,* works of diffuse authorship. Such works are becoming increasingly common and the fact of their existence leads him to agree with Carpenter (1981) that every attempt to define authorship in terms of the originator of a work is doomed to failure. While admitting that probably no definition of authorship can meet all needs, Wajenberg does not see this as cause for concern. In some cases, for instance for the above-mentioned works of diffuse authorship, maybe all that is needed is to be able to identify persons and corporate bodies whose relationship to the work in hand is bibliographically significant.

From the above observations, Wajenberg is not led to conclude that *authorship* should be left undefined; nor is he tempted to generalize that the concept of *bibliographic significance* should replace that of *author* universally. Instead he offers his own pragmatic definition of authorship: "an author of a work is a person identified as an author in items containing the work, and/or in secondary literature that mentions the work" (p. 24). While similar to previous definitions of authorship by attribution, Wajenberg's definition extends them in a very important way by allowing assumption of responsibility to be attributed by secondary sources. The extension is one that acknowledges a cataloging reality, *viz.,* structuring the bibliographic universe depends upon scholarly activity.

The essential pragmatism of Wajenberg's definition lies in the fact that it is based on a bibliographic rather than an existential reality. Thus, by his definition, spirits are regarded as authors if they are identified as such in the item being cataloged or in secondary sources. Wajenberg's view toward corporate bodies *qua* authors is also pragmatic: while he would have no objection to assigning them authorship status, he would rather prefer not to, since corporate headings are not much sought by users and are, moreover, time-consuming to establish.

Pragmatism is a time-honored philosophical stance which holds that the meaning of concepts is to be found in their practical bearings. No consideration of the conceptual foundations of descriptive cataloging would be complete without a cataloging practitioner's view of an appropriate meaning of *author,* that is, a view based on a wide knowledge of cataloging rules and acquaintance with the endless variety of bibliographic entities that populate the bibliographic universe.

The second chapter to address the question of authorship is by Anne Piternick, who presently divides her time between being Assistant Dean of the Faculty of Arts and Professor in the School of Library, Archival and Information Studies at The University of British Columbia. Her chapter, entitled "Authors Online: A Searcher's Approach to the Online Author Catalog," looks at the concept of author in descriptive cataloging from two points of view: from the view of how authors are handled by abstracting and indexing (A & I) services and from the view of how they might be handled if advantage were taken of computer capabilities.

The treatment of authors by A & I services differs considerably from their cataloging treatment. The most obvious difference is the lack of authority control in the former; but an equally dramatic difference, especially notable in the context of Wajenberg's chapter, is the regard of authorship attribution. To illustrate the A & I view of authorship attribution, Piternick cites a definition of *author* that is truly remarkable, one that will make the reader "gasp" (p. 31). Generally, the A & I services provide author indexing in depth, even when there are a great many contributors to an article; they differ, thus, from cataloging services whose assignment of author headings is limited by the rule of three.

Piternick suggests that the concept of author pervasive in the A & I services stems in part from a culture of giving credit. She elaborates the point that different purposes are served by assigning author names as index terms to periodical articles and assigning them as main or added entry headings to books. Nevertheless, she argues that additional author access would be useful in online catalogs. Following the A & I practice, entry might be provided for all those contributing signficantly to a publication. Further, the roles or responsibility functions of these persons might be designated; and, as is done with subject descriptors in ERIC and MEDLINE, these roles might be distinguished as major or minor. As to the expensive business of authority control, like Duke in his chapter in this volume, she argues that authority work need not be done for all such persons; their names might simply be made available in the notes section of a bibliographic record for free text searching.

Turning to the use of technology to improve author access in online catalogs, Piternick makes two recommendations. The first is to make name authority information easily available to catalog users in the form of online displays, in the manner, say, of the Company Thesaurus, which is used as an adjunct to the Predicasts databases. The second is to develop a workstation that would provide integrated access to A & I and catalog databases; thus, a user looking for the works of an author would be enabled to find them all, whether in the form of whole books, parts of books, or periodical articles.

Occasionally, it is necessary in considering the conceptual foundation of descriptive cataloging to look beyond present cataloging practice to methods of bibliographical control practices in other environments. Piternick offers such a perspective and leaves us to ponder the question whether we can achieve the technical and conceptual integration necessary to unify different practices of bibliographical control.

A Cataloger's View of Authorship

Arnold S. Wajenberg

It is with some trepidation that I approach this subject. Although I have spent my entire career working in academic institutions, I have always been a practicing cataloger, and a supervisor and trainer of catalogers. I am not an academician, nor a cataloging theorist. I have, of course, sometimes thought about the principles underlying my work, and Professor Svenonius is very persuasive. So here I stand.

Although Panizzi's code made extensive use of author headings, he found no need to define the term "author" (Panizzi, 1848). Soon, however, problems and controversies made it necessary to attempt a definition. Are compilers the authors of the anthologies they create? Are corporate bodies the authors of works that emanate from them? It was to resolve such questions that Cutter defined "author" as "in the narrower sense [to apply to] . . . the person who writes a book; in a wider sense it may be applied to him who is the cause of the book's existence by putting together the writings of several authors (usually called the editor, more properly called the collector). Bodies of men (societies, cities, legislative bodies, countries) are to be considered the authors of their memoirs, transactions, journals, debates, reports, etc" (Cutter, 1904, p. 14). Virtually every code since Cutter's has included a definition of authorship, often very like Cutter's. These definitions are set forth and studied in detail in Tait's *Authors and Titles* (Tait, 1969b). They have also been commented on extensively by cataloging theorists, notably Lubetzky and Carpenter (Lubetzky, 1969; Carpenter, 1981).

Often, the attempt to define authorship is frustrating and even irritating to one who spends his or her career working with books and who rather naturally feels that it is obvious what an author is. This irritation can be sensed in the wording of Lubetzky's definition of an author in his *Principles of Cataloging:* "The author is simply the person who produces a work, whatever the character of the work, whether or not it has any 'intellectual or artistic content,' and whoever may actually be 'chiefly responsible for the creation' of that content" (Lubetzky, 1969, leaf 26). The context of this definition is a criticism of the definition of "author" in the 1967 edition of *Anglo-American Cataloging Rules,* based on chief responsibility for the intellectual or artistic content of a work (AACR, 1967, p. 343).

Inevitably, Lubetzky's definition has also been examined and, by some at least, also found wanting. The problem lies in the ambiguity of the word "produce." A stenographer who transcribes dictation from a recording produces a document but is certainly not the author of the document so produced. Probably the most thorough and rigorously philosophical investigation of the concept of authorship made to date is to be found in the second and third chapters of Michael Carpenter's book *Corporate Authorship* (Carpenter, 1981). In it he proves, I believe conclusively, that every attempt to define authorship in terms of the origination of the work is doomed to failure. In the process he identifies a number of the special problems associated with identifying authors, most of them involved with what he calls multiple and diffuse authorship. It might be instructive to consider a few of them.

Translations provide a rather good test of definitions of authorship based on origination or production. How can Sophocles be considered to have produced a modern English translation of his play *Antigone?* The English language did not even exist when Sophocles was alive. Diffuse authorship is increasingly common. Carpenter mentions the classic example, the motion picture. Typically, a number of different people make quite divergent contributions to the creation of the work— performers, directors, producers, photographers, set and costume designers, as well as the writer of the screenplay. In fact, for such a work, the concept of authorship is usually unimportant from a cataloger's point of view. What the cataloger is properly concerned with is identifying names that are, to use the Library of Congress' phrase, "bibliographically significant"[1], and which should therefore be included in the description and used as access points. In fact, that is really the cataloger's primary concern, whatever the nature of the item being cataloged.

Printed material also is often the result of diffuse authorship. A technical report may display on its title page the names of a project director and several assistants, researchers, statisticians, sometimes even writers. For some works, the problem is simply the number of people functioning, or identified, as authors. It is especially common for scientific and technical works to have several people identified as their authors. In fact, Miranda Lee Pao has demonstrated statistically that scientific writers collaborate more often than writers on computational musicology and probably in other fields of the humanities (Pao, 1980). Even more depressing, her study confirms the findings of earlier researchers that people who collaborate are much more prolific than those who do not. There seems to be some justification for uneasiness in the presence of shared authorship. Denham and Broom, writing in *Scholarly Publishing,* warn: "An undesirable practice . . . is sharing of authorship out of gratitude, friendship, deference, or the requirement of a laboratory or project director for such credit in all publications from 'his' laboratory" (Denham and Broom, 1981, p. 251).

There are, of course, a number of other fascinating conundrums associated with the identification of authors. Is the composer or the librettist properly regarded as the author of an opera? Of the libretto of the opera? Why should the praeses of an early European academic disputation be regarded as the author, rather than the respondent, or even the "auctor"? (The answer is that the praeses or faculty moderator prepared with considerable care and attention to detail the points or "theses" to which the student seeking a degree was required to respond.) These are just a few of the annoying problems with which catalogers have struggled for years and which cataloging codes have attempted to solve in various ways and with varying degrees of success.

It is a very great pleasure to present a new authorship problem, which was not available to Lubetzky or Carpenter. It is revealed in an article by Meredith Merritt in the November 1, 1985 issue of *Library Journal* (Merritt, 1985). The title of the article is "Racter the Author?" It describes a computer program, Racter, which has written a book entitled *The Policeman's Beard is Half Constructed.* The book consists of computer prose and poetry and has been published by Warner Software/ Warner Books. Warner Software describes Racter as "the most advanced prose-creating computer program today" (Merritt, 1985, p. 60). (There seems little doubt that Warner Software markets Racter.) The question, of course, is whether or not a computer program can be considered an author. There is no question that it created the book and that the book is attributed to the program, even though the book does have an introduction by William Chamberlain, one of the two programmers who created Racter. The Library of Congress cataloging for the book has title main entry, which is probably a wise choice, as Mr. Merritt says. However, he is right to complain that there is no added entry for Racter. There is, of course, the problem of deciding which chapter of AACR2 to follow in

constructing the heading. In spite of the tendency to anthropomor-
phize computer programs, personal name is probably not appropriate.
However, a program does not seem to meet the definition of a corporate
body in 21.1B1. Perhaps "Racter" could be regarded as a sort of uniform
title, or perhaps AACR2 needs another chapter in Part 2, for computer
programs and other miscellaneous entities.

Delightful as it may be to consider the endless variety of problems
that books present to catalogers, the title of this paper clearly implies an
obligation to suggest a definition of authorship that is acceptable to
catalogers, or at least to this cataloger. The definition proposed here
grows out of my conviction that, whatever their interests and concerns as
human beings, catalogers as catalogers are concerned, not with the
existential universe, but only with the bibliographic universe. It is the
cataloger's responsibility to bring order to the bibliographic universe,
much as the physicist brings order to the physical universe. The cataloger
should therefore confine his or her attention to the published record, the
bibliographic universe. It is in this context that I recommend the following
definition.

> An author of a work is a person identified as an author in
> items containing the work, and/or in secondary literature
> that mentions the work.

The identification may occur anywhere within the item, e.g., in the
preface or introduction of a book, but it is usually found in formal
statements on the chief source of information or in other prominent
sources, using "prominent" as defined in AACR2, rule 0.8. Such formal
identifications require that the cataloger be familiar with conventional
usages and layouts of such sources as title pages. For example, Shakespeare's authorship of *Hamlet* may be indicated by the use of the genitive
(Shakespeare's *Hamlet*), or by the use of the preposition "by" (*Hamlet*
by Shakespeare), or by the placement of Shakespeare's name on the title
page, without any formal connection to the title. The cataloger must
always be prepared to use information from other sources, such as the
text of the item or secondary literature, to correct inferences based on
formal statements in prominent sources. In the vast majority of cases,
however, formally stated information is all the cataloger has, and it is
usually all that is needed.

In AACR2, rule 21.1A carefully defines "author" in such a way as
to include those responsible for all kinds of library materials, and not just
books. Carpenter questions the need to expand the meaning of the word
beyond its dictionary definition, and I share his reservation (Carpenter,
1981, p. 125). It would seem easy enough for the rules to require that
persons whose function in a nonverbal medium is analogous to that of

authors should be treated in the same way that authors are treated, as far as choice of access points is concerned. Authors could then, properly, be limited to those to whom verbal works are attributed. I am reluctant to tie the definition to writing, because some early works, notably the Homeric epics, may well have been created and transmitted orally for decades if not centuries before being recorded in written form.

It is not my intention to rule out the possibility of corporate authorship, and I would have no objection to expanding the definition to include corporate bodies with persons identified as authors. On the whole, however, I would prefer not to regard corporate bodies as authors, for reasons that have nothing to do with the concepts of authorship. Corporate headings are difficult and time consuming to establish. Furthermore, most catalog users experience difficulty in finding them; indeed, they seldom seem to look for them. If corporate bodies are authors, they are not very useful ones, and I would prefer not to give them that status.

The observant reader will notice that the definition here proposed is very similar to Carpenter's "authorship by assumption of responsibility" (Carpenter, 1981, p. 139–151). It goes beyond that view of authorship only in that it allows responsibility to be thrust upon a perhaps unwilling author by secondary literature. In this way, a rare book cataloger working with an anonymous 18th century English pamphlet can treat Daniel Defoe as the author if authoritative Defoe bibliographies, such as Moore's, list it among his works. Of course, the cataloger must decide what is an authoritative Defoe bibliography, but that sort of decision is the proper responsibility of the cataloger. The cataloger need not be concerned with such problems as the scholarly debate over whether or not Homer ever really existed. The *Iliad* and the *Odyssey* are regularly attributed to Homer and the cataloger's definition here proposed is really a definition by attribution. Racter is clearly an author by this definition.

A definition by attribution also clarifies a sometimes controversial provision of AACR2 calling for entry of "a communication presented as having been received from a spirit under the heading for the spirit" (rule 21.26). There is no question that such works are attributed to the spirit in items containing the works. Objections to entry under the spirit are always made on existential, not bibliographic grounds. Whatever a cataloger's personal beliefs about spirit communications (and this cataloger does not believe in them), he or she has no right to permit his or her personal beliefs to intrude upon cataloging decisions. These decisions should be based on the bibliographic record. When I was lecturing on AACR2 shortly after its publication and mentioned this point while speaking in Columbus, Ohio, a lady in the audience said, "Oh, you are trying to get away from the old-fashioned cataloger's arrogance." I consider that a wise, insightful statement, and I have a gloomy suspicion that the lady was a reference librarian, not a cataloger.

Of course, neither this nor any other definition of authorship will solve all cataloging problems. (If it did, we would not need catalogers.) If authorship is defined by attribution, there will be a problem every time attribution is uncertain. A good example of such problems is found in an article by Judith Milhous and Robert Hume in the Winter 1983 issue of *Harvard Library Bulletin,* entitled "Attribution Problems in English Drama." In it, the authors investigated the attribution of authorship for 82 plays from the 678 listed in a standard reference source:

> Annals of English drama, 975–1700 / compiled by Alfred
> Harbage; revised by S. Schoenbaum.—London: Methuen,
> 1964.

They regard 33 of these 82 questionable attributions as now settled "beyond reasonable doubt." In 55 of the 82 cases, their conclusion differs significantly from that found in the *Annals* and in another standard reference source:

> The London stage, 1660–1800. Part 1, 1660–1700 / edited by
> William Van Lennep, Emmett L. Avery and Arthur H.
> Scouten.—Carbondale: Southern Illinois University Press,
> 1965.

Milhous and Hume carried out their investigation because they are charged with preparing a revised edition of part 1 of *The London Stage.*

The following sequence of events is quite possible. A cataloger working on an English play published in 1689 consults both *Annals of English Drama* and *The London Stage* and selects an author heading on the basis of information found in these sources. A few years later, this or another cataloger has occasion to work with the same play; she or he consults the revised edition of *The London Stage* and discovers that the play is there attributed to a different person. If the cataloger is conscientious, he or she will make some change or addition to the catalog record. If she or he is fortunate, the catalog will be online and not burdened with unnecessary main-entry requirements. The change can then take the form of an additional author heading and an explanatory note added to the catalog record.

Such work does require time and a measure of scholarly ability. However, it is bibliographic scholarship that is required, and it is appropriate to expect this of catalogers. The cataloger is still interpreting and bringing order to the bibliographic universe.

I realize that, in a meeting devoted to the conceptual foundations of cataloging, I might justly be accused of dereliction of duty, if not heresy. I have no right to expect more than chains, the rack, and the stake, or, if my peers are merciful, the headsman's axe. Nevertheless, ''here I stand, I cannot otherwise.''

Notes

1. In its *Rule Interpretations,* the Library of Congress uses the phrase ''bibliographically significant'' to characterize persons or bodies that warrant being recorded in responsibility statements, e.g., LCRI 1.1F1 (Tseng, 1987).

Authors Online: A Searcher's Approach to the Online Author Catalog

Anne B. Piternick

Introduction

One of the results of the recent major study of online public access catalogs (OPACs) has been the emphasis on subject searching. This emphasis is not new among librarians: for many years there have been complaints about Library of Congress (LC) subject headings, considerations of PRECIS indexing as a replacement (Dykstra, 1978; Schabas, 1982), and experiments such as the "BOOKS" project (Atherton, 1978) to enhance subject headings. But the results of the OPAC study made librarians realize the importance the *users* themselves placed on subject access and the difficulties they were experiencing in locating works on subjects of interest. Bates, who has published widely on problems and methods of searching, has recently formulated a model of an OPAC based on principles which would enhance subject searching for the naive as well as the experienced user (Bates, 1986).

It is heartening to find that more attention has also recently been paid to the problems faced by the user in attempting to locate names of authors in an online catalog. Especially interesting is a series of papers emanating from the Graduate Library School at the University of Chicago (Dickson, 1984; Taylor, 1984; Elias and Fair, 1983; Shore, 1984) which have thrown some light on the character of mismatches between what the user has chosen as an access point and what the catalog has provided.

At the same time, several papers have appeared in the online searching literature which have focused on problems of searching for author and other names in online bibliographic databases, for example Pilachowski and Everett, 1985; Pilachowski, 1986; Everett and Pilachowski, 1986; Snow, 1986; Pasterczyk, 1985. Many of these databases have no name authority controls, or apply a minimum of control by reducing forenames to initials, and these papers focus on online searching strategies which will circumvent problems of nonstandardized names. Because of the cost of authority work, catalogers in the age of the OPAC have now become interested in the techniques and strategies used by online searchers and have been considering their use in OPACs as an alternative to at least *some* authority work or as an enhancement to the work currently performed by authority files in assisting the user (Taylor, 1984; Jamieson, Dolan, and Declerck, 1986).

Another recent area of interest involving authors has been the definition of "authorship." Experience with online bibliographic databases has highlighted approaches to author cataloging that are very different from the ones represented by library cataloging rules. Carpenter several years ago discussed different criteria and principles which have been, or might be, used to determine "authorship" (Carpenter, 1981). Arnold Wajenberg's chapter in this volume advocates the principle of "authorship by attribution" (Wajenberg, 1989).

Patrick Wilson has suggested abandoning the notion of "authorship" altogether and relying instead on title-page transcription with "the proper names in that transcription made searchable" as a means of recording names which a user might search for as "authors." Name authority files would still be provided, and a distinction would be made in searching for personal names as subjects and personal names as what he calls "nonsubject, bibliographical" personal names (Wilson, 1983, p. 13).

Elaine Svenonius and her colleagues here at UCLA have recently explored the idea of automatically creating access points for all names that appear on the title page or in other "designatable" locations in a monograph (Svenonius, Baughman, and Molto, 1986). They were looking at this approach as a means of studying the feasibility of simplifying access-point cataloging, "operationalizing" it so that it could be performed by low-grade personnel or automatically by machine.

An interesting finding of the study was the astonishing number, and the different categories, of names falling outside the major groups usually recognized as responsible for a work—that is, writers, editors, emanators, publishers, or illustrators. The authors note the difficulty not so much of deciding who should be included in the categories of responsibility, but of defining who should *not* be considered eligible for inclusion. It appears that defining a "nonauthor" is every bit as difficult as defining an author.

The Contexts of Authorship

My own earlier work on authorship has focused on what one might call the socioeconomic reasons why abstracting and indexing (A & I) services in science and technology emphasize personal authorship and attribute authorship to many individuals who patently cannot have written a word of the works to which their names are attached (Piternick, 1985b). It has, in fact, become a matter of grave concern to the scientific community that so-called "authors" have allowed their names to appear on papers to which they have contributed little and for which they are not willing to accept responsibility. I do not wish to go into the sad history of the Darsee case, the controversy over which has actually produced a new kind of author, the *honorary* author, a term invented to describe a collaborator who has not been directly involved in the work described in a paper.[1] I will note, however, that the American Council of Learned Societies last year felt it appropriate to issue an item on academic authorship in its *Scholarly Communication Reprint* series (Kennedy, 1985). Also those seeking a definition of *authorship* might be interested to read an editorial which appeared in the *Annals of Internal Medicine* in 1982. Some of us might well gasp to read rules for authorship set forth by the Editor, which include the strictures that:

> 4. An author should have taken part in the writing of the paper.
>
> 5. An author should have read the entire contents of a paper and assented to its publication before it is sent to a journal (*Annals of Internal Medicine* 97 (Oct.) 1982:613–614).

There have also been cases where individuals have actually been surprised to find their names included among lists of authors of published papers and have vigorously protested the attribution of responsibility for the contents of the papers in question. Not surprisingly, MeSH has recently added a heading for "Retraction of Publication," which applies to articles previously indexed in *Index Medicus* and later retracted by their authors.[2]

Publication is important in academia as a criterion in promotion and tenure decisions. It is also an important feature in applications for research grants. This has led to a concern to give credit to all who might have made some contribution, however small, to a particular piece of work. In the context of the humanities and most areas of the social sciences, credit has usually been given in an "Acknowledgement" statement at the end of an article. In the sciences, especially the experimental sciences, the practice has been to list the names of all contributors in the authorship position, following the title.

The A & I services have generally given support to these practices, especially in the era of computer processing, by including a large number of authors in the bibliographic description and the author index. Conventions used by scientific journals often require alphabetical listing of names, although where there is great imbalance the names of major contributors may be listed first.[3] Thus, the A & I services do not find it easy to follow a "rule of three" which would always favor those whose names fall at the beginning of the alphabet. Although some have set limits at, say, 10 authors, others, notably *Physics Abstracts,* have records with well over 100. The highest number of authors reported to date by the INSPEC database is 238.

The primary purpose of the A & I services has traditionally been directed at providing information on new developments in their fields. The arrangement of their printed products is by subject; titles are often translated or modified to bring out the content and may appear in entries before authors; abstracts are often provided. Authors are usually relegated to a secondary position, since the emphasis is on identifying content rather than bibliographic units. But author indexes have been increasingly used as a means of counting author contributions and, thus, the A & I services also function as an important mechanism in what one might call the "culture" of giving credit.

The point I am trying to make here is that the *context* of authorship in the scientific and technical A & I services is a different context from that of the library catalog. The functions of the catalog, as they have been reaffirmed at this colloquium, are to identify works held by the library and to make it possible for the user to find all works by the same author. They do not include, or have not so far included, the allocation of credit.

Authorship in the Electronic Era

Many libraries now are planning or implementing the integration of online databases with their catalogs, either by downloading selected records, such as analytics for serials held by the library or articles by faculty authors (Quint, 1987), or by the provision of workstations which provide access to the catalog and to a whole range of other online databases.[4] We all like to think of the system which will result from such integration as a seamless whole, with the transition to and from different databases and systems being transparent to the user. We are well aware, however, of the technical problems of such integration. Where we have the application of standard formats and indexing vocabularies, as in the case of both the National Library of Medicine catalog and the *Index Medicus* online (*MEDLINE*), the merging of records can be expected to proceed smoothly. But there is a lack of standardization in many databases which do not use name authority files. There are also differences in the approach of database vendors to the problems of format and bibliographic role. Record formats are standardized by the database vendor and may be different from what is supplied by the database producer. Corporate names are often gathered into one field, whether they are corporate authors, author affiliations, sponsors, or emanators (Burress, 1985; Piternick, 1985). Other chapters in this volume deal with the problems of integration, so I will leave further discussion to them.

What we must be aware of is the possibility of problems arising from the contextual differences between databases. Does it make sense to preserve the traditional goals of the catalog? Or should we extend them to accommodate the goal of giving credit by removing some of the restrictions on entry of author names which we commonly accept in cataloging through the application of the infamous "Rule of Three"? Since an online computer file can easily accommodate more author entries than allowed for in card files, why impose such restrictions (Lin, 1985)?

I ask this in part because the anxiety about claiming and giving credit which we see in the sciences seems to be spilling over into other areas. The causes may be different: some authors may fear claims for damages or charges of plagiarism. For example, I was given a new cookbook for Christmas on the title page verso of which the author ascribes specific recipes to other chefs. One has often found an acknowledgment in such books that recipes have been borrowed, but there seems to be something excessive about putting this "up front," so to speak, where it could conceivably cause grief to some catalogers.

At present, we are being faced with a whole variety of new kinds of documents which we are trying to describe in our catalogs but which require new definitions of "authorship" to cope with. It is not difficult to see that there might be some disagreement as to which persons involved in the creation of these documents could be described as authors, or which of their names should be made access points in an online catalog. Take the example of films mentioned by Arnold Wajenberg: comparatively few of the people whose names flash by on the screen at the end of the movie are included in an LC record. Is the LC record adequate? And adequate for what?

Compare the results of AACR2 cataloging with *Magill's Survey of Cinema,* a reference source which is up on DIALOG. Leaving aside the actors, *Magill's* provides search access to the director, producer, screenplay author, cinematographer, and editor, with a separate field for each. There is also a field for "Other Credits" which, in the DIALOG sample record, displays names of those responsible for art direction and music. If one regards the name of the releasing studio as equivalent to the name of a corporate author, we still have less than 10 author roles represented.

Now take a look at the list of abbreviations for entries in the *British National Film and Video Catalog*. This indicates coverage of around 20 different roles of individuals involved in creating and producing a movie. Moreover these do not include actors and a variety of other performers: people like commentary speaker, interviewer, narrator, and no fewer than three kinds of music performer—a plain and simple music performer, a performer who is a member of the cast, and a performer who is only heard on the soundtrack. Names of all these people appear in a "Production Index." One may well ask "Why?"

It seems clear that we are dealing here with three different contextual approaches to film: the cataloger's approach, the approach of the compiler of the reference work, and the approach of the librarian or historian operating in the film research culture. The existence of databases with a much greater number of access points does mean in this case that we can switch to their records if our own are not full enough. But is there an argument for changing our approach?

How should we approach electronically produced documents? If we look at such documents we find that new kinds of authors are beginning to appear on title pages (or the equivalent for nonprint works). Consider, for example, a printed *Directory of Leisure Scholars and Research, 1984,* which was reviewed in a recent issue of the *Library Association Record*. This was entered in the journal under the names of the compiler and the processor. Should we regard the processor as an author, or at least worthy of an added entry? Increasing use of electronic publishing methods may give prominence to processors and programmers, not to mention programs, who help to construct a work. In such cases we should be asking ourselves whether or not we need the name of such a contributor to identify a work and, if not, what purpose it serves. Would anyone wish to find other works processed by the same processor, for example?

My example here was of a printed directory, but we could find similar cases if we looked at other kinds of electronic products, for example, computer software. Deanne Holzberlein's examples of computer software cataloging include, in the "Notes" section for statements of responsibility, categories for persons such as coordinator, developer, programmer, editor, producer, author, and for those responsible for the program, for documentation, and for a particular version of a program, for example, one that will run on a Commodore. She notes that OCLC includes notes such as these because "people have asked to have this information included" (Holzberlein, 1982–83, p. 8–9). AACR2 permits inclusion of such names "if they are not named elsewhere in the bibliographic description and are judged necessary for the bibliographic description" (p. 212). It is obvious that some people think they are needed for some purpose or other.

Works like computer software are comparatively new in library collections and there may be a feeling that name access should be provided to all persons who have some responsibility for software programs because librarians are not really sure how users will search for them in a catalog or how the lack of such access will affect, say, the compilation of author bibliographies. Such uncertainty is understandable. A report issued by the U.S. Office of Technology Assessment in April 1986 commented on the difficulty, or even the impossibility, of awarding copyright in the case of some new electronic products. One issue highlighted in the report was the difficulty of establishing authorship or share of authorship in an article, piece of software, or database compiled by a group of authors using personal computers linked by an electronic network. Another example pointed to possible conflicts between man and machine in copyright claims. A music-writing program exists which a musician can modify to suit his individual style. If the musician uses the program to help produce a popular song, who can claim copyright: the author, the program, or the programmer? (U. S. Congress. Office of Technology Assessment, 1987). If the copyright lawyers find things so difficult, is it any wonder that some catalogers are opting for both belt and suspenders in recording the names of anyone who has some responsibility for a work?

Fears have also been expressed that authorship of an item may not stay stable, that a work in electronic form by one author may be modified by others subsequent to its "publication," whatever that may represent. If changes are acknowledged, we may be able to identify revisions and their relationships to an original, but only at the cost of records involving a whole string of names.

Catalogers may also be facing increased problems in the future because of the difficulty of controlling publications produced with desktop systems. A recent note by Duane Nystrom, the Director of Publications of the Joint Committee on Printing of the U.S. Senate, predicted that desktop publishing will lead to decentralization and the breakdown of control of the publications of federal government departments and agencies (*Society for Scholarly Publishing Letter* 8(1986):1,4). We can imagine what that will mean. A study done for the European Communities in 1979 on the bibliographic presentation of "grey literature" found that such reports and other items produced informally were sometimes woefully lacking in standard bibliographic information (Knowles, 1979). If desktop items are considered worth cataloging, it may be that nonconventional methods may have to be used to identify, record, and retrieve the names of those considered to be authors in some way responsible for the documents.

Compilers of general library catalogs have not in the past felt it necessary to include the names of those making minor contributions to works or contributing only parts of works. They have left the task of recording names of authors of parts of works to the A & I services[5] or to more specialized libraries which operate in a context which requires such analysis. The specialized contribution of these libraries is what makes it so valuable to have, for example, access to several art library databases on RLIN. It is to be hoped that the same division of labor that has existed between general and special services in the past will continue for new kinds of works, especially where authorship is a problem. Perhaps certain libraries or bibliographic agencies would formally agree, as others have done in the past, to sharing in a very full recording of names of those contributing to particular types of works. In some areas, this may suggest the kind of cooperative project which provided analytical cataloging of microform sets. (We should hope that the situation which made such a project necessary will not be repeated when libraries begin to acquire collections of material on various kinds of optical or laser disk.)

The inclusion in a record of all names of contributors would not necessarily imply that they all would be given the full cataloging treatment, e.g., given added entry status or subjected to authority controls. I am assuming that they could be entered in a "Notes" field, together with the terms which designate the nature of their contribution, and that they could be retrieved by keyword or free-text searching methods. The inclusion in the record of the terms designating the nature of their contribution might make it possible at some later stage to retrieve certain categories of names for full cataloging treatment if it seemed desirable.

If full records of the kind described were made accessible in some bibliographic files, the end result would be to give assurance of finding names not covered in one's own catalog through searching such files. This is the kind of alternative searching routinely carried out in the Interlibrary Loan (ILL) Division in my own library and surely this is typical of other ILL operations. An item not found in our own catalog is often searched, for example, in the NTIS or ERIC files: these may reveal that a monographic item is a report, a parapublication, or a piece of "grey literature" which we own as part of a microfiche set, but have not analyzed in our own catalog. Or it might be searched to see if it is a single paper in a conference volume or part of a multiauthored work (Piternick, 1985a).

Authors Online

I originally approached this chapter very much from the point of view of an online searcher looking at the problems of searching author names in an OPAC and in the searching systems offered by database vendors. It gradually took on other, more conceptual aspects, more in keeping with the thrust of the title of the colloquium, and in this final version I am abandoning some of the contents of earlier drafts. To those interested in some of the problems experienced by users I suggest a reading of papers by Dickson, Everett and Pilachowski (and Pilachowski and Everett), Pasterczyk, Shore, Snow, and Taylor. I would, however, like to make four suggestions which relate more to concepts than to the technical aspects of searching.

The first is the idea of designating authors as "major" or "minor." This would be a way of distinguishing in a search between the different bibliographic roles played by a particular person—author, editor, collaborator, compiler, etc. The model here is the designation by databases such as ERIC and MEDLINE of subject descriptors as "major" or "minor." I suggest that any name appearing as an added entry might be categorized as "minor" and all names used as main entries as "major." A default author search would be a search for all entries attributed in any way to a particular author, whereas a sophisticated searcher might limit a search to major or minor authors, depending on requirements. The results of a default search should, however, clearly differentiate between different roles by showing first all works for which the name was the main entry, then those for which the person was a joint author, editor, compiler, etc.

Many authors are also subjects; for this reason, libraries have sometimes opted for the "Name" catalogs to bring all author and subject names together. It is no help to a searcher, however, to look for works by an author and be presented with works *about,* rather than *by.* I would like therefore to suggest that catalogs follow the example of the online searching systems, which provide for searching specific fields individually or as a group. That is, searching would be permitted for a name in an author index, in a subject index, or in a name index, which would include names from both those indexes. I can see a name index as having certain advantages:

- It would give confidence to searchers who were not sure whether or not to consider, say, a performer or composer of a piece of music, or a photographer or illustrator of a book, as authors for searching purposes.
- It would provide two searches for the price of one, where the searcher genuinely wanted books *by* and books *about.*

The display resulting from such a search should, of course, distinguish between works by and works about an author.

I have noted above that names of some of the persons involved in creating a variety of electronic or nonbook materials might be placed in the "Notes" section of the record and searched using full-text searching methods. It would obviously be advantageous to be able to limit searching of such names to that subset of the catalog database which described a particular type of material. This implies the capability of using the General Materials Designator as a "limit" operator, in the same way that DIALOG permits limiting of searches of the LC machine-readable cataloging (MARC) file to English or non-English, or fiction or nonfiction, publications. It is true that this is a technical matter, but what I am visualizing here is the concept of the OPAC as a group of subfiles as well as an integrated file.[6]

My final suggestion relates to the name authority file. The MARC authority file format already accommodates the specification of "earlier name," "later name," "official name," and so on. I would like to suggest modification of the authority file into a somewhat more user-friendly form so that it might be displayed online as a kind of online thesaurus. An example of such a thesaurus can be consulted online as an adjunct to the Predicasts databases on DIALOG: this is a Company Thesaurus which indicates relationships between a company and its affiliates, parent company, wholly owned subsidiaries, old and new names, and so on. Even without modification, the authority file should be able to generate more explicit messages to the user than "see" or "see also."

Conclusion

I have been trying to identify here some of the problems and prospects of Patrick Wilson's virtual catalog (Wilson, this volume)—the OPAC as one of a whole range of bibliographic files accessible to the user.

The ideal user workstation should act as a gateway to the OPAC and a full range of integrated bibliographic databases. The user trying to locate publications by or about a particular author should be able to switch comfortably from the library's catalog to union catalogs or bibliographic files such as RLIN or OCLC, to *Books in Print* or *British Books in Print,* to abstracting and indexing services, or even to the *LCMARC* and *REMARC* files on DIALOG or similar files on other searching systems. Not only would this offer the advantage of access to fuller records or to analytics: it could also offer the possibility of access to a fuller range of searching features. In online searching, a searcher may opt to search a particular database on one system rather than another, because of the ease of certain procedures on the one or the presence of certain fields on the other. In this way, a wide range of possibilities is open to the searcher.

To make all this possible, technical integration is necessary, so that a record in one file could be identified in another by mapping a standard number or other bibliographic element from one record onto a corresponding record in another file. But conceptual integration is also necessary, so that the purpose and context of the OPAC and other files is recognized and the limitations of one compensated for by the richness of another.

Acknowledgments

If I were to nominate an "honorary author" for this chapter, it would be Ann Turner, head of Catalog Records at the University of British Columbia Library, who gave me much information and advice on cataloguing and catalogs. I am also grateful to Jocelyn Foster (also of the UBC Library) for insights into user needs, and to Leah Gordon for "walking me through" the developing UBC OPAC. Finally, I am grateful to Elaine Svenonius for persuading me to take a look at the searching of catalogs and online databases from a conceptual point of view.

Notes

1. See the following articles in *Nature (London)* **325** (15 Jan. 1987): Stewart, Walter N. and Ned Feder, The Integrity of Scientific Literature, 207–214; Braunwald, Eugene, On Analyzing Scientific Fraud, 215–216 (a rebuttal to Stewart and Feder); and "Fraud, Libel and the Literature," 181–182 (an editorial introducing the above two items).

2. For an example of a protestation against attribution of responsibility, see Broad, William J. The Publishing Game: Getting More for Less. *Science* **211** (13 Mar. 1981): 1137–1139. See also the following articles: Milanese, Claudio, Neil E. Richardson and Ellis L. Reinherz. Retraction of Data; and Culliton, Barbarra J. Harvard Researchers Retract Data in Immunology Paper, both in *Science* **234** (28 Nov. 1986): 1056 and 1069 respectively.

3. For an interesting reference to the allocation of credit implicit in the ordering of authors' names, see Bernstein, Jeremy, Personal History: The Life It Brings—II. *The New Yorker* (2 Feb. 1987): 36–39. See also Zuckerman, 1968.

4. It was announced at the ALA Midwinter 1987 that OCLC and RLIN terminals now have gateway connections to DIALOG.

5. The Wilson Company, in fact, has traditionally based the amount of a library's subscription to its printed periodical indexes on the cost of indexing only those periodicals which the library holds. This is an overt acknowledgment that the indexes are complementary to the library's catalog.

6. Another candidate for "limit" might be *location*. Location could be used to produce custom catalogs for branch libraries, of course, but it might serve other purposes, such as limiting an OPAC search in a branch library to material immediately to hand. Libraries

III

Standardization and the Proliferation of Rule Interpretations

The value of standardization as a means to avoid the duplication of cataloging effort and to facilitate the exchange of bibliographic data has long been recognized. In 1853 Jewett envisioned a union catalog of all holdings in American libraries. Immediately he perceived that if such a catalog were to be realized a uniform style would have to be followed in recording bibliographic information. His pronouncement that "nothing, so far as can be avoided, should be left to the individual taste or judgment of the cataloger" (Jewett, 1853, p. 8) epitomizes an extreme view of standardization. It is a legalistic view, one that sees virtue in subservience to rules.

The value of standardization, while deeply entrenched in the Anglo-American cataloging tradition, has not gone unchallenged. Cutter, always ready to place the convenience of the user before the ease of the cataloger, argued that "strict consistency in a rule and uniformity in its application sometimes lead to practices which clash with the public's habitual way of looking at things" (Cutter, 1904, p. 6) and "when these habits are general and deeply rooted, it is unwise for the cataloger to ignore them, even if they demand a sacrifice of system and simplicity" (Cutter, 1904, p. 6). Unlike Jewett, Cutter preferred to view cataloging as an art needing only a few high-level rules or principles that could be applied by analogy to a variety of situations.

Another of the eloquent voices challenging the legalistic view was that of Lubetzky in his celebrated "return to principle" (Lubetzky, 1953, p. 1):

> At the same time, one could hardly view with equanimity the continuous proliferation of the rules, their growing complexity, and the obscurement of the objectives and design of the code as a whole. One is impelled to ask: Are all these rules necessary? Are all the complexities inevitable? Is there an underlying design which gives our code unity and purpose?

A question worth pondering is whether the antilegalistic position represented by Cutter and Lubetzky is in eclipse today. Over the last several decades, in part as a concomitant of increased cooperative cataloging, the pressures to conform to a bibliographic standard have increased. At first sight, it would appear that we are once again entering a period of legalistic cataloging, enmeshed in a proliferation perhaps not of rules but of rule interpretations. However, a deeper analysis of the consequences of standardization might well reveal the dualism that opposes the view of Jewett to that of Cutter and Lubetzky to be somewhat simplistic in today's complex cataloging environments.

Two chapters look at aspects of standardization. The first is by Ben R. Tucker, Chief of the Office for Descriptive Cataloging Policy at the Library of Congress and Library of Congress member of the Joint Steering Committee for the Revision of AACR. His topic is the Library of Congress rule interpretations and his title, "Ask Me No Questions and I'll Write You No RIs." Cutter observed that it was difficult for any rule to promote complete uniformity in practice. Yet the drive toward uniformity persists and, in the United States at least, has led to the referral of unresolved cataloging decisions to the taste and judgment of the catalogers at the Library of Congress.

Tucker begins his paper by examining exactly what is meant by a Library of Congress Rule Interpretation (LCRI). It would seem that many of the statements encompassed under the rubric "Library of Congress Rule Interpretations" are not interpretative at all, but represent either rule revisions or LC decisions that pertain to application or documentation. From an eyewitness vantage of more than a quarter of a century at LC, Tucker describes a fascinating history of how the procedure of issuing answers to cataloging questions evolved from a casual, uncoordinated, and private process to one that has become formalized, centralized, and public. Significant in this fascinating history, and in the history of standardization generally, was the concession in 1970 by the Library of

Congress to make its some of its cataloging decisions available to the public.

An interesting question arises: what if, for earlier rules, the Library of Congress disseminated its interpretations to the same extent it does today for AACR2—would there be more or fewer rule interpretations? Tucker's answer to the question reveals AACR2 in a new light (p. 49). He concludes his chapter with the observation that one really cannot lament the proliferation of rule interpretations; they are a fact of cataloging life.

A well-founded philosophy of catalog code development must take cognizance of the past, particularly of those factors which have affected and may continue to affect code design. As regards rule interpretation, Tucker makes a valuable, knowledge-based contribution to such a philosophy.

The second chapter on standardization is by Tom Delsey, Director of the Acquisitions and Bibliographic Services Branch of the National Library of Canada and, since 1985, Chairman of the Standing Committee of the IFLA Section on Cataloging. In this chapter, entitled "Standards for Descriptive Cataloguing: Two Perspectives on the Past Twenty Years," he discusses the technological and economic forces contributing to bibliographic standardization. Unquestionably it would be an economic good if only one bibliographic record per item were created worldwide, but, Delsey observes, there are obstacles preventing this, notably differences in audience and purpose, all the more considerable as they are solidly entrenched by the weight of historic precedent. To overcome such obstacles requires the establishment of political mechanisms to distribute the work of cataloging and to coordinate decisions about rules and their applications. It is important to realize that cataloging rules cannot be developed in a theoretical vacuum, but must be shaped by political and economic considerations. For instance, rules must be written to minimize changes that would have to be made to existing catalogs and options must be provided to anticipate conflict.

In discussing the effect of computer technology on standardization, Delsey delineates three waves of development, each characterized by a striving toward a different kind of consistency. First there is striving for consistency in the recording of cataloging data, a requirement imposed by computer literalness, which does not allow for the "silent correction" of errors. Second, there is striving for consistency in bibliographic description across different material-specific formats. Third, there is striving for consistency in conceptualization. Achieving this last sort of consistency is ambitious and entails removing the numerous logical anomalies that afflict the definitional and classificatory elements of present codes. According to Delsey consistency in conceptualization can be achieved only by the development of formal structures, for instance of the kind defined by the entity/attribute logic of data models.

Like Patrick Wilson, Delsey sees a future in which the conceptual foundations of descriptive cataloging will undergo profound changes. However, for Delsey these changes will stem not so much from a revision of the objectives of a code for bibliographic description, but from a reconceptualization of its logical structure.

Ask Me No Questions
and I'll Write You
No RIs

Ben R. Tucker

The Library of Congress has been distributing all its rule interpretations to other libraries since the adoption of the *Anglo-American Cataloguing Rules,* second edition (AACR2). This chapter discusses this phenomenon from my own point of view. As an introduction, it is useful to explain the phrase "Library of Congress Rule Interpretations" (LCRIs), which appears in *Cataloging Service Bulletin* as the caption for statements prepared by the Office for Descriptive Cataloging Policy at the Library of Congress. In order that Library of Congress catalogers may have one series of statements that are outside of AACR2 but are related to these particular rules, "Library of Congress Rule Interpretations" encompass not only interpretations, but also other types of statements. Principally, these noninterpretative statements are the following:

1. Decisions on options and alternative rules;

2. Decisions on a few rules either not to be applied (e.g., statements in LCRI 11.0A negating AACR2 provisions requiring microforms of books, etc., to be cataloged as microforms) or to be applied differently from the way the rule is stated (e.g., the second paragraph of LCRI 12.0B1, which prevents a title page "published later" from ever being the chief source for a serial);

3. Documentation of routines related to the rules (e.g., many statements about verification of geographic names in LCRI 23.2A and statements in LCRI 26 about evaluating existing reference structures, adding data for content designation to worksheets, etc.); and

4. Official revisions of rules, as determined by the Joint Steering Committee for Revision of AACR.

The first and last of the categories listed above constitute at least 50% of the statements found under the caption "Library of Congress Rule Interpretations." If one concentrates on the genuinely interpretative statements, one can quickly note that any superficial impression of the quantity of "interpretations" is exaggerated by at least 50%. The number of those statements that may properly be called "interpretations," however, is still large enough to merit some close consideration, as this chapter will demonstrate. Such a close consideration must begin with an explanation of the development of interpretations at the Library of Congress, and thus as further preamble the following personal and institutional history is offered.

When I started cataloging at the Library of Congress in 1960, one of the many things I learned early is that the *Rules for Descriptive Cataloging in the Library of Congress* (RDC, 1949) and the *A.L.A. Cataloging Rules for Author and Title Entries* (ALA Rules, 1949) only answered some of the cataloger's questions. The daily work of cataloging brought to light many issues either not addressed by the rules or addressed inadequately. My reviser's copy of the rule books had all the margins filled with handwritten notes and also had slips of paper and 3 × 5 cards tucked between the pages. Other catalogers in my section had their own personal versions of such an apparatus. As a neophyte I had the only clean copy of the rules in the section. During training I learned to note certain points I doubted I would easily remember and after some time I had my own personal version of this apparatus to the rules. Still, there simply was not enough space in margins to write in everything, and tucking notes or cards into the rule books also had a limit. I found that many of my colleagues also relied on a personal file of 3 × 5's on which were written, under rule numbers or topic names, answers to questions; directions from revisers, editors, or section heads; and interesting examples of titles, imprints, etc., copied from books cataloged. As long as the neophyte was under revision there was a good deal of coordination of these answers, etc., between the personal apparatus of the reviser and that of the trainee. There was no comparable attempt at coordination among members of a section, or indeed among the various sections—at least not normally. Of course in the case of major disagreements or the discovery of really major decisions, word was passed around a section by the section head or to all the section heads by the principal descriptive cataloger.

Seven years later in 1967, a new code, the first edition of the *Anglo-American Cataloging Rules* (AACR1) was adopted. The practice of developing a personal apparatus to the rules was continued under these rules. In preparation for the adoption of AACR1, the then chief of the division made a vain attempt to end the practice by asking all catalogers to turn in their copies of the rules and replace them with clean copies. But there was no change apparent in the number of answers to be written and preserved in some form. In 1966, on the eve of the adoption of AACR1, something else had happened at the Library of Congress: the Shared Cataloging Division was founded due to the considerable expansion of our cataloging under the National Program for Acquisition *and Cataloging* [my emphasis]. This meant a new division with a chief and assistant chief of a status equal to the officials of the formerly single Descriptive Cataloging Division. The divisions for descriptive cataloging of books are divided into sections according to language or language family. With two such divisions there was suddenly considerable overlap of identical responsibilities[1]: two sections cataloging publications, for example, in English, in German, or in Romance languages. Then in 1968 the picture was further complicated by the removal of all serial catalogers, responsible for all languages, from the Descriptive Cataloging Division to the Serial Record Division and the consequent increase in the number of serial catalogers. The principal descriptive cataloger had a major problem of communication, with three divisions requiring answers, many of which were language specific rather than division specific and therefore applicable to more than one section. The *new* rules generated *new* questions. The combination of the adoption of new rules and what might be termed a *scattering* of the catalogers had become a potent force for improved intramural communication by 1968. Contradictory advice easily came to light, with recriminations and hard looks among the divisions, in *one* of which in pontifical splendor sat the sole principal descriptive cataloger. Finally in 1968 the assistant chief of the new Shared Cataloging Division made a dramatic proposal: the principal descriptive cataloger should begin to write the answers to questions and distribute them in exact copies to all the sections of both divisions. It should be emphasized at this point why a written version of answers was necessary, because it is in these written answers that we can recognize the precise origin of the documents we today refer to as *rule interpretations*. Even before the establishment of the Shared Cataloging Division in 1966 the Library of Congress had a large staff: approximately 125 descriptive catalogers. This staff was almost doubled on the creation of the new division. Because of their number, it had always been something of a problem to "talk with the catalogers," and this difficulty quickly escalated to impossibility. The situation has never changed: communication remains the largest challenge that faces us. With the normal approach of using staff meetings for handling questions an impossibility, the Office for Descriptive Cataloging Policy has no means of general communication with all the staff at the Library of Congress, for whose work the office is in a sense responsible, other than the written word.

To return to our history, the principal descriptive cataloger did decide to begin writing the answers to questions in 1968. This shift in communication was also appropriate because of other happenings. The building of the MARC database had also begun in 1968, causing an unprecedented dissemination of LC records. On their own, more and more catalogers in other libraries were switching games: giving up their soloing for the greater sport of second-guessing LC. Earlier we had successfully ignored the manifest need of other catalogers to know LC policies, which could then roughly be defined as the sum of answers to all significant questions posed by LC catalogers.

For a long time I had to say to those catalogers outside the Library of Congress requesting copies of our internal cataloging documents that these were not available for distribution outside the Library of Congress. These documents were primarily for the purpose of creating a national record worth distributing to other libraries. Other libraries did not have such a responsibility and so were free even to promote specialized policies at some variance from the national ones as they attempted to be responsive to the needs of local users, rather than be all things to all people, as attempted by the Library of Congress. In crass terms, I could actually say to petitioners, "If you are not producing national records, be happy about *not* having to ring yourself round with restrictions: if only your own patrons are looking at your own records, you need not follow LC policies."

In November 1970 excerpts from the LC internal documentation were published in *Cataloging Service,* bulletin 96, and this was the tentative beginning of the end of the concept of internal documentation at the Library of Congress.[2] We have gradually learned and even embraced the proposition that any rule interpretation or other policy statement in the hands of Library of Congress catalogers should also be made available to other libraries. It is probably fair to say that the adoption of AACR2 in 1981 really put the finishing touches on the reversal in attitude, a natural result of the gradual process begun as described in 1970. Thus it has happened that under AACR2 we have shared all of our internal documentation, which naturally has tended to reflect on AACR2 as being possibly a poor code, since it needed so much interpretation. Actually it has been the only new code adopted during the period of increased dissemination of Library of Congress statements of policy and practice.

Had the Library of Congress disseminated its internal information to the same extent as at present during the periods 1949–1967 (under the RDC and the ALA 1949 rules) and 1967–1981 (under AACR1), it would have been possible to evaluate the three sets of rules that have governed descriptive cataloging since 1949 by asking: under which of these sets of rules did the Library of Congress have to produce the most rule interpretations for its catalogers? In the absence of hard information, one can only offer subjective judgments. My own memory tells me that at least within the Library of Congress, the rules in use during 1949–1967 would be the clear winner in a contest that would name the most fertile source of rule interpretations. The rules applied during that period were extremely specific, with principles often not stated, causing each new case to need special consideration.

It is useful to look at the current process of formulating interpretations at the Library of Congress. Today the technical administration of the current rules and policies for descriptive cataloging is handled at the Library of Congress by the Office for Descriptive Cataloging Policy. Since this office is at the Library of Congress, it does both more and less than the head or chief cataloger in an ordinary cataloging department. It does less in the sense that its activities do not encompass any administration either for classification or for subject headings, which are within the provinces of the Subject Cataloging and the Decimal Classification Divisions of the Library of Congress. On the other hand, the office exceeds the scope found elsewhere in the following ways:

1. It must deal with the full range of materials processed under the regular Library of Congress cataloging programs that result in published catalog records. These include books, serials, audiovisual materials, music, cartographic material, microforms, etc., regularly in about 70 languages and occasionally in about 400 others, coming from all countries of the world.

2. It must as well respond to the comparable needs of processing the archival collections of the Library of Congress, which include film, prints, photographs, manuscripts, etc.

3. It must respond to any of the needs mentioned above when institutions and organizations outside the Library of Congress express them.

It is fair to say that most of the questions brought to the office do not result in written directives, that is, in rule interpretations. Even the minority of questions that do generate such directives is large over a period of time, however, given such a rich source of questions as sketched above. The questioners are many and include not only individuals and institutions in North America, but also others from as far away as Papua New Guinea or New Zealand. Also they encompass many organizations acting in a more or less official capacity for a special community, such as Online Audiovisual Catalogers, the Music Library Association, the Australian Bibliographic Network, etc. To a certain extent it is standardization that drives the questioning, a standardization driven in turn by the fact of machine catalogs, utilities, networks, etc.

When interpretations are created, changed, or abolished, the reason can always be found in the rich source of questions arising in practice under forces of standardization. In conclusion, it must be accepted that interpretations of the cataloging rules are a fact of cataloging life, and therefore as a general proposition it is hardly worth discussing whether there should be any interpretations or how many there should be or should not be. Instead, the Library of Congress welcomes the kind of continuing specific input it has been accustomed to for some time now, according to which interpretations are created, revised, re-revised, or cancelled on the basis of catalogers' experience either at the Library of Congress or elsewhere.

Notes

1. See *Cataloging Service Bulletin* 29 (Summer 1985:23–27) for more details on the organization of descriptive cataloging at the Library of Congress as well as some of the recent history. See Smith (1985) for more historical information, particularly concerning 19th century origins of cataloging at the Library of Congress.

2. *Cataloging Service Bulletin* 96 (Summer 1970: 1) carried the following explanatory note: "In June 1968 the Library of Congress began to make its cataloging decisions available in processed form for the use of its descriptive catalogers but not for general distribution. By this means the catalogers are informed of official LC interpretations and decisions relating to the application of the *Anglo-American Cataloging Rules* together with directives relating to cataloging routines. With the thought that some of this material may be of considerable interest to other libraries, the following excerpts are published in virtually unedited form. The decisions are arranged according to the number of the pertinent Anglo-American rule, with several which do not fit neatly under a rule at the end, arranged alphabetically by topic."

Standards for Descriptive Cataloguing: Two Perspectives on the Past Twenty Years

Tom Delsey

Standards for descriptive cataloguing have existed in one form or another for well over a century now and have been subject to change—occasioned either by the evolution of cataloguing theory or by force of practice— throughout the entire period of their existence. During the last 20 years there have been two factors that have had a particularly significant impact on the development of cataloguing standards: the first is the economics of shared cataloguing, and the second, the application of computer technology to the cataloguing process.

Economics of Shared Cataloguing

In its logical extreme the economic argument for standardization in descriptive cataloguing asserts that a single standard description for any published item created by an authoritative agency with responsibility for its cataloguing will serve for use in any catalogue requiring a record for that item, thus eliminating the need for any duplicative effort. That premise underlies the International Federation of Library Associations' (IFLA) program for Universal Bibliographic Control; it forms the basis for the cataloguing programs of most national bibliographic agencies; and it is the operative assumption on which scores of cooperative cataloguing projects are based. In practice, of course, the ideal is seldom fully achieved. At the international level, differences in language and cultural context tend to work against the straight transfer of a record from one country to another for use without modification. At the national level, differences in audience and purpose for various catalogues will often dictate at least some degree of modification or adaptation of the record to the local context. And because virtually all catalogues carry with them an historical cumulation of past practices and idiosyncracies there will almost always be some degree of reconciliation with the existing file to be dealt with. Nonetheless, the degree to which a standard catalogue record can be achieved does have a real bearing on the potential for inter-changeability of records, and consequently on the degree of economic benefit that can be derived therefrom.

Recognition of such benefits and demonstrations of how they can in fact be realized have given a greatly increased impetus to efforts at standardization over the past two decades, both nationally and internationally. On a formal level, the result has been a much more broadly based approach to the development of cataloguing standards. On a practical level there has emerged a much more extensive and elaborate network of supporting mechanisms to assist in the standardized application of cataloguing rules.

With respect to the standards themselves, the last two decades have been the first in which we have seen efforts to establish an international base for descriptive cataloguing standards take concrete form and begin to have a significant impact on national standards. Within IFLA we have seen the development of a program for standardizing bibliographic description expand from a relatively modest beginning with the first draft of an International Standard Bibliographic Description (ISBD) for mono-graphs (ISBD, 1971) to encompass a whole array of standards covering everything from antiquarian books to computer files. As the chief catalyst for the development of international cataloguing standards, IFLA has also been responsible for elaborating the principles adopted in Paris in 1961 (Paris Principles, 1961) and for the embodiment of many of those same principles in internationally accepted "standards" governing the form and structure of corporate headings, personal names, ministerial bodies, etc. Not only have these standards received international approval, but more importantly they have gained acceptance through incorporation into regional and national standards and cataloguing codes and through implementation in the programs of numerous national bibliographic agencies. Closer to home, the last 20 years have taken us from the inauguration of a cataloguing code that was the first in many years to attempt to bridge the Anglo-American world (AACR1)—though not with complete success—to a new edition of that same code that managed not only to combine in a single text a set of rules to be used on both sides of the Atlantic, but at the same time to incorporate extensively international standards for both description and access (AACR2). The second edition of the *Anglo-American Cataloguing Rules* also enjoys the distinction of having been translated into numerous languages and of having been adopted either directly or indirectly as the national standard for cataloguing in many countries well beyond the Anglo-American sphere. One could argue, in fact, that AACR2 has been as effective as the ISBDs themselves in propagating international standards for descriptive cataloguing.

As mentioned at the outset, the major impetus for broadening the base of formal cataloguing standards and for attempting to achieve international compatibility of standards has been a recognition of the economic benefits to be derived from standard cataloguing. However, those benefits cannot be realized from standardization of rules alone. To optimize the interchangeability or exchange value of cataloguing records one has to ensure as far as possible standardized application of those rules and to minimize the tendency of the file within which one catalogues to exert its own influences on the catalogue record. Restrictions in scope and content of the file against which one catalogues and the weight that is given to historical precedent in that file can have a significant effect on the application of the cataloguing standard and can often negate the efficacy of the standard to produce a record that is compatible with records produced under the same standard but in the context of a different file. Consequently, we have seen over the last several years an emphasis on matters relating to the implementation of cataloguing standards that has been as great if not greater than the effort expended on the development of the standards themselves. Even a cursory glance at the implementation of AACR2 will reveal a great panoply of mechanisms external to the rules themselves designed to support uniform application of the rules and compatibility of records originating from different sources. The national bibliographic agencies of Britain, Australia, Canada, and the United States—the ABACUS group—began long before day one of AACR2 implementation to coordinate their decisions on options and alternative rules within the new code. This effort was required at least in part because the reconciliation of differences between British and North American practice had not been fully realized in the rules themselves. Nominally AACR2 represented a single code: there were no longer separate British and North American texts. But through options and alternative rules the code provided opportunity not only to continue many of the divergent practices of the past, but to increase their number to legion proportions.

To forestall that, and to complete the unfinished business of reconciliation, the ABACUS libraries have engaged themselves in several rounds of coordinating decisions on options and alternatives and have progressively narrowed the differences that separated them. Similar efforts have been made to standardize the application of rules through the development and promulgation of rule interpretations, again on both a national and international level through coordination among the ABACUS libraries. Other mechanisms, such as division of jurisdictional responsibility for name authorities and cooperative file building have been implemented on an increasingly large scale, particularly in North America through programs such as CONSER, NACO, and the National Coordinated Cataloging Program.

All this effort to ensure standardized application of cataloguing rules appears to have had a residual effect on the rules themselves. There has been a tendency, where options are concerned, to move progressively toward the acceptance of options that minimize the potential for the scope and content of existing files to impact the formulation of headings. Increasingly the favored options are those that anticipate conflict rather than those that are contingent on actual conflict. There is a similar trend in rule revision to rewrite rules so as to minimize the impact of existing files on decisions affecting the form and structure of new headings. Through refinement and revision many rules are becoming increasingly restrictive and designed quite clearly to lend themselves more readily to uniform application. What we are seeing in the evolution of cataloguing rules is the logical extension of efforts to realize the economic benefits of shared cataloguing and of measures to neutralize as far as possible those factors that can run counter to achieving compatibility of records.

Application of Computer Technology

The application of computer technology to the cataloguing process has brought with it increasingly exacting demands for precision and logic in the recording of bibliographic data. Twenty years ago, in the context of the technology reflected in the card catalogue the major constraint on the catalogue record was the 3 × 5 format of the card itself. As long as the catalogue record was formatted within those overall dimensions there were no physical impediments to its inclusion in any card catalogue of standard design. The layout of the record on the face of the card was not of critical importance. Granted, the more or less uniform placement of elements such as the call number and the heading under which the card was to be filed would facilitate easy use of the catalogue by both patrons and library staff. But we have all seen and used card catalogues that accommodated a wide variety of peculiarities in the formatting and placement of call numbers, underlining of filing elements placed elsewhere than at the head of the record, corner-marking, etc., without seriously degrading the useability of the catalogue. The card catalogue and the manual processes involved in its maintenance also exhibited a relatively high tolerance for deviation from literal and logical norms within the catalogue. Typographical errors or inconsistencies in headings could be silently corrected in the process of filing the card; added entries that did not match exactly the corresponding main entry on the card to which they were related could nevertheless be placed in their proper sequence in the file; dashed entries inscrutably found their proper place adjacent to their parent record; and of course sno-paque and lining out served to mask thousands of faults.

With the advent of the machine-readable catalogue record and computerized processes for record matching, filing, and indexing, the level of tolerance for variations in format and for literal and logical inconsistencies within the catalogue was radically diminished. The parsing of a unit record into its constituent parts, which had been reflected in a general but less than precise way in the card layout, was done in much more exacting terms as analysis was undertaken for the development of a structure and scheme of content designation for the machine-readable cataloging (MARC) formats. Once the machine-readable formats began to be standardized and to converge around a reasonably consistent norm, the standards for the cataloguing data themselves began to reflect the same kind of precision in the demarcation of constituent elements within the record, most notably with the development of a scheme of prescribed punctuation for the first of the ISBDs and its incorporation into the Anglo-American and other national cataloguing codes. The parallels between the ISBDs and machine-readable record formats run much deeper of course than the correspondence between content designators and prescribed punctuation might suggest: underlying both the record format and the standard description is a more or less congruent formal structure based on an analysis of the catalogue record into a hierarchy of constituent parts, represented as fields and subfields in the format or as areas and elements in the description.

Historically, the analysis of record structures and data elements began with an exclusive focus on records for printed monographs and serials: the first MARC formats, the first ISBDs, and the first revisions to the AACR1 incorporating the ISBD provisions all followed the same sequence, addressing printed monographs first and shortly thereafter printed serials. Developments in that first phase served to meet the immediate demands of the new technology by bringing a sufficient degree of logical analysis and standardization to bear on the catalogue record to facilitate its adaptation to a computerized environment. It was not long after, however, that the technological imperative began to force a second wave in the standardization process, one which was characterized by what might be called a horizontal rather than vertical focus.

In the earlier phase the analysis had been centered on a record structure that was specific to the type of material being described: printed monographs in the first instance, serials in the second. Although there were naturally many parallels between the two, those parallels emerged more as a result of the common ground from which the two had evolved than from any deliberate effort at logical consistency. There were in fact in the early drafts of both the formats and the ISBDs instances of fairly obvious and significant inconsistencies between records for monographs and serials that would not likely have occurred if the analysis and development of specifications had not been so specifically focused on the type of material.

The pressures of technology soon brought about a redirection of focus and initiated a wave of horizontal standardization. Ironically, the first move in this new direction was taken not in the direct context of machine-readable record formats but in the cataloguing rules themselves. As the authors of the second edition of AACR began their work in the mid-1970s, they were quick to recognize that the very characteristics of computer technology that had demanded precision in the analysis of record structures for monographs and serials would bring a demand for a consistent record structure across material-specific formats, especially as databases began to integrate records for items in various media and as approaches to the development of application software became increasingly modular and highly structured. Recognizing the need for what I have called a horizontal approach to the standardization of record structures, the Joint Steering Committee for Revision of AACR took the lead in proposing the development of a General International Standard Bibliographic Description [ISBD(G), 1977] that would serve as a framework for the description of all types of material: print and nonprint, monographic and serial, published and manuscript. The immediate objective of the Joint Steering Committee (JSC) was to establish a consistent base for the development of the various chapters on description in the new Anglo-American code. But inasmuch as they had adopted as principle the objective of conformance with international standards for bibliographic description, specifically as reflected in the ISBD(M) 1974, they had a vested interest in ensuring that their own work on the description of materials of other types and formats would be consistent with parallel work being done at the international level within IFLA. Hence the initiative on the JSC's part to establish the structural framework for bibliographic description as an international standard. The result of that initiative was the development of the ISBD(G) and an agreement between the JSC and the IFLA that the general framework would be adhered to both in the AACR2 rules for description and in all the ISBDs.

The ISBD(G) has on the whole proven to be an effective underpinning for the standardization of bibliographic description. For a full decade the framework has been subjected to the scrutiny associated with the development, harmonization, and revision of ISBDs for monographs, serials, cartographic and nonbook materials, printed music, antiquarian books, and most recently, computer files. It has survived intact under the formulation at an even more detailed level of a whole set of rules covering an even wider range of materials in AACR2. And it has stood the test of application in literally millions of catalogue records produced at the national and local level worldwide. The standards and cataloguing rules based on the ISBD(G) have undergone a number of revisions at the level of detailed specification; extensions have been made within the parameters set by the framework to accommodate a wide range of newly emerging media; and adaptations have been introduced to facilitate the recording of data from a broad range of scripts and linguistic conventions. But throughout this continuing process of incremental refinement at the detailed level, the structure imbedded in the framework has proven sufficiently flexible to accommodate the necessary changes in detail without requiring any major change itself.

A parallel to the horizontal standardization initiated with the ISBD(G) and the formulation of a consistently structured body of rules for description of various types of material in AACR2 can be seen in the arena of machine-readable formats as well. The major thrust in that arena, in fact, came closely on the heels of the publication of AACR2 with a thoroughgoing review of the various MARC formats aimed at minimizing irregularities and inconsistencies between formats and reflecting more faithfully the structural parallels that informed the new cataloguing rules. With varying degrees of success, the concept of horizontal integration was extended beyond those portions of the format that encompass the elements of bibliographic description to other elements in the MARC record as well, particularly those comprising the so-called "fixed fields." The net result was a significant increase in compatibility between the various material-specific formats that has gone a long way toward supporting and facilitating the kind of file integration and structuring of application software originally envisioned by the authors of AACR2 when they first conceived the ISBD(G).

While there have been significant differences both in approach and in results between the early phase of vertical focus and the later horizontal focus in bibliographic standardization, it is essential to note that both have operated basically on the same plane. That is, the analysis of bibliographic data thus far, regardless of whether it has centered on the description of a specific type of material or whether it has attempted to draw parallels between descriptions of various types, has to a very large extent confined itself to the formal structures of the conventional catalogue entry. The ISBDs, AACR2, and the MARC formats have all taken as their starting point the traditional unit entry; they have analyzed its constituent parts more from the perspective of form than of function; they have developed a kind of taxonomy of the unit entry and have marshaled into a reasonably uniform structure many previously existing anomalies within and between various types of entry. But they have not to any significant degree carried the analysis of bibliographic data beyond that formal plane.

We are now beginning to see new developments in computer technology and the analytical methodologies associated with it that are likely to bring new pressures to bear on the formal structures that have been developed for bibliographic data over the last two decades, and as a consequence we may expect to see yet another new direction emerge in the standardization of descriptive cataloguing. Gradually the flat-file, unit-record approach that has dominated the design of bibliographic databases for the last 20 years is giving way to the technology of the relational database and analytical theories of data modeling incorporating such concepts as the third normal form and canonical synthesis. The differences between the conventional form of analysis that we have seen reflected in the MARC formats and these newer data analysis techniques are analogous to the differences in the field of linguistics between the traditional approach to prescriptive grammar that we all labored under as schoolchildren and the more recent theories of descriptive grammar as reflected in concepts such as Chomsky's deep structure in language. These newer approaches to data analysis penetrate the formal structures embodied in the conventional catalogue entry and other similar user views to identify the basic entities for which one compiles data, to map attributes to their associated entities, and to define relationships between entities. Applying these modeling techniques one derives sets that consist not of elements such as main entry, added entry, imprint, collation, etc., but rather of entities such as work, item, piece, author, etc. The taxonomy of uniform title, descriptive title, dependent title, etc., gives way to the logical mapping of attributes such as titles to the related entities of work, item, etc. The net result is a level of analysis that is qualitatively different from that we have been accustomed to and a rigorous precision that leaves little room for ambiguity or nebulous definition of the relationships between entity and attribute or between one entity and another.

Within this new context formal structures such as those embodied in the ISBD(G) will be subjected to intensive scrutiny of quite a different order than that we have seen in the past: questions of adaptability and consistency of form will yield to questions pertaining to entity/attribute relationships and consistency of logic. One will have to deal with the anomalies of a material-specific area that throws together in more or less haphazard form attributes of physical entities (i.e., of the publication medium) with those intrinsically related to the intellectual entity (i.e., of the work itself, independent of its physical carrier). Logical anomalies pertaining to the so-called general and specific material designations and to their coded counterparts in the fixed fields of the MARC formats will also be brought to the fore. At a deeper level, such analysis is likely to expose the logical problems inherent in the ambivalent stance of our conventional formal structures vis-à-vis the object of bibliographic description and to force an examination of issues pertaining to the description of materials transcribed from print to special formats for the visually handicapped or reproduced in microform, etc., in quite a different light.

My reason for highlighting these inconsistencies is not to reopen debate on the issues that underlie them, but simply to point up the fact that the structures we have developed to date are not altogether compatible with the logical models that are likely to emerge with the application of the newer methodologies of data analysis associated with the design of normalized and relational databases. The impediments posed by those incompatibilities may not be so severe as to precipitate a radical redesign of our formal structures for the representation of bibliographic data, our conventional user views, but I would suggest that as the data models emerging from the analytical design of state-of-the-art bibliographic databases begin to converge in a more or less uniform logical pattern there will be a steadily increasing pressure to revisit the formal structures and align them more closely with the logic of the data models.

The signs of change are already with us. The revamping of the AACR2 rules for the description of machine-readable files and the development of a new ISBD for computer files has brought to the fore the whole issue of physical versus intellectual entity attributes and their relative positions in the formal structure of the bibliographic description. The effort to extend the MARC formats to accommodate serials in nonprint form and multimedia items have stumbled against the inconsistent grouping of attributes related variously to intellectual form, physical medium, and publication type. And the interrelated questions of original versus reproduction and multiple carriers for the same intellectual entity, despite the pro tem stance on microform reproductions, are still very much with us and are being viewed from a new perspective as efforts are

IV

Main Entry

Underlying most cataloging codes is the concept of main entry. In the past, the main entry has been seen as essential to the performance of the collocating, ordering, and citing functions of the catalog. Today, however, with the advent of online catalogs, the need for the main entry is being questioned. Why, it is asked, in a computer environment where all access points are equal, is there a need to distinguish any one of them as primary or main? To those who want a main-entry-free code, the preface of AACR2 offers an apology. The framers of the code say they did not have time to deliberate on the considerable implications of an alternative entry or main-entry-free code (AACR2). They advise those who wished to develop catalogs not based on the main-entry concept that AACR2 might be adapted to that purpose.

It has been suggested that AACR2 is "the last main entry set of cataloging rules" (Gorman, 1980, p. 46). Can this be true? An answer to the question requires that the considerable implications of abandoning the main entry be explored. Among such implications are the following: If the main entry were to be abandoned, what would replace its role in the construction of uniform headings? What would take its place in structuring displays in online catalogs? How would abandoning the main entry affect single-entry and minimal-level catalogs?

Two chapters address the implications of a main-entry-free code, one by demonstrating an actual working main-entry-free code and the other by disentangling the several different meanings that attach to the concept of main entry. The first of the two chapters, "The Japanese No Main-Entry Code," is by Tadayoshi Takawashi, Associate Professor at the Shizuoka Prefectural University Junior College in Hamamatsu,

Shizuoka, Japan. Takawashi explains that Japanese cataloging practice uses two codes, the Nippon Cataloging Rules and AACR2, the former for materials written in Japanese, the latter for materials written in other languages. The Nippon Cataloging Rules, introduced in 1977, is a main-entry-free code. Its origins can be found in the Description Independent System (DIS) proposed 22 years earlier by Mori (1955). In the DIS, a unit card composed of a description and as many traced headings as are needed is used to create multiple entries. Mori argued that in such a system there is no need to designate an author or title or subject card as main, since all cards contain the same information. A point to note is that this argument for a main-entry-free code does not make any reference to computerization.

Takawashi continues by addressing some of the objections posed to a main-entry-free code. The objection that call-number formulation is thwarted in a system without main entry he counters by observing that the first of the traced headings for a book can be used in the construction of the book's book number. The objection that main entries are needed for single-entry catalogs he meets by suggesting that single-entry catalogs might be designed so that records, ordered by record number, are accessed by author, title, and subject indexes.

In 1983 work began on a new Japanese main-entry-free cataloging code. Designed to be in conformity with the ISBDs and UNIMARC, it has an additional feature which, in light of suggestions made in several chapters in this volume, is forward-looking and desirable. This is a concept of bibliographic hierarchy in which the work is taken as the basic unit of description and the physical manifestations of the work are subordinated to it.

Takawashi performs a useful service to Anglo-American cataloging theorists by presenting them with a broad, international perspective and giving them empirical data, derived from a working main-entry-free code, with which to assess some of the implications of abandoning the main-entry concept.

"Main Entry" is the title of the second chapter in this section. Its author, Michael Carpenter, a faculty member at the School of Library and Information Science, Louisiana State University, observes that the conflicting claims over the value of the main entry in online catalogs cannot be rationally assessed until the term *main entry* is unambiguously defined. He then sets about to do just that. *Main entry* can be explicated in terms of its referents or in terms of its functions. Referentially, *main entry* can be defined as a portion of the text of a bibliographic record, as the record itself, or as a search or sorting key. Text portions that have conventionally been designated main entry in the past include the text represented by the heading for a record, the text in the author and/or title fields of a record, and all text in a record needed for complete description of the item in hand. Carpenter finds inadequate definitions of *main entry* that point to text portions on a bibliographic record in that they fail to provide for the role of main entry in retrieval. Similarly, he dismisses as being inappropriate for the design of cataloging rules the definition of *main entry* that refers to the record itself, by which he means the text proper of the bibliographic record enhanced by data such as tracings and the various identifying numbers associated with a book.

Another approach to defining *main entry* is in terms of keys that can be used to search a catalog or to sort records in a display. A promising key for this purpose is one that specifies author/work/edition; Carpenter calls this an *AWE entry*. Such a key, which incidentally itself can be defined as a portion of the text of a bibliographic record, would be particularly useful in performing a main-entry function if it sufficed to uniquely identify bibliographic items at the edition level.

Carpenter then turns to the role of the main entry in fulfilling the objectives of the catalog. Consensus opinion holds that the main entry finds its chief function in providing for collocation of works and editions in display. An obstacle to achieving this function, however, is the ambiguity surrounding the key concepts of *author, work, edition,* and *related work.* Carpenter suggests attempts be made to operationalize the definition of these concepts. He concludes with the suggestion that an AWE-defined main entry might well serve as the sort key by which default displays are arranged in online catalogs.

In unraveling the various meanings of *main entry* and in suggesting a meaning particularly appropriate for the online catalog Carpenter is led to affirm categorically the continued need for a concept of main entry. Thus, he contributes to the literature on descriptive cataloging a position statement on one of the most fundamental concepts underlying the Anglo-American code. It is a position which those seeking to understand the implications of a main-entry-free code are obliged to address.

The Japanese No Main-Entry Code

Tadayoshi Takawashi

The Nippon Cataloging Rules (NCR) is the standard for cataloging in Japan, but the preliminary new edition (NCR, 1977) mainly deals with Japanese books published after the Meiji period, i.e., the mid-nineteenth century. Thus, it is almost impossible to catalog all library materials with NCR, especially materials in foreign languages. The reason Japan needs AACR2 is that most academic libraries have to catalog materials written in languages other than Japanese. Actually, Anglo-American cataloging rules have been used in Japan for about 100 years.

Features of Japanese Materials Cataloging

In Japanese books, the heading and description in a bibliographic record are usually given in *kanji* (Chinese characters). In order to file entries, however, *kana* (the Japanese syllabary) must be written above the kanji headings to provide for filing entries in sequence (see Fig. 1). In other words, both kanji and kana, or romanization, must be used in a double-decker arrangement. However, a heading for an added author may be shown only in the kana or romanized form written above the kanji main-entry heading, with the corresponding name in kanji in the descriptive portion of the record underlined in red. The Japanese are forced to do this since there is usually insufficient space left on the unit card for another set of double-decker headings. Such an added entry card (Fig. 2)

Shiomi, Noboru ...Romanization of main heading
塩見　昇 ...Main heading (in kanji)
　学校図書館と児童図書館　塩見昇 ...Title: School libraries and children's libraries
　間崎ルリ子共著 ...Joint author
　　東京　雄山閣　1976 ...Imprint
　　265p 24cm（日本図書館学講座 5) ...Series (in parenthesis)
　　内容：　学校図書館　塩見昇著 ...Contents
　　児童図書館　間崎ルリ子著 ...(Continued from previous line)
　　1.Masaki, Ruriko 2.Gakko ...1. Romanization of added author heading
toshokan to Jido toshokan ...2. Romanization of title

Figure 1
Author main-entry card.

looks peculiar to users since kana and kanji are usually written parallel to each other, as shown in the case of the main-entry card in Fig. 1. For added author entries, the main-entry heading is not an appropriate second-order filing element, which is the same in the case of Western books.

A Description Independent System

Under the influence of both AACR and the Paris Principles, Japanese catalogers used codes based upon the main-entry principle until 1977, at which time a new code of Nippon Cataloging Rules (NCR, 1977) was compiled. In 1955 Mori had already challenged the main-entry system, advocating a description independent system (DIS), which was later modified and called a description unit card system (DUCS). A DIS is fundamentally the same as a system employing alternative headings (Freedman and Jeffreys, 1967; Jeffreys, 1967).

　Masaki, Ruriko ...Joint author (added entry)
Shiomi, Noboru ...Romanization of main heading
塩見　昇 ...Main heading(in kanji)
　学校図書館と児童図書館　塩見昇
　間崎ルリ子共著 ...Joint author (underlined)
　　東京　雄山閣　1976
　　265p 24cm（日本図書館学講座 5)
　　内容：　学校図書館　塩見昇著
　　児童図書館　間崎ルリ子著
　　1. Masaki, Ruriko 2. Gakko toshokan
to Jido toshokan

Figure 2
Added author entry card.

According to Mori, an essential characteristic of a DIS is that multiple entries for an item are created by reproducing the unit card made for it. He argues that a main entry is meaningless in a DIS catalog when author, title, and subject cards contain the same bibliographic information.

The main features of a DIS are listed as follows.

1. A unit card is composed of a description and tracings. There are no main-entry headings (see Fig. 3). In the tracings are recorded as many headings as are needed. Headings are typed on the upper part of the reproduced unit cards. Cards with author headings are filed in an author catalog, title headings in a title catalog, and subject headings in a subject catalog. In such a system there is no concept of main entry.

2. The formatting of a title main entry on a 3×5 unit card uses a hanging indention and is different from that of an author main entry. In a DIS, where there is no concept of main entry, there is only one formatting required on unit cards. Thus, standardization in the formatting of the description is achieved. Also all headings can be typed at the same indention and standardized.

There are several advantages to a DIS. First, in a DIS a unit card is created without regard to headings, a procedure which is practical, efficient, and even theoretical. Second, there is no need to be distressed any longer in the choice of main entry, the difficulties and contradictions of which are well known (Osborn, 1963).

On the other hand there are some perceived disadvantages to a DIS. First, the main-entry heading is utilized when giving an author or book

学校図書館と児童図書館　塩見昇
間崎ルリ子共著
　東京　雄山閣　1976
　265p 24cm（日本図書館学講座 5）
　第1部：　学校図書館　塩見昇著
　第2部：　児童図書館　間崎ルリ子著
1. Gakko toshokan to Jido
toshokan 2. Shiomi, Noboru.
3. Masaki, Ruriko 4. Gakko toshokan
5. Jido toshokan 6. 017 7. 016.8

...Title: School libraries ...

...4,5.Subject headings
...5,6.Classification marks on NDC

Figure 3
DIS card (unit card).

number to a book, but this cannot be done if no main heading appears on a DIS unit card. This objection can be met by utilizing in the book number the author's name record in the first tracing. Second, it is argued that a DIS is not effective for creating a single-entry catalog. We may suppose, as Mori states (Mori, 1955, p. 199), that the concept of main entry is *only* valuable in a single-entry catalog, such as the NUC. However, in the age of computer catalogs even a union catalog in hard-copy form can support multiple entry. For example, the COM Union Catalog produced by WLN is composed of a register arranged by record number and author, title, and subject indexes. There is no concept of main entry.

The DIS has caused great disputes between those who support it and those who support main-entry systems. Nippon Cataloging Rules 1965, however, adopted the main-entry principle, based upon the Paris Principles. It was not until the 1970s that the Cataloging Committee of the Japan Library Association (JLA) sincerely began to think of adopting the DIS in the compilation of the new NCR.

Code Drafts, NCR 1977, and the New Edition

In 1970, the JLA Cataloging Committee proposed a no heading unit card system (NHUCS), which was a compromise between the main-entry system and the DIS. According to the NHUCS, the descriptive part of a bibliographic record is to be created independently of the headings, and all the headings are to be recorded as tracings, including the "main entry," which is recorded in the first position without numbering (Fig. 4). In short, the proposal attempted to be applicable to both the main-entry system and the DIS.

After several national conferences, the JLA Cataloging Committee compiled and published NCR 1977, based on the no main-entry principle. Instead of recording headings in tracings, as in the NHUCS, a DUCS was adopted in which there is no main-entry heading, not even as a tracing (Fig. 5). NCR 1977 was established as the standard cataloging code in Japan being utilized for both Japan/MARC and the Japanese National Bibliography.

In 1983, a new JLA Cataloging Committee, chaired by Shojiro Maruyama, began to revise the code, which was in only a preliminary edition. The Committee is aiming to compile such rules as will be completely compatible with both the ISBDs and UNIMARC. The Committee published the first draft of the standard edition in 1984, the second in 1985, and the third in 1986. The new edition, NCR 1987, was published in September 1987. This edition also adopts the no main-entry principle, although the name of the entry method changes from DUCS to descriptive

学校図書館と児童図書館　塩見昇　　　　　...Title: School libraries...
間崎ルリ子共著
　　東京　雄山閣　1976
　　265p 24cm （日本図書館学講座 5）
　　第 1 部：　学校図書館　塩見昇著
　　第 2 部：　児童図書館　間崎ルリ子著
Shiomi, Noboru 1. Masaki, Ruriko　　　..."Shiomi, Noboru" is for main heading
2. Gakko toshokan to Jido toshokan
3. Gakko toshokan 4. Jido toshokan
5. 017 6. 016.8

Figure 4
NHUCS card (unit card).

unit system (DUS). Two further features of this edition are worth noting:
its handling of headings and the concept of bibliographic hierarchy.

Headings

Since the adoption of NCR 1977 in Japan, great importance has attached
to the finding list function of the catalog, while the collocation function
has been treated lightly. In addition, the principle of uniform headings for
authors has been adopted, even though the making of uniform titles is not
generally prescribed. Provisions for the choice and form of heading are
simplified. For example, in the assignment of a corporate heading, it is
prescribed to choose the name of the higher body, even though the work
was published by a body subordinate to it. This causes inconvenience,
especially for large libraries. In the new edition of NCR, an option
is provided which allows the addition of a subordinate body to the corpor-

学校図書館と児童図書館　塩見昇　　　　　...Title: School libraries...
間崎ルリ子共著
東京　雄山閣　1976
265p 24cm （日本図書館学講座 5）
　　第 1 部：　学校図書館　塩見昇著
　　第 2 部：　児童図書館　間崎ルリ子著
1. Gakko toshokan to Jido toshokan
al. Shiomi, Noboru a2.Masaki, Ruriko　　...."a" meaning author
s1. 学校図書館(Gakko toshokan)　　　　　..."s" meaning subject
s2. 児童図書館(Jido toshokan)
① 017　②016.8

Figure 5
DUCS card (unit card).

ate heading. Though limited to anonymous classics, sacred scriptures, and musical works, application of uniform titles is also provided as an option.

The Bibliographic Hierarchy

A novel feature of the new edition of NCR, incorporated in preparation for online catalogs, is its provision for bibliographic hierarchy. The concept of bibliographic hierarchy is derived from the *Reference Manual for Machine-Readable Bibliographic Description* (UNIBID, 1981). The provision in question is "mainly devoted to showing how bibliographic data is [sic] organized at different levels in a record" (Maruyama, 1986, p. 29). Integral to the concept of bibliographic hierarchy is that the work, not the physical piece, be taken as the basic unit of description. This is another novel feature of the new NCR, since NCR 1977 views a physical unit as the basis for description.

The concept of bibliographic hierarchy is required in the computerized cataloging age for the purpose of displaying bibliographic information. In a card catalog, the format of input and output is almost the same; therefore, the concept is not necessary. The Committee is still reviewing the concept of bibliographic hierarchy to make it suitable for the forthcoming online catalog.

In the draft of its statement on bibliographic hierarchy issued in January 1987, the Committee defined *bibliographic unit* as "a unit that is defined as a set of data elements belonging to the same bibliographic level and constituting a bibliographic record with or without other units of a different bibliographic level" (Maruyama, 1986, p. 29). The bibliographic hierarchy then is constructed of the following units.

1.1 Basic bibliographic unit
    Monographic bibliographic unit (Fig. 6)
    Serial bibliographic unit

1.2 Collective bibliographic unit (Fig. 7)

1.3 Component part unit (Fig. 8)

2. Physical unit: "a unit that describes a physically independent part of a larger item (Fig. 9).

In case of a physical unit, we have added a numeric or another designation (usually a volume number) for each physical part as an independent bibliographic data element, because, without this designa-

学校図書館と児童図書館 / 塩見昇,　　　…Title: School libraries…
間崎ルリ子共著
東京 ： 雄山閣, 1976
265p. ; 24cm. -- (日本図書館学講座 ; 5)
第1部: 学校図書館 / 塩見昇著
第2部: 児童図書館 / 間崎ルリ子著
t1.Gakko toshokan to Jido toshokan
a1. Shiomi, Noboru. a2. Masaki, Ruriko
s1. 学校図書館(Gakko toshokan)
s2. 児童図書館(Jido toshokan)
① 017　② 016.8

Figure 6
NCR 1987 monographic unit, normal style (unit card).

日本図書館学講座 / 椎名六郎 [ほか] 編
東京 ： 雄山閣, 1975-1978
10冊 ; 24cm
1 ： 図書館概論 / 椎名六郎; 岩猿敏生著
                　.
                　.
                　.
10 ： 図書および図書館史 / 小野泰博著

t1. Nihon toshokangaku koza a1. Shiina, Rokuro
s1. 図書館学(Toshokangaku)　①010.8

Figure 7
NCR 1987, collective level (unit card).

児童図書館 / 間崎ルリ子著. -- (日本図
書館学講座 ; 5 ： 学校図書館と児童
図書館 / 塩見昇, 間崎ルリ子共著.
 -- 東京 ： 雄山閣, 1976. --
265p. ; 24cm. -- 第1部. -- p.155-263)

Figure 8
NCR 1987, analytical level (unit card) (component part unit).

Ｃｏｓｍｏｓ 下 ／ カール・セーガン著 ： 　　…Author:Carl Sagan
木村繁訳　　　　　　　　　　　　　　 … 下 meaning "No.2 of two":Translator
東京 ： 朝日新聞社, 1980　　　 …Tokyo: Asahi Newspaper Co., 1980
383p. ; 20cm

t1. Kosumosu a1. Sagan, Carl a2. Kimura, Shigeru

Figure 9
NCR 1987, physical level (unit card).

tion, we would not be able to identify each physical part of the larger item.

The physical unit is used in the following cases: (1) to show publishing information on a multivolume publication within a given period; (2) to show a physical part of a host document containing a component part; and (3) to show holdings for local housekeeping and for reporting to union catalogs'' (*ibid.*).

Acknowledgment

I would like to express great gratitude to Mr. Tsutomu Shihota and Mr. Zensei Oshiro for helping with this chapter.

Main Entry

Michael Carpenter

> If there is confusion in the term or in the use of the term *entry,*
> it is because we do use that term in different senses.
> —Lubetzky, 1979, p. 19.

Main entry, so the story goes, has no place in an online catalog. Instead, main entry has been replaced by retrieval of records through any of a number of equal access points, free text search, and combinations of terms selected from data fields within a record. Even so, some writers state that the abandonment of main entry leads to an important loss in the catalog, that of the ability to bring together the editions of the works of an author, along with other works related to them. One cannot tell which viewpoint is correct, for it is far from clear that the term *main entry* is used in an unambiguous sense.

To make matters worse, several types of catalog display are often confused when the role of main entry in library catalogs is discussed, making for puzzles about the correct application of the term *main entry*; not all types of catalogs require main entry, and some catalog displays do not use a main entry in the same way others do. Through a description of the various referential definitions of main entry, a discussion of the functions of main entry, and a treatment of online catalog displays, many puzzles about the application of the term will be solved. In the end, when viewed as a catalog display containing the elements of author (or originator), name of a work, and details specific to an edition, main entry will be seen to be (1) completely consonant with at least one type of online catalog, and (2) suitable as a device to bring together the editions of a work, the works of an author, and related works.

Definitions of *Main Entry*

Most discussions of main entry have been concerned with the functions of main entry rather than what main entry is. That is, most writers have been concerned with functional rather than referential definitions.[1] Before the role of main entry in an online catalog can be considered, it is best to have an idea of what main entry is. As it turns out, the literature is sparse; most of what is available is found in the glossaries attached to cataloging codes. A transcription of most of the key glossary definitions is attached in an appendix to this chapter. Outside of the glossary definitions, catalogers are prone to speak of main entry in print and in conversation in ways not wholly consistent with the glossary definitions. Some of these ways are summarized in the discussion below.

The main uses of the term *main entry* can be captured in the following five categories.

1. Portions of the text of the record of a bibliographic entity

2. The record of a bibliographic entity

3. Search keys in a bibliographic record

4. Primary keys in a bibliograhic record

5. Sort keys in bibliographic records

Portions of the Text of the Record of a Bibliographical Entity   Main entry is often seen as a portion of the text of a bibliographical record. The portion of text may range from the heading alone of the base record to the full text of that record. As the text varies in length, so do the functions ascribed to it. For convenience in presentation, it will be assumed that a normal bibliographical record, be it on a catalog card or in the MARC format, is being examined.

Main Entry as the Heading of a Bibliographical Record   The leading line on a catalog card that has not yet had added entries prepared for it or the equivalent contents of a MARC record (a field in the 100s, or by default, the 245 field) is often considered the main entry, or if one is speaking reflectively, the main-entry heading. Because it is often not clear in common speech among catalogers whether one is thinking of the main entry or the main-entry heading when speaking of the heading as the main entry, it should be noted that the same uncertainty is mirrored in at least two definitions from glossaries of cataloging codes.[2] The definitions of main entry in the glossaries for the 1949 and 1967 codes state that one of the referents of the term is the heading under which the complete catalog record is represented. The other referent is the record itself. It is not entirely clear whether it is the main-entry heading or the main entry that is ultimately described in the glossary and, in turn, discussed in the rules.

One possible consequence of considering main entry to be the author heading for a base record is that main entry can do little more than assemble the works of an author or a literary unit. Because there is no normalization of titles for those works whose titles vary from manifestation to manifestation, bibliographical units are assembled on a chance basis alone.[3] Before uniform titles were first employed on a wholesale scale in the 1920s for musical works, uniform titles were rarely provided for materials entered under author or originating body. Failure to provide uniform titles still pervades many catalogs. The only assembling device has generally been some sort of author heading, so main entry without assembly of the bibliograpical units of an author is often the rule.

If there is no reason besides custom to choose any one heading as the main entry in catalogs such as those just described, one might just as well use the title proper as a main entry of sorts. Advocates of title main entry, or title unit entry, are quite correct in asserting its ease of use; one doesn't have to cogitate about complex rules for deciding on main entry when the title proper becomes the preferred entry.[4] Nevertheless their viewpoint is based on a restricted definition of main entry and a similarly restricted view of the nature of the catalog.[5] Title unit main entry does not assemble the editions of a work, and the tasks of the catalog have been restricted so as to delete that of showing which editions of a work are available; as noted above, many library catalogs have in fact failed to assemble editions of works or bibliographical units. This crude approach to title main entry does not provide for the use of uniform titles when there are multiple editions of a single work represented in the catalog. One important change in the functions of main entry occurs when titles are used as the sole main-entry headings; an oft-stated function of main entry, that of identifying the principal author, is dropped.

Main Entry as the Combination of the Author and Title Fields of a Bibliographical Record, or in Default of the Author, a Title Field If defining main entry as the heading for a base record leads one to the use of title main entry once the function of indicating principal authorship is dropped, the addition of more text of a record to the author heading, namely the title, can lead one to another definition and set of functions for main entry. The combination of the author and the title of a record can be thought of as the identification of a work. When there is a situation in which the titles of the various editions of a work vary, one of the solutions in traditional catalogs has been the employment of a uniform title. Uniform titles are generally interposed between the author heading and the title proper so as to ensure that the filing element next in importance to the author heading is the uniform title. If there is no author heading, the uniform title still takes precedence in filing arrangements over the title proper, the title as stated on the piece. Sometimes there are qualifications, such as language, version, or date following the title portion of the uniform title. Uniform titles are not always in brackets, located between the author heading and the title proper. Instead, temporary filing titles or corner marks have occasionally been employed as substitutes for uniform titles.[6] Other times, only notes are provided, relating the various titles under which a work has appeared; when in notes, such information does not generally play the role in filing enjoyed by those entries having uniform or filing titles. If information about varying titles were confined to notes, entries for those works would generally not be arranged in such a way as to bring together the various editions of a work even though the information is available.[7]

Depending on whether uniform titles or similar arrangement devices are to be found in a display of bibliographic records, two sets of consequences for a library catalog ensue which we now consider.

1. Where uniform titles are provided, the text of the main entry, in the sense of a combination of author and title fields, consists of the author heading plus the uniform title. If there is no author, there is a uniform title alone. Works, or bibliographical units, are assembled through the use of uniform titles, which is why main entry in the sense of the combination of author heading plus uniform title may be thought of as having the function of naming a work. A catalog in which uniform titles are provided for some bibliographical records may, as a practical matter, not provide them for all. For example, they need not be provided for works appearing in a single manifestation. Yet for such works a uniform title would still be considered to be logically or implicitly present in the record.[8]

In addition to the requirement of the 1949 rules that the main entry provide information sufficient to identify a work,[9] both the 1967 and 1978 versions of AACR require that the main entry be in the form in which the work is to be cited.[10] Whether the citation is internal to the catalog or is instead intended for general use in bibliographical citations is not clear from the way in which the code definitions are written. If the citation is internal to the catalog, then the uniform title need not be made explicit until another manifestation of the work, under a differing title proper, makes its appearance. Since new editions of works carrying new titles may appear with substantial frequency in a large-scale bibliographical database, it will be necessary to revise cataloging entries to include the new uniform titles.[11] If the citation were intended for general use, and I don't think it is, the ambiguity of the AACR phrase "presented in the form by which the entity is to be uniformly identified and cited" notwithstanding, the strangeness of many catalog headings and choices of entry would seem to be counterproductive.[12]

In an effort to alleviate the ambiguity attaching to the use of the term *main entry,* Michael Gorman uses the term *standard citation* to denote the standardized form of the name of a work. Because Gorman does not completely define the term, I am not sure whether a standard citation includes sufficient identification to include a description of the edition (Gorman, 1979). A standard citation appears to fulfill many of the functions performed by uniform titles were uniform titles (usually in conjunction with author headings) applied to all materials.

2. When uniform titles are lacking in a catalog, even in an implicit sense, then it is only by accident that the various editions of a work are assembled. It may be a matter of intrinsic empirical interest how often the title proper alone suffices to identify a work, but the statistics will have no logical relevance to the design of a set of cataloging rules, even if the title proper fulfills the role of the uniform title in the vast majority of cases.

It may be argued that one can construct a substitute for a uniform title or otherwise bring together the various editions of a work using notes as found in a catalog about the bibliographical history of an item. However, two points about the use of this information should be noted. First, if the information is included in the "Notes" fields, then the identification of the two items as being copies of differing editions of the same work has already been made. It is merely the formatting of the information that has to be changed in order to provide a display demonstrating the presence of the multiple editions of the common work. Second, because of the lack of unanimity as to what is an acceptable level of cataloging, the information may often not be provided. One cannot generate identifications on the basis of records too short to include vital information that would permit distinction of the various editions of a work. How lengthy the record must be to be sufficient varies from case to case.

In any case, the editions of a work appearing in multiple manifestations are not explicitly assembled when the titles of varying editions differ. Where main entry consists of the main heading plus title proper, only a partial identification of an edition has been achieved. It is partial because many works appearing in multiple manifestations have common headings and title statements. Therefore editions are not completely identified in such cases; something additional is required to complete the identification. We have identified a necessary but not sufficient element in the bibliographic description of editions in general.

Main Entry as that Portion of the Text Completely Describing the Bibliographical Entity   When all the record except the tracings and record identifiers (record numbers, ISBNs, Library of Congress card numbers, etc.) are taken as the main entry, it is clear that an edition will have been identified as well as can be according to the rules set up in the catalog.[13] In some catalogs, descriptive information can be omitted that is provided in another record, the differences from the primary record alone being made clear. For example, the dashed records of the British Museum *General Catalogue* which specify "another edition" provide elements distinguishing their editions from that described by the primary record. Nevertheless the whole record is implicitly repeated in each main entry. Similar abbreviations in description are found in many printed book catalogs. It is quite possible that a new MARC format could be derived in which editions were made part of the holdings statement for a record identifying a work.

Abbreviated descriptions might be found in catalogs other than those like the British Museum were there a set of rules setting forth a uniform set of necessary and sufficient conditions for the description of editions. The distinguishing characteristics of editions might then be noted after the heading for the uniform title; the uniform title would thus identify both the work represented in the entry as well as its edition. For example, the uniform title might read: "[Author heading.] [Name of work.] [Date and other characteristics distinguishing this edition from others]." The AACR2 rules for entry of the Bible do this to a certain extent. But such a perfect set of rules of description does not appear possible because there is little agreement as to what constitutes an edition. Controversies over what constitute duplicate records indicate that a consensus definition of "edition" is not likely soon. Furthermore, there are wide variations in publishing conventions and title-page terminology; for example, what some rules call a printing is occasionally described on title pages, especially French and Spanish, as an "edition."

The arrangement of the elements of the main entry that is seen as the whole text of the record seems to be relevant to the utility of the record. For example, if a record were arranged so that the collation came first, followed by (say) the price, followed by imprint, the record would lose bibliographical interest for us; our custom of citing materials would make the novel arrangement uninteresting. Usual citation order prescribes an arrangement in the order: author (if any), work (name of the work, such as title), and edition. This arrangement will hereafter be called AWE. The AWE order for bibliographical records does have some bibliographical use as a filing element, if for no other reason than the fact it reflects our customary citation order. The AWE display is occasionally used as a subarrangement; the date of publication might come first, followed by AWE. Arrangements not employing AWE are likely to be generally useless.

In summary, while portions of text of a bibliographical record are used for filing purposes, or as devices for arrangement in a catalog display, they do not provide a description of "main entry" sufficient to match the traditional requirements of what constitutes a main entry. Portions of the text of a catalog record, like headings and partial descriptions, are no longer the devices by which one always retrieves materials in an online catalog, though they can serve to arrange the materials that have been retrieved. Arranging materials is an important function, for what is retrieved together is not always meaningfully arranged or displayed together in the output from an online catalog.

Main Entry as the Record of a Bibliographical Entity   Since the days of the fourth edition of Cutter's rules, there has been substantial unanimity in deeming the main entry in card catalogs to be that entry on which all the tracings have been recorded. Cutter speaks of the tracings being recorded on the main-entry card, a lead followed in the glossary for the 1908 rules. The definition in the 1941 rules speaks in addition of the main entry being a master card. As will be seen from the collection of definitions gathered in the appendix to this chapter, codes up to AACR2 repeat the requirement that the main entry be the complete catalog record of the item cataloged.

There are two kinds of records in a catalog. The first is a logical record, which is composed of a set of fields. The second is the physical record. In card catalogs, it is possible to identify the physical record as the main entry; the logical record and the physical main record are only conceptually distinguishable. In practice they are not distinguished.

In contrast to a card record, the physical location of a record in an online catalog is of no relevance in the design of cataloging rules. If the logical record in an online catalog is the master record, then it is also the main entry per the 1941 definition.[14] Of course, it makes just as much or as little sense to call the MARC record a main entry as it does to call the record in a single-entry catalog a main entry.

Search Keys in a Bibliographical Record   Search keys, roughly speaking, are fields, portions of fields, or combinations thereof in bibliographic records that can be employed as access to a record or group of records.[15] Examples of fields in bibliographic records are headings, title statements, statements of responsibility, etc. These fields are given numerical names in the MARC format such as 110 and 245.

It has been claimed that it is better to discuss permitted access strategies, or search keys, rather than entries in the environment of the online catalog (Wilson, 1983). If "entry" is defined as a means or point of access to a particular record, then the claim is correct. In this sense, "entry" might be equated with (say) "OCLC search key" because a search key is also a means of access to a record.

"Entry" has sometimes meant more than a means of access to a record. When the word *entry* is employed in the term *main entry,* it has, as noted earlier, also stood for the citation of a bibliographical record. When used in the term *added entry* it could also stand for an alternate means of citation or identification for the same bibliographical entity. It would not be legitimate to infer that an OCLC search key can become a means for identifying a bibliographical entity; entry as search key is clearly different from entry as citation of a bibliographical record. Part of the difficulty appears to originate in the ambiguity of entry in denoting (1) a record, (2) the act of entering a catalog to find a record, and (3) the act of making a record for a file.[16] A search key becomes an entry *to* a record in a file; it is not an entry (record) *in* a file.

There is a further problem connected with the use of *entry* to denote *search key.* In so-called single-entry catalogs, the sole search key becomes not so much the *main* entry as the *only* entry for the record. The search key affects the very purposes to which the file can be put. This means that the key must be designed so that the one most likely to be used under the circumstances is selected. For example, for interlibrary loan purposes, given the lack of uniformity in citations, especially to editions of works whose titles vary, entry under author appears to be preferred. For those libraries still maintaining an in-process file on cards, there is a certain attraction to entry under title as given on the piece, just because the searcher is likely to have the physical copy of the book at the time search is being made of the file. The disability from which single-entry files suffer is that they often have to serve conflicting demands and have only one means of meeting all of them. As in all situations involving conflicting demands, the best or optimal solution is not necessarily good for every purpose. Specifically, the filing order selected for a given file answers only some of the demands placed on it. It is the best catalog available under the circumstances, yet it is still a poor substitute for a multiple-entry catalog.

Primary Keys in a Bibliographical Record   Often in conversations about main entry it will be claimed that, with respect to some types of catalog, the identifying part of a record, such as a record number (OCLC Record Number, Library of Congress Card Number, etc.), can be treated as the main entry for the record. The number uniquely identifies the record and its presence is associated with the record which contains the tracings and/or permitted access points. If the claim is taken seriously, a catalog could be organized by record numbers. It would contain a register of full records and an index of entries that refer either to the record number or to a combination of a short form of the record with the record number.[17] One can find the full record only by looking in the register.

In his discussion of database structures, Dagobert Soergel provides an example of a structure characterized by a main file giving full records for the main entities, with "one or more index files providing different avenues for access" or an index-register file (Soergel, 1985, p. 196). As Soergel says, this structure is common to many bibliographical retrieval systems such as abstracting services. It does not appear to be characteristic of most library catalogs. The main file of the retrieval system is sorted by the *primary key,* which is the identifying name for the main entity. The primary key might be an accession number, a call number, or some other identifier; it is generally not the AWE display. On the other hand, in a library card catalog, the primary key is generally the main entry, while in a shelflist it is the call number.

In his discussion of primary keys Soergel indicates that the primary key may be an arbitrary element of the main listing. What counts is that the primary key provides a unique identification of the record. How much of the record is required to form a unique identifier for the record? The author heading alone is clearly not sufficient. Nor is the combination of the author and title proper. However, the combination of the author, work, and edition would be sufficient to qualify as a primary key. On the other hand, a record identification number may also be a primary key. Until the purpose of a catalog has been determined, we have no primary keys, only candidate keys.

Evidently, bibliographical records generally have multiple candidate keys, e.g., the call number, ISBN, ISSN, OCLC or other network, or LC card numbers, in addition to that portion of the text identifying the item being cataloged. Primary keys can be composed of combinations of fields. Unique combinations of fields, or candidate keys, in addition to those just mentioned, could include the set mentioned earlier of the collation, price, and place of publication. Which of these candidate keys will make the best primary key? A primary key of interest to a bibliographic searcher or library catalog user would be the AWE text.

In any discussion of the optimal primary key, one consideration is that in an online catalog the transition from an access point or search key to display of the record is usually transparent. If the primary key is numerical, the search as it proceeds from the search key through the record number, or primary key, to the record itself, is not visible. All a user sees, or should be required to see, is the appearance in some form of the record. The niceties of database structure are probably not relevant in a discussion of optimal primary keys, unless the user is made to see the transition through the key. In some catalogs, both printed and online, the user is made aware of the transition by being compelled to request the item number before the record appears. In order to keep this double look-up from happening, short records, containing, say, author-title information in addition to the identification number of the full record, are often provided as an aid to the user. If a user finds merely a collection of record identification numbers under a given heading, he or she may well abandon the search even for a known item for lack of time to follow through on all the identification numbers.

When main entry is defined solely as the primary key and no further definition of the primary key is available, it would appear that the main entry has no essentially bibliographical function. It does not necessarily provide a description of the item underlying the record. If *main entry* is not defined in any other way than the identifier, or name, in a manner of speaking, of a record, it can be synonymous with *primary key*. It has no bibliographical interest because it can be something other than AWE. On the other hand, when the primary key is defined as the combination of those attributes sufficient to identify an item on the edition level (AWE), then there is a possibility of duplicate records in a file, a possibility that can be avoided only through carefully constructed cataloging rules that provide entries sufficiently well defined to permit easy identification of duplicates. Then the holdings of duplicate records can be merged and one or more records suppressed.[18]

Sort Keys in Bibliographical Records   It is frequently claimed that one of the advantages of main entry is its use as a tool for arrangement and subarrangement of entries. The assumption behind this is that main entry is a device for filing, pure and simple, in short, a sort key.

A sort key is a string that can be used as an ordering device for positioning a given record in a file. Some sort keys are used as primary sort keys, while others are used for subarrangement, as secondary sort keys. Further levels of subarrangement are possible with tertiary, quaternary, etc., sort keys. AWE displays can function as three levels of sort key. In a catalog, card or online, there could be display of materials under a given subject heading. The subject heading would be the first-level, or primary, sort key. The second level would be the author or emanator (A), the third-level sort key the work name (W), and the fourth-level sort key the edition information (E). If the work were anonymous, so that the only two elements of the display were W and E, W would be the second-level sort key and E the third.

Not all sort keys are visible. Until recently, many cataloging codes as well as filing codes had procedures for filing "as if" the component parts of a heading or filing element were arranged differently than they appeared to the user of the catalog.[19] Criticism abounded of these rulings in the library literature of the 1940s and 1950s. Writers would claim that "file as if" procedures were excessively complex; filers would have difficulty in interpreting the filing code. Yet problems always emerged from the mechanical or so-called strictly alphabetical filing codes; although cards could be filed easily, the entries could not be readily found by users who had grown accustomed to so-called classified arrangements. A classified arrangement is evident in some sets of filing rules for the arrangement of the collected works of an author; in a classified arrangement, the collected works would appear at the head of the file, followed by selected works, and finally by individual works alphabetically arranged. Some problems undoubtedly had to do with a failure to integrate heading structure with filing codes; the placement of "Sir" in a heading prior to the forename, even though the "Sir" is ignored in the filing arrangement, is an example of a failure to integrate heading structure with filing arrangements. Other problems originated with the fact that a classified order of filing was usually easier to use than an alphabetical one.

Instructions to file "as if" are essentially instructions to file by a hidden sort key. The visible sort key, the main entry as displayed, is not the arranging element; some other text or key is used for arrangement. Because the main entry, as constructed, is not always used as an arranging device, it seems safe to claim that not all main entries are used as sort keys.

Take another example. Thanks to a change in cataloging rules, or perhaps some slight change in the bibliographical conditions of a certain publication, the first through third editions of the publication have been cataloged with main entry under an issuing body. The fourth edition, let us say, has been cataloged under title, with only an added entry for the corporate body. Using a heading, whether main or added, possessed by the records of all editions of the publication as a search key, we can retrieve the records for all four editions. Yet if other records intervene and the printout is single entry, not an uncommon state of affairs with the usual online catalog, the various editions of the work have been dispersed. A dramatic instance of a similar situation can be found in the records for the annual institute of the Graduate Library School of the University of Chicago. Some are entered under the name of the editor, some under the title, some under the heading for the institute, and others under the heading for the school. Clearly they can all be retrieved together, but they will not be displayed together if their main-entry headings are used as the arranging device. If main entries are used as sort keys, a certain amount of predictability in their content is required, or else there must be some sort of facility for readjusting all main entries to follow a certain pattern, a facility available at the time the display is generated.

Summary   The various uses of the term *main entry* are not necessarily mutually exclusive. If main entry is defined as that portion of the text of a record sufficient to identify an edition, it can also serve as a primary key.

The main-entry heading of a record can serve as a search key; it often does. Conversely, in a catalog of any substantial size, the heading cannot be a primary key because it is not unique to a single record. To state that the entire record could be a primary key would make the catalog unwieldy to use. The selection of an appropriate definition of main entry rests substantially on the function of main entry.

Functions of Main Entry

If main entry is to have any function, it must be in the context of fulfilling an objective of a catalog. Seymour Lubetzky's formulation of the objectives of a catalog was canonized in the "Statement of Principles" adopted by the International Conference on Cataloguing Principles at Paris in 1961. In short, the function of the catalog is to be an "efficient instrument for ascertaining . . . whether the library contains a particular book specified" by its author, title, or substitute therefor, as well as for ascertaining which works of a particular author and which editions of a given work are available (International Conference on Cataloguing Principles, 1963, p. 91: "Statement of Principles" paragraph 2–2.1). To carry out these functions the principles require that at least one entry be made for each book cataloged, and if required, more than one entry. Multiple entries are required when the author has more than one form of name and when the work contained in the book is known by more than one title.

The *Paris Principles* do not mention the assembling of the various editions of a work in multiple manifestations in one place, under main entry. Because of objections raised by some of the conference participants, the assembling function of main entry was deleted (International Conference on Cataloguing Principles, 1963, p. 33–34). Lubetzky had originally stated that the second function of the catalog is

> to relate and display together the editions which a library has of a given work and the works it has of a given author. (Lubetzky, 1960, p. ix).

The function of assembling the editions of a work and the works of an author in a display is carried out by means of the main entry.

Other functions of main entry of historical interest are as follows:

1. Naming a work (dealt with above as that portion of text which provides a uniform title)

2. Providing credit to the principal author[20]

3. Providing the only full entry (this has been dealt with above)

4. Being the entry to which all others refer (irrelevant in an online catalog)

For the purposes of this chapter, the discussion of the functions of main entry will be confined to the one for which there has been an international consensus. The following assertion is offered as a summary of that consensus.

The function of main entry is to display together the various editions of a work, the works of an author, and works related to one another in a catalog.

The possible loss of this function in a main-entry-free catalog was pointed out at the beginning of this chapter.

Because the physical location of records is irrelevant in the database of an online catalog, we shall confine ourselves to a discussion of the display of catalog output. Because of the limitations of space, we cannot discuss the ambiguities of "author," "work," "edition," and "related" other than to provide a few examples. In general, suffice it to say that insofar as the component parts of the function of main entry are ill defined, the function itself is ill defined.

"Author" is ill defined; an author with multiple pseudonyms often constructs several *oeuvres* for his pseudonyms. Should the catalog bring together the various works comprising an *oeuvre* or should it assemble the works of the author as a natural person? There has been division on this point in the provisions of many cataloging codes.[21]

"Work" and "edition" have an ill-defined boundary. Should Chapman's Homer be considered a translation of Homer or a work in its own right? Sometimes the case is unclear; one of the purposes of cataloging codes is to prescribe rules to enable us to make consistent decisions. For example, the *Prussian Instructions* treat Ulfila's Gothic translation of the Bible as an independent work rather than as a translation of the Bible Ministerium, 1915, p. 32, section 43).[22] On the other hand, AACR2 would treat the translation as a version of the Bible.

When concepts are vague and one must operationalize definitions, two choices are generally open. The first choice is to stipulate definitions of the concepts, noting that the stipulated definitions do not fully capture the concept, and compose a set of cataloging rules. The second choice is to seek a wholly new analysis.

Traditional cataloging codes have taken the route of stipulating definitions. The purpose of rules is to help the cataloger distinguish cases that will be treated as, say, instances of separate authorship from those that will not. As codes have been revised, so too have the stipulative definitions. Sometimes code revision has been accomplished through the imposition of policies by a given library rather than formally for the profession at large.[23]

The path of one new analysis can be taken by first noting that catalogers have in practice behaved differently from what a cataloging code prescribes. Patrick Wilson, a proponent of the new analysis, claims that catalogers do not in fact examine the authorship of materials they are cataloging. Instead, he notes that catalogers are simply recording names found on the piece in hand (Wilson, 1983). Stipulative definitions of authorship in a cataloging code are beside the point. In rebuttal, it may be noted that the new analysis does not appear to explain how catalogers delude themselves into thinking they are examining the authorship of an item to be cataloged.

Because of the problem connected with the new analysis, and given the new possibilities of catalog display opened up by the online catalog, it may be preferable to stipulate definitions that fit the concepts underlying all types of catalogs generally better than just older types of catalog. Accordingly, the function of main entry as an assembling device will be examined to see how it works with the various types of catalog display now at least conceptually available. In that way the role of main entry in an online catalog can best be evaluated.

Main Entry in an Online Environment

The role of main entry in an online environment varies from catalog to catalog. Since the creation of a taxonomy of catalogs must await another occasion, I shall limit my discussion of the role of main entry in the online environment to one particular type of catalog. The catalog I am envisioning represents an evolutionary advance over that conceived by Gorman in his 1979 paper.[24]

There may be several forms of name for a given person or corporate body in a catalog. Traditionally, one particular form of name has been chosen as the standard for establishment, or authorized use, in the catalog. References were to be created for the other forms of the name to the one that was chosen for use in the file. Similarly, for those works having varying titles in their several manifestations, a particular form of name was established as the uniform heading, with references of some sort to that uniform title. The uniform title may have been invariably cited in combination with a uniform heading for the work's author or originator. Together the heading and title formed the uniform means of identifying and citing the item being cataloged. Thus we have one of the traditional conceptions of main entry. The form of citation of headings is fixed or established in the traditional catalog.

What happens if the form of heading is not static or fixed? We could have a catalog in which the user would select the form of name being used in the AWE display. No one of the variant forms of name would be established; they would all refer to a common nexus, the particular author, or the particular work. No one heading would be selected as the standard citation.

Let us take an example. In 1955 and 1959 the two volumes of a history of library classification were published. The citation in the original language reads as follows:

Е. И. Шамурин, Очерки по истории библиотечно-библиографической классификации

The first of the two editions of a 2-volume translation into German was issued by VEB Bibliographisches Institut Leipzig in 1964 and 1967, while the second was issued by Verlag Dokumentation München-Pullach in 1964 and 1968; the title pages (recto and verso), the dates of the second volume, and the bindings appear to be the only differences between the two editions. The title leaves of the München-Pullach edition are cancellans leaves. On the title page of the translations, the author's name is given as E. I. Šamurin. On page v of the first volume, the author's name is given as Evgenij Ivanovič Šamurin, Jewgeni Iwanowitsch Schamurin, as well as the form on the title page.[25] On the Library of Congress record for the book, the name in the main entry heading is "Shamurin, Evgenii Ivanovich." These three forms of the author's last name stem, of course, from the varying schemes of transliteration used. In a catalog using the Roman alphabet, it seems reasonable that a user might approach the catalog with any of the forms of the author's names just given. In a display in which the relative location of entries is determined by the beginning combinations of letters, the arrangement of entries will be substantially different for each form of the name.[26]

The writer composed other works of interest to theoreticians of cataloging. In that capacity we would like to retrieve the records for them and have those records displayed together in a predictable location on a large printout. Given the widely differing forms of name, the best form of name for our purposes is the one under which we made our original request, rather than a form established as standard by a code of rules and a code of transliteration whose details are not clear to us as users.

With respect to the name of the work, the above remarks apply *mutatis mutandis*. The first word of the title might be transliterated as

Ocherki, Očerki, or Otscherki, with substantial variations for the title in a filing arrangement. Additionally, the title proper of the German translation, *Geschichte der bibliothekarisch-bibliographischen Klassifikation,* might be used as the name of the work, with references from the Russian forms. However, in the type of catalog envisioned here, any of the three transliterations or the German title could equally be used as a uniform title for the work. For a library holding both the German translation and the Russian original, one might have an arrangement of entries under a heading for the author and the uniform title in German. The German-language uniform title for the Russian original would be qualified with a term indicating that the language was the Russian original. It must be remembered that the uniform title could be any of the variant names of the work.

What are the common elements in a main entry in a catalog capable of accessing any one of a particular set of variant forms of name for heading? For reasons of citation order, if no other, we would still have the AWE display. There is no established form for the A or W parts of the display when variant names exist. Standard or uniform means of citation are gone. Even so, the function of main entry survives in AWE display; the editions of a work, the works of an author, and related works are all brought together through AWE display. One form of name is used in the display, but it is the name under which the search is made.

Even though variant forms of name may be equipotent in AWE display, one may question if any particular element has to be the A part of the display. Traditionally, one of the tasks of cataloging rules is to determine which of several claimants to a principal position in a bibliographical record is placed in that position. In card catalog terms, the question is which entity is to be given main entry. A traditional catalog requires that no more than one name be associated with a work name.[27] The group of the variant forms of name for a given author or work will be linked together into what Gorman calls a package (Gorman, 1979). There will also be links between work packages and author packages.[28] Links between work and author packages could be classified, and only particular forms of links need be sought in bibliographical displays. For example, one may call up displays of the records only for those works in which a person is listed as editor. The editor would form the A part of the display, even if the work contained chiefly the writings of another. The link between the author and work packages would be different than the one in which the only allowable authors were the writers of the work.

Turning to the question of multiple pseudonyms, one may wish to call up only those works ascribed to a particular author using a certain pseudonym. Or it may be desired to call up all those materials related to Chapman's translation of Homer rather than to Homer in general.

Conversely, one may wish to generate a display of all works of the author who has multiple pseudonyms. Given that various classes of links are possible, it is possible to deal with the vagueness inherent in the concepts "author," "work," and "edition." Stipulative definitions can now be prepared which will capture the ambiguities inherent in the concepts. A study of the nature of the classes of links must await another occasion.

Most online catalogs do not have the capabilities just described. The vast majority rely on a fixed or established form of name for both the A and the W parts of the display. They generally require that elements from the established headings be used in searching. Only a few catalogs will permit access from a referred-from form of name and then provide information about the established heading. In these catalogs, main entry is more than mere AWE display. It is still the uniform means of identification of a bibliographical entity and, within the catalog, the standard citation for the item.

For the catalog just described authority work is performed; the various names of an entity must be brought together. The only difference between the catalog being described here and older types is that no one particular candidate heading is established as the authoritative or standard heading. Catalogers must add information to the file; this added information might be called Cataloger Information Added, or CIA. The identification of the various forms of Shamurin's name as being variant forms of the same name is an example of CIA. The identification of varying manifestations of the same work as being instances or editions of the same work is another example of CIA.

The implications for the MARC formats of the type of catalog display described here are two. The first is that the bifurcation between the MARC formats for bibliographical data and the MARC format for authority data must be overcome for the linking process to work; there must be some sort of link of authority record numbers (the identifier of an author package as described above) and the names found in the headings for bibliographic records.

Since the catalog envisaged here would be capable of changing default displays, it would always be possible to have an AWE display arranged by, say, personal names only, or title only. What would be constant is the identification of the material represented completely down to its edition statement. Citation order or AWE would thus represent not a record storage format, but a display format.

The recent rule revision providing for the use of multiple headings for authors whose various *oeuvres* are entered under a series of multiple pseudonyms indicates that the provision of multiple access under various forms of an author's name is now being accepted ("Joint Steering Committee," 1987).[29]

Conclusion

The justification for citation order (author-title, and/or title alone) as a default display is to be found in our cultural traditions. Just a look at a bibliography arranged by titles alone, such as that found in Hamdy's book, will demonstrate what happens if traditions are violated; it becomes very difficult to find materials of interest (Hamdy, 1973, p. 145–155). Of course, a bibliography of citations is a sort of single-entry listing. This tradition is ancient indeed, going back as it does at least to the library of Ashurbanipal (Wendel, 1949, p. 2–7). And as we see, even with the computer, matters have stayed the same, with only some slight variation. We can now physically separate various phenomena that were only logically distinguishable earlier. Discussions about main entry have changed focus from records to useful displays; we can be sure that they will continue.

Does main entry have a place in the online catalog? Properly defined, it does. If not, and if nothing else fulfills its function, then an online catalog either meets new objectives or fails to meet our expectations.

Appendix: Definitions of Main Entry

The definitions of main entry prominent in the English-speaking tradition from 1904 are summarized below. Most of the definitions are extracted from glossaries attached to cataloging codes.

Although there are no definitions of the term in the first (Cutter, 1876) and second (Cutter, 1889) editions of his rules, Cutter does define main entry in the fourth (1904) edition in the following way:

> the full or principal entry; usually the author entry.

> In Full it consists of the author's name, the title and the imprint. In a printed catalog it is distinguished from the added entries by having the *full* contents, which may be abridged or omitted in the subject entry, and all the bibliographical notes, most of which are left out in the added entry.

> In a printed-card catalog the entries are of course all alike. Main entry in that case means the one on which is given, often on the back of the card, but sometimes by checks on the face, a list of all the other entries of the book (author, title, subject, reference, and analytical). (Cutter, 1904, p. 21)

(The middle paragraph of the definition is reminiscent of Cutter's earlier definitions of "entry" in a printed catalog. Entry for Cutter refers to a single entry in a catalog, a dictionary catalog being an interfiled combination of several catalogs.)

The 1908 rules follow the first and third paragraphs of Cutter's definition almost word for word (Catalog Rules, 1908, p. xv).

The 1941 preliminary code says that main entry is

A full catalog entry, usually the author entry, giving all the information necessary to the complete identification of a work ["work" is not defined in the glossary]. This entry bears also the tracing of all the other headings under which the work in question is entered in the catalog.

The main entry, used as a master card, may bear in addition the tracing of related references and a record of other pertinent official data concerning the work. (American Library Association, 1941, p. xxvi)

The 1943 *A. L. A. Glossary of Library Terms* (p. 85) repeats the 1941 wording.

The 1949 rules state that main entry is

1. The basic catalog card, usually the author entry, giving all the information necessary to the complete identification of a work. This entry bears also the tracing of all the other headings under which the work in question is entered in the catalog. It may bear in addition the tracing of related references and a record of other pertinent official data concerning the work.

2. The entry chosen for this main card, whether it be a personal or corporate name, the title of an anonymous work, a collection, composite work, periodical or serial, or a uniform title. (ALA Cataloging Rules 1949, p. 232)

Ranganathan states in his *Heading and Canons* that main entry is the

Specific entry giving maximum information about a whole document. All other entries, specific or general, relating to the document in question, are derived from the main entry.

. . . In a dictionary catalogue, main entry begins with the name of the author of the book or a substitute for it, or the title in the case of an anonymous book and periodical publication. In other words, it is a word-entry.

. . . In a classified catalogue, main entry begins with call number in the case of a book, and a class number in the case of a periodical publication. (Ranganathan 1955, 48–49)

The last paragraph is reminiscent of Cutter's definition of "entry" in multiple catalogs. Ranganathan then proceeds to analyze main entry into the successive sections of Leading Section (usually the author statement), Title Section, Note Section, Collation and Imprint, Location Section, Call number, and Accession number. Nothing is mentioned about the tracings (Ranganathan, 1955, p. 50–51).

In the "Statement of Principles" adopted at the International Conference on Cataloguing Principles, Paris, 1961, the following is stated with respect to main entry:

4.1 One entry for each book—the *main entry*—must be a full entry, giving all the particulars necessary for identifying the book. Other entries may be either *added entries* (i.e., additional entries, based on the main entry and repeating under other headings information given in it) or *references* (which direct the reader to another place in the catalogue).

6.1 The *main entry* for works entered under authors' names should normally be made under a *uniform heading*. The main entry for works entered under the title may be *either* under title as printed in the book with an added entry under a uniform title, *or* under a uniform title, with added entries or references under the other titles. . . . (International Conference on Cataloguing Principles, 1963)

In Section 7, it appears that the uniform heading should reflect the title most commonly accepted for a work appearing in multiple editions.

Main entry is defined as follows in AACR1 (1967):

1. The complete catalog record of a bibliographical entity, presented in the form by which the entity is to be uniformly identified and cited. The main entry normally includes the tracing of all other headings under which the record is to be represented in the catalog.

2. The heading under which such a record is represented in the catalog or, if there is no heading, the title. (p. 345)

In his *Online Public Access Catalogs*, Charles R. Hildreth defines main entry as follows:

In traditional cataloging practices, the fullest description of a work to be entered in a card catalog. The main entry point is usually the author, and this entry (card) includes all the other headings under which the work is entered in the catalog. Obsolete in online bibliographic database searching where many equal access or entry points are provided for one record. (Hildreth, 1982, p. 234)

Finally, the glossary to AACR2 (1978), provides the following definition:

The complete catalogue record of an item, presented in the form which the entity is to be uniformly identified and cited. The main entry may include the tracings of all other headings under which the record is to be represented in the catalogue. (p. 567)

Notes

1. Freedman (1983) contains a summary of the ways in which Panizzi, Jewett, Cutter, and Lubetzky perceived the functions of main entry.

2. Baughman and Svenonius (1984, p. 5) contains an awareness of the ambiguity associated with the definition of main entry as a heading when there is an attempt to bind "main entry" to "heading."

3. Examples of works whose titles vary from manifestation to manifestation include translations, revised editions appearing under a new title, and works with a common text appearing under differing titles in differing countries.

4. Because of the lack of a stable definition in the literature, we shall assume that title unit entry and title main entry (when not used as a default for author-title main entry) both refer to the same thing, namely the use of some title as the beginning text in a bibliographic record or master card in a catalog.

5. Hamdy (1973) contains the most cogently argued case for title main entry I have seen.
   The background for Hamdy's theory goes back at least as far as Mortimer Taube's catalog of technical reports for the Science and Technology Project in the Library of Congress in the 1940s. Taube realized that the heading chosen for main entry need only be a matter of policy. Although Taube chose to use corporate main entry, he could have used title main entry just as well. Cataloging codes descending from the practices codified by Taube, e.g., the COSATI standard, do use a form of title main entry in printed catalogs.

It is still possible to assemble bibliographical units if provision is made for uniform titles. Since his collection of technical reports did not contain many works appearing in multiple manifestations, Taube did not find it necessary to assemble bibliographical units (works) in his catalog. Hamdy makes few provisions for uniform titles even though Hamdy's paradigm of a library, a research library, does contain works appearing in multiple manifestations.

Tate (1980) does provide for some uniform titles, specifically for parts of the Bible, in her presentation of a case for title main entry.

6. Library of Congress practice for years was to create so-called filing titles in the form of typed corner marks. Corner marks were visible in the Library of Congress main and official card catalogs only, and not in the printed versions thereof, although they were implicit in the filing arrangements used in the massive book-form catalogs of LC printed cards.

7. Practice in AACR2 is not to provide uniform titles for revised editions of works where the revision carries a title different than the original. Although it might be assumed that the editors of AACR2 deemed varying titles for revised editions of work to be evidence that the new editions were in fact new works, such assumptions cannot be absolutely assured because of the lack of rationales provided in AACR2.

8. It might be claimed that the title proper is the uniform title by default. For a work appearing in a single manifestation, the title proper would fulfill the function of the uniform title. But in those cass where the title proper varies from edition to edition of a work, the title proper has a different function than that of the uniform title.

9. See the first part of the glossary definition for *main entry*: "The basic catalog card . . . giving all the information necessary to the complete identification of the work' "

10. See the glossary definitions presented in the appendix.

11. Practicing catalogers often say that uniform titles are difficult to formulate. With the notable exception of serial titles, the uniform title will consist of little more than the title proper. It is only when there is actual bibliographical complexity that the formulation of uniform titles is difficult.

12. But see AACR2's rule 0.5, which says in part, "the concept of main entry is considered to be useful . . . in promoting the standardization of bibliographic citation."

13. Items such as the LC card number, ISBN, record header, and LC call number are not of themselves descriptions of an edition, even though they may in some sense be said to identify or name it. These indicia alone do not provide a meaningful description of a book or an edition. They can act as names; they are not descriptions.

14. In some online catalogs, using relational databases, the record may be decomposed into its component parts. Yet bibliographically important pieces are reassembled in the display. On the other hand, the decomposed record can generally be recompiled into a record suitable for the communications format. The recompiled record would be the master or single record here.

15. A frequently used search key is to use the first few characters of the author or main-entry heading in combination with the first few characters of the title; a variation on this is used in OCLC. The fields may or may not be unique to the record, with the result that a group of records will be retrieved. One can also search a file by various identifiers such as price or acquisition date. Search on such fields is not bibliographically interesting. It does not relate to the functions of a catalog, which are, more or less roughly, to provide an instrument for informing the user of a catalog what books or works a library has on a given subject or by a given author.

16. The following dictionary definition of *entry* will demonstrate the ambiguities:

      entry. . . . 1: the act of entering: ENTRANCE 2: the right or privilege of entering: ENTREE 3: a place of entrance; as a: VESTIBULE, PASSAGE b: DOOR, GATE 4a: the act of making or entering a record b: something entered: as (1): a record or notation of an occurrence, transaction, proceeding (2): a descriptive record (as in a card catalog or an index) (3): HEADWORD (4): a headword with its definition or identification (5): VOCABULARY ENTRY 5: a person, thing or group entered in a contest. (*Webster's New Collegiate Dictionary,* 1979 ed. s.v. "entry" 378)

17. See Crestadoro (1856). Crestadoro uses a complete transcription only once and that is in the numerical register. Entries under various headings in the index are made to numerical entries. A modified version of this procedure has been adopted for the microfiche version of the *National Union Catalog.*

18. Hunstad (1986) contains a discussion of the use of ISBNs and LC card numbers as criteria for the merging of duplicate records. These numbers are not reliable indicators of duplicate records, because there is often no one-to-one correspondence between catalog entries and materials bearing the numbers.

19. Cutter's rules have sections on arrangement incorporated into the cataloging rules. Codes such as the 1908 and more recent codes have generally not included filing rules. Instead, many codes of filing rules were published. Up through the late 1960s, most filing codes contained significant amounts of "file as if" instructions. Since 1970 most codes have emphasized filing arrangements based on the actual wording of the heading.

20. Cf. Tait (1969). Tait summarizes Rule 3A of AACR1 by saying that it assigns principal responsibility for the item being cataloged.

21. See, for example, the varying treatment in the provisions of AACR1 (works brought together under a single heading, per rule 42) and AACR2 (names linked by references per rule 22.2C3, and since January 1987, an added entry is provided under the heading for the writer's real name).

22. The main entry is "ULFILAS Gothische Bibelübersetzung" with a reference from "BIBLIA [goth.]."

23. The role of national library rule interpretations and policies is not to be underestimated. The imposition of a policy of limited cataloging by the Library of Congress in the early 1950s seems to have led to a change in the nature of cataloging and library catalogs. The boundaries between cataloging policy, cataloging rule interpretation, and cataloging rule revision are likely to remain vague.

24. It is not clear who should receive credit for the following conception of an online catalog. Certainly, conversations with Michael Gorman have had their share of input. So have conversations with other catalogers. I believe it is an idea that is "in the air." While Gorman has had much to do with the ideas adumbrated here, he should not be criticized for the errors in my presentation.

25. The title page of the second volume of the Leipzig edition has the háček ("hook") over the "a" rather than the initial "S," thus, Sămurin. This error might seem of little significance were it not for the fact that the title page transliteration is based on the Czech alphabet: Czech dictionaries treat "š" as a different letter than "s," words beginning with the modified letter filing after all entries beginning with the unmodified letter.

26. Cataloging tradition has it that the fastest growing part of the average library catalog is that portion where the headings begin with the letter "S."

27. There might be no name associated with the work; the display would have to be W (work name or title) followed by E (information specific to the edition).

28. The links discussed here are not necessarily those characteristic of hierarchical databases. By "link" is meant a pointer or some device relating two entities.

29. According to this article, "JSC approved the Australian proposal for a change in rule 22.2C, so that certain authors will have multiple headings in the catalog, when multiple names are used and one of these names is a pseudonym."

Added June 1988: See Abbay (1987) for an account of the development of AACR2 rule 22.2C2.

V

The Impact of Technology on Code Design

One of the guidelines purported to be followed in the design of AACR2 was that "particular attention [should be paid] to developments in the machine processing of bibliographic records" (AACR2, p. vii). There are those, including several authors in this volume, who have questioned whether the code is really geared to take advantage of machine capabilities. As was noted in the introduction to Part IV, a frequent charge is that the code has failed in this respect in remaining a main-entry code. Other aspects of the code that have been subject to question on the grounds of technological adaptation are access and display. In card catalogs, access and display are both tied to a single linear ordering of bibliographic records. Online catalogs, however, permit a variety of alternative orderings and nonlinear modes of access. How to build into online catalogs enhanced possibilities for access and display and how these possibilities will affect code design are perhaps the most central questions posed by technology's potential. But there is another side to technology as well and that concerns its potential negative impact. An example of a case where the impact of the computer seems quite the reverse of what seems desirable—where the tail (the computer) wags the dog (the code)—is the rule to transcribe uniform titles without articles (LCRI 25.3A). Code design is affected not only by code designers but by system designers.

Consequently, the danger exists that computer ease will be put before user convenience. There is the further danger that code designers and systems designers will be unable to coordinate their work, causing decisions to be made at cross purposes and like situations to be handled differently. An example of the latter is the 240 field for uniform titles, which by the code is not recognized as an access point but which, nevertheless, is indexed in some online catalogs. Possibly neither group sees the full picture: systems designers may be unschooled in the conceptual foundations of the code and code designers may not clearly understand machine capabilities.

Two authors consider the impact of technology on code design. One looks at technology in relation to the general principles which have guided code design in the past; the other looks at technology from the point of view of its impact in providing enhanced access to bibliographic information. Both chapters touch on the question of the validity of AACR2 in the online environment.

The first chapter, entitled "The Impact of Technology on Cataloging Rules," is by Helen F. Schmierer, Bibliographic Database Coordinator in the Systems Office at the University of Chicago Libraries and ALA Representative to the Joint Steering Committee for the Revision of AACR. Concerns about the continued appropriateness of AACR2 can be approached in different ways. Schmierer's approach is to take the past as a guidepost to the future, her assumption being that only by understanding the past will we be able to look into the future and see what will stay the same and what will change.

In an historical review Schmierer demonstrates how present-day bibliographic practices in the Anglo-American world are a product of industrialization and technology. She describes a tradition, which while employing various technologies in catalog construction, including handwritten slips, typed cards, printed cards, printed book catalogs, microform catalogs, and machine-readable catalogs, has nevertheless pursued a steady course toward conceptual systematization. Schmierer's theme throughout is a reiteration of Panizzi's convictions about the integrity of bibliographic records and catalog structure. She allows that technology can affect catalogs in minor ways. For instance a difference between manual and online catalogs is that in the former storage and display are identical, but in the latter they are not. Another effect of technology is that it accelerates the drive toward standardization and the mass production of bibliographic records. One recent effect of technology on code design can be seen in the AACR2 adaptation of rules for form of entry to the file-as-is algorithm. But technology cannot have a significant impact upon catalogs in the sense that it cannot alter principles. It cannot, therefore, affect the conceptual foundations of cataloging.

Technology can, however, beguile. Schmierer questions Gorman's declaration that the main entry is "an idea that has been overtaken by technology" (Gorman, 1980, p. 46). She also questions the wisdom of providing keyword access to bibliographic data, suggesting that it could produce bewildering results. She then observes that we may be tempted to believe that the way the computer stores data is the most productive way to think about bibliographic data; but the consequence of this may be that we lose sight of what we want to do with the data. It is not technology she warns but practice, by the way it dictates the collection and manipulation of data, that unwittingly alters and even undermines the fundamental principles that ensure the integrity of the catalog.

Schmierer's view of a catalog that maintains its essential identity through time represents a definite position on the central question addressed in this volume, *viz.*, whether changes in technology call for changes in the conceptual foundations of cataloging. It is a view that construes a particular and lofty meaning to the bibliographic practice of cataloging. It is also a view that is challenged by other writers in this volume.

The second chapter on the impact of technology on code design is by John Duke, Head of Bibliographic Services at Virginia Commonwealth University. In his chapter, "Access and Automation," he tackles directly the problem of how to exploit computer technology in the design of rules for access. He begins by observing that keyword search strategies, which make enriched access possible, have the effect of blurring the distinction between description and access. In a manual environment the only windows to a bibliographic record are the headings, titles, or other information, e.g., call numbers, under which a copy of the record is filed; but in an automated environment the entire record is transparent, enabling it to be viewed from a number of different windows. But questions arise here. Is our code to be designed for the automated environment alone? Is it necessary to have two different codes for the two different environments? Duke's answer to these questions is no: the economics of shared cataloging dictates that there be only one cataloging code and, therefore, that code must be designed to produce bibliographic records that fit into either environment.

Given the possibilities of enriched access together with the important constraint that one code must serve in different environments, how are bibliographic records to be structured? This is the design question Duke addresses next. He proposes a tripartite record structure, consisting of (1) a document surrogate, (2) a document guide, and (3) a document text. The document surrogate he characterizes as being rather like a present-day bibliographic record, incorporating the usual data elements needed in bibliographic description as well as conventional access points.

The document guide extends the bibliographic description by incorporating enhanced data, such as contents notes and summary notes. The document text goes beyond description to incorporate the described object itself in the database, i.e., the full text of the document. The advantage of a tripartite structure like this is that it permits successive levels of access to be adopted optionally. A code that embodies such a structure would be independent of any particular kind of catalog; at the same time it would serve to define minimal conditions for necessary and sufficient access to bibliographic records.

Duke then considers the question of controlled versus uncontrolled access to bibliographic records. While recognizing that the second objective of the catalog requires authority control, he suggests that perhaps something less than universal authority control might be acceptable. In particular, he suggests that access to the portions of the document records enriched by document guides be limited to keyword access. While this represents a compromise, it is one that could be justified by the provision of additional access, for instance analytic access, which would contribute not only to fulfilling the second objective but also Cutter's often ignored third objective, "to assist in the choice of a book."

Duke's constructive proposal is a very positive contribution to this volume on the conceptual foundations of descriptive cataloging. In depicting what is possible by way of enhanced access he gives our imagination the stuff it needs to address an important aspect of the question of the implications of technology for code design.

The Impact of Technology on Cataloging Rules

Helen F. Schmierer

As a social institution, the library is inevitably affected by the conditions of the community. Libraries, their users and their staffs, have for so long been affected by technology that much of its contribution to our successes is accepted unacknowledged, although in our failures we are often prey to, and wonder at, its powers. The contemporary American library is a product of industrialization and technology—first and foremost, of course, the technology of printing, but also those of finance, manufacturing and mass production, transportation and distribution, communication, and data processing. Working in today's American library, possibly in air-conditioned comfort and probably in the midst of typewriters, photocopiers, microforms, and computer terminals, it is staggering to be reminded 'twas not ever thus. Forty years ago the electric fan, the typewriter, and perhaps the mimeograph were the obvious machinery in libraries. Such products of technology as the typewriter and air-control systems were only becoming regular fixtures in industry at the turn of the century and likely were not found in many libraries.

Although the history of libraries may be said to extend from the third millennium B.C. and rooms of clay tablets in the temple of Nippur (*Encyclopaedia Britannica,* 1976), the creation of book lists from a Sumerian tablet dated 2000 B.C. (Strout, 1956, p. 255), and the formulation of cataloging instructions from Trefler's work in 1560 (Strout, 1956, p.

263), the Anglo-American ideas of the library catalog and catalog construction are generally viewed as following from the early nineteenth-century activities of Antonio Panizzi at the British Museum. Among the inquiries into the management of the British Museum undertaken in 1836 by a Select Committee of the House of Commons was an investigation into the state of the Library's catalog and cataloging.

In 1837 when Panizzi was appointed Keeper of Printed Books at the British Museum, he fell heir to a trustee order of 1833 that a catalog of the Library should be published. The work on the creation of the catalog was underway but proceeding without much coordination. Initially, Panizzi was not permitted to devise cataloging rules for the enterprise; subsequently,

> With the help of his assistants J. Winter Jones, Thomas Watts, Edward Edwards, and John Parry, . . . [Panizzi] compiled the rules and presented them to a Committee of Trustees where they were discussed, amended, and then approved in July 13, 1839.

> The Trustees also ordered Panizzi to complete the catalog by the end of 1844. Under pressure, he did produce Volume A in 1841 in which the 91 Rules were published for the first time. (Brault, 1972, p. 3)

Reading the 91 *Rules for the Compilation of the Catalogue* (Rules, 1841) without reference to the Trustee hearings, one comes to appreciate the nature and content of Panizzi's envisioned library catalog: an alphabetical catalog (e.g., Rule II), with entries carefully chosen and formulated (e.g., Rules III–LIII) augmented by references (e.g., Rules LIV–LXVIII). Consider these 91 *Rules* for a moment, not as a description of a catalog and its construction, but from the point of view of technology; the 91 *Rules* are notable for the first of their number that reads: "I. TITLES to be written on slips, uniform in size" (Rules, 1841, p. v).

This inaugural rule speaks to the use of a particular mechanism for creating the physical catalog. The 90 rules that follow make obvious that Panizzi was a man with a mission. His standards were such that being ". . . dissatisfied with the inadequacies of . . . [the first volume of the catalog published in 1841], he persuaded the Trustees to suspend their order for printing until the entire catalog could be completed in manuscript form" (Brault, 1972, p. 3).

The delay in publication of the *Catalogue* was not without its critics, and Panizzi's persuasion of the Trustees was realized only after lengthy engagement. A series of communications and miscommunications passed between the Trustees and Panizzi over the matter of the *Catalogue* and its publication, and in the early 1840s the Trustees considered more than one resolution to resume publication (Miller, 1967, p. 123–151). As Miller reports, "At last, on November 27, 1847, Panizzi's moment of triumph came." At a meeting of the Sub-Committee, a Trustee proposed that

> . . . Panizzi "be directed to proceed with the utmost dispatch in the compilation of a full and complete catalogue, in manuscript, of the books in his custody, in such a manner as may appear to him most consistent with correctness and accuracy and adhering, as closely as the circumstances will permit him, to the rules laid down and approved by the Trustees on the 19th July 1839." This, and a subsquent motion that Panizzi should inform the Trustees of any means by which the completion of the catalogue might be speeded up, were passed . . . .

> A fortnight later these two resolutions were put to a general meeting and carried. Panizzi had won. (Miller, 1967, p. 147)

In that same year, 1847, once again the management of the British Museum was subject to an inquiry; this second investigation continuing into 1849 was conducted by Commissioners Appointed to Inquire into the Constitution and Government of the British Museum (Brault, 1972, p. 3). Also, once again, the British Museum's cataloging rules and catalog were the object of commentary. While the testimony of these hearings as it bears upon the content of the 91 *Rules* remains instructive to this day, the forces impelling the discussion from 1836 onward arose not from fascination with cataloging per se, but from the collision between Panizzi's envisioned catalog and the Trustees' mandate for its printed, mass distribution. Had Panizzi's convictions about the integrity and organization of the catalog and the content of its records not been held with such certainty and expressed with such eloquence, the British Museum's catalog begun in 1839 would have been but another example of an inventory listing.

Panizzi's command of the subject of catalog construction is demonstrated in a letter filled with cataloging examples and details written in 1848 to the Earl of Ellesmere, presiding officer of the Commission. Panizzi argues his views:

> My Lord, I beg to call the attention of your Lordship and of the other Commissioners appointed to inquire into the state and management of the British Museum to a subject of the highest importance and not less difficulty—the new Alphabetical Catalogue of the collection of printed books preserved for public use in that institution. (Panizzi, 1848, p. 18)

. . . The question is: What is the best plan of completing in a uniform and consistent manner, within the shortest time, . . . a full and accurate alphabetical catalogue of a collection of printed books for public use, containing not less than 500,000 works, and being the amalgamation of three or four separate large libraries, each of which has a catalogue drawn upon distinct plans, by various hands, at various times. (Panizzi, 1848, p. 19)

I trust, my Lord, that you will agree with me that no catalogue of a large public library, like that respecting which the Royal Commissioners are to inquire, can be called "useful" in the proper sense of the word, but one in which the title[s] are both "accurate," and so "full" as to afford *all* that information respecting the real contents, state, and consequently usefulness of the book which may enable a reader to choose, from among many editions, or many copies, that which may best satisfy his wants. . . . (Panizzi, 1848, p. 21)

By an alphabetical catalogue it is understood that the titles be entered in it under some "headings" alphabetically arranged. Now, inasmuch as in a large library no one can know beforehand the juxtaposition of these headings, and it would be impossible to arrange them in the requisite order, if they cannot be easily shifted, each title is therefore written on separate "slips" of paper . . . , which are frequently changed from one place to another as required. It is self-evident, that if these "slips" . . . be not uniform, both in size or substance, their arrangement will cause mechanical difficulties which take time and trouble to overcome. . . . (Panizzi, 1848, p. 21)

If it be determined to print such a catalogue, it seems to me that it must in the first place be drawn up in manuscript on slips, that the slips must be arranged for press in the precise and exact order and form in which they are to be printed, and lastly, that they be sent to press. . . . [Y]et, my Lord, it has been contended that a catalogue might and ought to be printed as fast as the titles could be got ready in manuscript. Therefore it is that I urge again and again that no alphabetical catalogue can be sent to press until the whole of the titles from A to Z are not only written in a consistent, full, and accurate manner, but until they are consistently and accurately arranged for press. The correctness of the very first entry may depend on that of the last. . . . By beginning to print before, we are certain to bring out a hurried, ill-digested, disgraceful mass of titles of more or less of the works forming a library . . . a mass destined to mislead the public, both by what it contains and by what it omits. (Panizzi, 1848, p. 41)

Once again, Panizzi's vision of the catalog was upheld by the Commissioners, reinforcing the Trustees' 1847 decision, although the "disadvantages, the immense, unmanageable size to which a manuscript catalogue could grow and the very high cost of maintaining it, were, as yet, not apparent" (Miller, 1979, p. 11).

The arguments against untimely publication of a catalog, however, lose their potency when it is possible to publish and distribute singly the records of a catalog, an enterprise undertaken by the Library of Congress (LC) at the turn of the century. The initial impetus for the 1908 *Catalog Rules: Author and Title Entries* was to create ". . . a code of rules which should be in accord with the system governing the compilation of catalog entries at the Library of Congress" (Catalog Rules, 1908, p. viii). The preface to the 1908 rules notes that although the American Library Association (ALA) had published rules in 1883, their compilation and issue had

. . . not, however, prevented considerable divergence in the practice even of libraries organized subsequent to 1883.

Questions of coöperative cataloging continued to engage attention, and coming to the front at the Montreal meeting of June, 1900, finally resulted in definite action by the Association. One of the first matters to be considered by the Publishing Board was the means of introducing more uniformity into the size and style of type, the size and quality of catalog cards, and the rules governing entries. As soon as the agreement had been consummated between the Publishing Board and the Library of Congress whereby the latter was to supply printed cards for current books, beginning, if possible, with January 1, 1901, the appointment of the present Catalog Rules Committee was decided upon. (Catalog Rules, 1908, p. v)

The ALA Catalog Rules Committee was charged

. . . to consider the catalog rules in force—especially the points on which American libraries had hitherto failed to reach an agreement.

Special efforts were to be made to secure agreement between the
rules of the Library of Congress and the new A.L.A. Rules. In
case of disagreement, the variations on the part of the Library
of Congress rules were to be specified. . . . (Catalog Rules,
1908, p. v).

At its initial meeting in March 1901, the ALA Committee first considered
and agreed upon matters related to the application of the printing
technology, viz. typography and layout:

a) The entire heading to be printed in 12-point heavy-faced type,
exceptions being made for titles, explanatory phrases, etc.

b) The author's name or the heading to be printed on a line by
itself.

c) The title to be printed in 12-point.

d) The imprint to be in roman type.

e) Series note to be printed at the end of the collation.

f) For collation, notes, and contents, the largest type that the
32-size card will permit is to be used, and if the 8-point type is the
largest, to use that.

g) The position of the collation and series note to be on a
separate line immediately after the date and preceding other
notes.

h) Notes as a rule to be placed before contents. (Catalog Rules,
1908, p. v–vi)

The agreement to this standard for the presentation of data on a catalog
card is hardly, in the scheme of all things, the equal of the ASTM
Specifications for Hollow Load Bearing Concrete Masonry Units. It is not
uninteresting, however, that typography and layout were the first matters
the Committee addressed, these possibly being the only particulars of LC
cards that the Committee might affect, as LC's card distribution was well
underway by the time the cataloging rules were published.

Also at its first meeting the Committee determined what cataloging
rules would be the basis for further consideration. The results of this
meeting were presented at the ALA Annual Meeting of July 1901 and the

Committee was given ". . . further instructions to continue the work and to cover the whole ground of the catalog rules" (Catalog Rules, 1908, p. vi). The ALA activities, which in 1904 were joined with similar work of the Library Association, produced in 1908 the publication of the first Anglo-American rules.

These rules, the anticipation of their publication, and the product of the powerful cataloging engine they described led as well to the demise of other rules. In the fourth edition of his rules published in 1904, Charles Cutter comments:

> In the last two years a great change has come upon the status of cataloging in the United States. The Library of Congress has begun furnishing its printed catalog cards on such liberal terms that any new library would be very foolish not to make its catalog mainly of them, and the older libraries will find them a valuable assistance in the cataloging of their accessions, not so much because they are cheaper as because in the case of most libraries they are better than the library is likely to make for itself. (Cutter, 1904, p. 5)

In the preface to his rules, Cutter identifies differences between his rules and those of the Library of Congress, urging that libraries accept the LC practices (Cutter, 1904, p. 5–6), an admonition not unexpected from a member of the ALA Catalog Rules Committee, which Cutter was, but curiously poignant advice in a competing compilation of rules.

In the years that followed the 1908 *Rules,* they a mere 61 pages, sans glossary, appendices, and index, the accretion of additional rules was such that when in 1941 only the rules for choice and form of entry were published as a Preliminary American Second Edition (ALA Catalog Rules, 1941) they extended to 371 pages, not counting the glossary, appendices, and index. This and other cataloging conditions of the period were pronounced to be The Crisis in Cataloging (Osborn, 1941) and prompted during the next quarter-century a sustained inquiry into and a recommitment to the objects and principles of the catalog that are generally embodied in the 1967 *Anglo-American Cataloging Rules* (AACR), particularly in the rules for choice and form of entry.

During the period when the creation of AACR was in its final stages, the Library of Congress inaugurated the National Program for Acquisitions and Cataloging (NPAC) that included the Shared Cataloging Program, an enterprise soon to illustrate that a bibliographic record "Made in the U.S.A." could include components elsewhere constructed. NPAC and the Shared Cataloging Program, authorized by the Higher Education Act of 1965, were directed toward the acceleration of LC's nondomestic acquisitions and cataloging, and both projects depended upon a series of arrangements LC made with foreign national libraries and bibliographic agencies. These arrangements included agreement that LC would incorporate into its cataloging records without change the title, edition, imprint, collation, series, and notes from bibliographic records created by such libraries and bibliographic agencies, although LC would adjust main and added entries to agree with cataloging rules used in the United States (Cronin, 1967, p. 40). Thus, it was that the mass distributor of bibliographic data became also a mass consumer.

At the same time that the LC Shared Cataloging Program demonstrated the practicality of utilizing foreign national bibliographic data in LC bibliographic records, the International Federation of Library Associations (IFLA) was assessing the practicability of a similar strategy for cooperation through activities of the IFLA Committee on Uniform Cataloging Rules that was working toward ". . . the establishment of an international standard for the descriptive content of catalogue entries" (IMCE Report, 1970, p. 106). The 1969 International Meeting of Cataloguing Experts, financed by the Council on Library Resources, brought together IFLA, LC, and other parties to discuss cataloging matters of mutual interest. Those assembled considered the potential for an international standard and agreed that ". . . the creation of a framework for bibliographical description that would serve the needs of both catalogues and bibliographies should be possible" and also concluded that such ". . . framework should be designed to accommodate all the descriptive data commonly required not only in catalogues and bibliographies but also in other records used in libraries and elsewhere in the control and handling of books" and that ". . . a fixed order for the main elements of the description was desirable . . ." (IMCE Report, 1970, p. 111–112).

The LC Shared Cataloging Program was the subject of a subsequent session of the 1969 Meeting; a published summary of this session reads in part:

> . . . In giving some account of the operation of the Shared Cataloguing [!] Program, he [Spalding] emphasized the great saving in time and money that had already been made in American libraries; but he drew attention to the dependence of the Program on the co-operation of national bibliographies. . . . The participants agreed that the Shared Cataloging Program had shown that variations in descriptive detail could be accepted and so had encouraged a more flexible attitude among cataloguers towards changes in their own systems, but that greater uniformity was nevertheless desirable, as variations could lead to uncertainty in identification. The Shared Cataloging Program, in making

cataloguers more aware of existing variations, had also increased their willingness to work towards uniformity. It became clear in the course of the discussions that the Shared Cataloging Program and the progress of mechanization were both strong influences favouring the creation of an international standard bibliographical description. All the subjects under consideration by the Meeting were therefore aspects of a single problem: the objective in view was the establishment of an international system of bibliographical communication. In such a system the national bibliographies would have the fundamental role of providing standard descriptions of new publications which could be used both for cataloguing in the libraries of their own countries and for international communication. (IMCE Report, 1970, p. 113–114)

The first of the International Standard Bibliographic Descriptions (ISBD) was published in 1971. The Foreword establishes the ISBD's *bona fides*:

The text now issued, which represents the final recommendations of the Working Group, was preceded by three drafts on which comments were invited from the participants in the Copenhagen Meeting and from many others associated with national bibliographical organizations in all parts of the world. Their comments have been fully taken into account.

and describes ISBD's purpose and scope to be

. . . primarily as an instrument for the international communication of bibliographical information. By specifying the elements which should comprise a bibliographical description and by prescribing the order in which they should be presented and the punctuation by which they should be demarcated, it aims at three objectives: to make records from different sources interchangeable; to facilitate their interpretation across language barriers; and to facilitate the conversion of such records into machine-readable form. (ISBD, 1971, p. iii)

Three years later the "first standard edition" of this document was published. This 1974 text, now called ISBD(M), declares

The ISBD(M) can be regarded as an essential instrument in the implementation of the long term policy of Universal Bibliographic Control, which in its essence was formulated in the following

resolution of the International Meeting of Cataloging Experts . . .
in 1969: "Efforts should be directed towards creating a system for
the international exchange of information by which the standard
bibliographic description of each publication would be established
and distributed by the national agency in the country of origin
. . . The effectiveness of the system would depend upon the
maximum standardization of the form and content of the
bibliographic description." (ISBD(M), 1974, p. vii)

The 1974 edition retains much of the 1971 text, ". . . but a considerable
number of verbal amendments have been made for the sake of clarity and
precision. The new text includes more detail and so leaves less to the
discretion of bibliographic agencies; this meets the wishes of the majority
of those who had made comments, but is a departure from the original
intention of the Working Group to provide a framework without making
detailed rules for its contents" (ISBD(M), 1974, p. viii).

Likewise the "first standard edition, revised" of 1978 retains much
of the 1974 text and reiterates the ISBD's purpose as an international ideal:

> The primary purpose of the ISBD(M) is to aid the international
> communication of bibliographic information. It does this by (i)
> making records from different sources interchangeable, so that
> records produced in one country can be easily accepted in library
> catalogues or other bibliographic lists in any other country; (ii)
> assisting in the interpetation of records across language barriers,
> so that records produced for users of one language can be
> interpreted by users of other languages; and (iii) assisting in the
> conversion of bibliographic records to machine-readable form.
> (ISBD(M), 1978, p. 1)

The 1970s were a fertile decade for the student of catalogs and
cataloging. This period produced the maturation of machine-readable
cataloging (MARC), the second edition of the most widely used cataloging
rules of any time, the *Anglo-American Cataloging Rules,* and four new or
revised ISBDs in addition to ISBD(M): G, the General ISBD (ISBD(G),
1977), S for Serials (ISBD(S), 1977), NBM for Nonbook Materials
(ISBD(NBM), 1977), and CM for Cartographic Materials (ISBD(CM),
1977). From its earliest beginnings, the second edition of AACR, published as the *Anglo-American Cataloguing Rules* (AACR2), was considered as but a continuation of the first, ". . . having the same principles
and underlying objectives as the first edition, and being firmly based on
the achievement of those who created the work, first published in 1967"
(AACR2, 1978, p. v). The second edition sought *inter alia* to reconcile

into a single text the separate North American and British texts of the first edition, to continue conformity with the *Paris Principles* and ISBD(M), to direct particular attention to machine processing of bibliographic records, and to develop further the rules for nonbook materials (AACR2, 1978, p. vi–vii).

Participants in the adventure that produced the second edition can attest that "developments in the machine processing of bibliographic records" (AACR2, 1978, p. vii) were not ignored (although, in fairness, it must be added that what these "developments" were or might be was a matter of individual assessment, not collective agreement). An awareness of machine processing, particularly common computer filing, affects the content of some rules. Nonetheless, the salutary influence of developments in machine processing of bibliographic records upon the second edition of the *Anglo-American Cataloguing Rules* is that these developments did not alter the principles upon which the rules are based.

The rules for description of all types of material follow the ISBD framework. The rules for form of entry accept the file-as-is principle, not only to simplify machine processing but also in the interests of common sense. The rules for form of entry also prefer the predominant form of name, and for corporate names prefer the predominant form even if that form is an acronym or initialism or includes arabic or other numerals, instructing that references lead from spelled-out forms. Similarly, titles are transcribed as found with added entries providing access to spelled-out or numeral forms. In addition, numeric elements in some heading forms are located to take best advantage of common computer filing practices. For example, the order of elements in a conference name is "name, number, date, place" so that numeric information is the primary subfiling element. In music uniform titles, the expression of medium of performance including a number is in the form "medium (number)," e.g., "pianos (2)" rather than "2 pianos."

Now, nearly a decade after the publication of AACR2, many libraries have or are soon to have online catalogs. We know that the records in many, if not all, of these online catalogs are machine-readable renderings of records earlier prepared for library catalogs in book or card form. Let us postulate, then, that these online catalogs have as their objects the finding and gathering functions of the library catalog. And, as with any library catalog, let us grant that the online catalog may be very large, that the statistical probability of any record's being consulted may be quite low although every record in the online catalog must always be available, that each record in the online catalog contains a variety of data elements whose inter- and intrarecord relationships may be very complex, and that those who use the online catalog will come to it with a variety of needs and expectations, not the least of which being that the online catalog will be orderly and intelligible (Cf. Hagler & Simmons, 1982, p. 157).

How might this online catalog be different from its predecessors?

First we must accept that just as previous technologies have their limits, so does computerization. A computer is merely a programmable electronic device that stores, retrieves, and processes data and that has the capacity to perform simple calculations and to follow instructions very rapidly. Two applications of computer processing will affect most online catalogs: the machine's tireless power to search, match, and retrieve, and its speed in reformatting data into large numbers of different displays. The computer's powerful capacity to search is such that any piece of data, no matter how small, be it a character, characters, word, or words, may be an access point and be used as the arranging or subarranging element in a response.

With these capabilities in mind, often the conclusions next reached, *post hoc, ergo propter hoc,* are that because word access is available the cataloging exercise of choosing entries is not required, possibly with the concomitants that the main entry is obsolete and authority work is not necessary. Librarians and users will soon discover in online files of only moderate size that word access, while powerful, produces some bewildering results. The question put by the Earl of Ellesmere in 1849 is wholly appropriate today: "Have you ever heard it proposed that each book should be catalogued under the form of name appearing on the title without any regard to uniformity and without regard to the different forms of name adopted by an author, or arising from the different languages in which works by the same author may be printed?" (Strout, 1956, p. 270).

Choosing headings, establishing their forms, and creating authority data are critical to transforming an amalgamation of records into a catalog. These activities make possible the gathering function, ensure that the works by a given author, on a given subject, or in a given kind of literature are collocated, and also enhance the finding function, enable the location of an item for which the author, title, or subject is known (Cf. Cutter, 1904, p. 12). As long as finding and gathering remain the functions of the library catalog, the selection of entries will continue and the authority work of establishing them and recording information about them, their variations, and their relationship to other headings will persist.

Can the assertion that the main entry is obsolete be refuted? Gorman makes the following case for the demise of the main entry:

> . . . Put at its simplest, in an online catalog, where any access point gives equal access to bibliographic information, what is the point of the main entry? Even in the card catalog that uses alternative heading entries, what is the point of the main entry?

. . . I would like to advance the view that the important functions of the main entry can be carried out in a non-main-entry catalog or data base. In other words, the idea of doing away with main entry rules does not mean that the useful functions that the main entry performs will also be done away with. . . . [T]he notion of doing away with author main entry does not imply replacing it with title main entries. This harmful proposition has obscured much of the argument about main entries.

In my view, what should be proposed, and what fits the emerging realities of the machine-readable cataloging age, is that the catalog record should be viewed as, first, a kernel of standard bibliographic description, based on the physical object, and second, a number of appropriate and equal access points derived by considering the authorship of, and/or responsibility for, the work of which the physical objects are manifestations united by the standard title (or uniform title). In other words, for general purposes, all entries will be main entries. (Gorman, 1980, p. 45–46)

Malinconico maintains that technology has not and cannot overtake the concept of main entry:

The objectives of bibliographic control and the functions to be served by a library catalog exist independently of the medium chose to achieve those objects. . . .

. . . The effects of automation on bibliographic control will be made evident in the formats for machine representation of bibliographic data, and the nature of the system implemented to manipulate those data, not in the codes developed to record and control bibliographic data. Computers will simply make it easier to accommodate principles that can only be developed in isolation from them; they cannot create new principles or modify existing principles. . . . This is not meant to imply that the those principles [articulated by Cutter and refined by Lubetzky] are immutable, only that they exist independently of any technology and hence cannot be modified by changes in technology. (Malinconico, 1980, p. 26–27)

To say that technology cannot change principles does not mean that technology may not have an effect on the catalog. Cataloging rules from Panizzi through the 1967 edition of the *Anglo-American Cataloging Rules* were created with the knowledge that catalogs and catalog records were available and distributed in print. A difference between print technology and computer technology is that in the former information storage and display are identical, while in the latter, in database systems, storage and display are typically not the same. Machine-readable data may be stored in various ways not for the convenience of users but for the convenience of operating systems and protocols or programs that update, retrieve, communicate, or display data, and the storage of data may be changed whenever required or desired. There is great temptation to believe that the way a computer stores data is the most productive way to think about data, a mode of thinking that obscures our responsibility to determine what it is we want to do and what data are necessary to permit our expectations to be met.

Even more alluring temptations are to assume that a group of records called a "catalog" is a "library catalog" constructed according to rules based upon principles and to believe that any group of records will unambiguously permit the objects of the library catalog to be realized. If our cataloging principles—those of Cutter and the *Paris Principles* (International Conference on Cataloguing Principles, 1963)—truly represent what is required and desired, does the fault lie with the rules that do not carry forward these principles? Or, is it the case that practice does not follow the rules and principles?

Why would practice not follow rules and principles? The possibilities are endless: because there is not enough staff to do the work and shortcuts are taken, because the 3×5 card is too small, because the designers and programmers of an online catalog are unaware of or do not appreciate such rules and principles. It is at the point of practice or implementation, however, that a particular technology may work to erode principles. Because many librarians and users are accustomed to only one catalog, that file and the practices it incorporates too often shapes their views and determines their prejudices about what a "catalog" may be. Why, otherwise, should one hear with increasing frequency "The system can't do that," "The terminal doesn't display that field in citation displays," "That field is too long for the computer."

A library, in the most rudimentary definition, is identified as a place in which books, manuscripts, musical scores, pamphlets, periodicals, prints, newspapers, or other literary and artistic materials are kept for use, or as a collection of such items. Libraries assemble collections for the greater good and as collectors and holders of information are decidedly passive compared to census bureaus, insurance agencies, and industries that collect information to control, for example to manage work flows, monitor production, or track the flow of goods. More than the collections themselves, it is the surrogates, catalogs, for these collections that are the focus for library control mechanisms. It is not surprising that the expressions "bibliographic control" and "authority control" have come to describe cataloging activities; these phrases merely acknowledge that libraries are not immune to the Control Revolution and what Beniger perceives as the "expanding economy of information as a means of control" (Beniger, 1986, p. viii).

The catalog rules and codes from Panizzi's day to the present manifest the symptoms of regulations for information control. The rules and codes are directed toward creating catalogs that are predictable, and both the rules and the catalogs they describe are products of bureaucratic organizations. The prefatory statements in the various ISBDs leave no room for doubt that the intent of the ISBD specifications is to maximize the interchange and processability of data by applying objective criteria to determine the content of bibliographic descriptions and by demarcating the elements with prescribed punctuation.

A basic article of belief in the realm of control technology is that in order to increase control two conditions must be met: increase in the capability to process and decrease in the amount of data to be processed (Beniger, 1986, p. 15). Any vision that conceives the library catalog as more than an amalgamation of processable data runs counter to this tenet of control technology, and it is on this point that the tussle is joined between data for control and informed judgment as the basis for catalog organization and construction. The library catalog as envisioned by Panizzi, Cutter, and the *Paris Principles* is not proclaimed a success by virtue of processability. Instead, the library catalog succeeds when it admits not only of locating an item but also of collocating clusters of works by the same author or on the same subject. The library catalog is not a rude inventory of items; it is an organization of records designed to provide access to knowledge.

In our cataloging tradition there has been a steady movement toward systematic catalog construction: first, Panizzi's 91 *Rules* crafted to create consistent treatment of conditions found in collections of one library; later, in Cutter's rules and the 1883 ALA rules development of rules for a broader audience of libraries, those of a nation; in 1908, the codification of rules first undertaken to describe a product, LC cards that because of their wide distribution and subsequent use became, and are to this day, a substantial component of virtually every catalog in the United States; and, in the 1960s and 1970s, the further extension of uniformity to catalogs worldwide through agreement to the *Paris Principles,* international use of the *Anglo-American Cataloging Rules,* and acceptance of the International Standard Bibliographic Descriptions.

While developments in systematic catalog construction have progressed, libraries have used various technologies for catalog presentation: handwritten slips and cards, typed cards, printed cards, and printed book, microform, and machine-readable catalogs. Although these specific means of representing the catalog have affected the form of library catalogs and to some extent the manipulation of library catalogs, the technologies have not altered or changed the defined functions of the library catalog; the pervasive effect of technologies on catalogs and rules for catalog construction has been to foster uniform results, mass distribution, and mass consumption. The seductive powers of uniformity and control encourage the doable, not the useful. Technologies and techniques that promote the former at the expense of the latter undermine the functions of the library catalog; those who do not comprehend the value of organizing information or appreciate the intellectual aspects of library use are unlikely to devise or implement useful ways of gathering and categorizing knowledge.

Access and Automation: The Catalog Record in the Age of Automation

John K. Duke

Introduction

The economics of computing have been a tremendous incentive to the growth of online catalogs, often making it more expensive *not* to install online systems. Libraries have the potential to store more and larger records and the processing power to manipulate those records in new, creative ways because of rapidly advancing technology.

Librarians have not ignored the promise of automation and its implications for catalog records. New technology has prompted suggestions for enriched records[1] that include complete tables of contents, back-of-the-book indexes (Enser, 1985), a greater number of access points (Lin, 1985), and, in more visionary speculations, the complete text of a book. The purpose of this chapter is to explore how automation and the notion of enriched records might change our perception of access in the catalog. My assumption is that the technological means will eventually be available to add enriched data economically as a normal part of the catalog record. If this is true, automation will significantly alter the structure of catalog records and the problem of controlled access points.

For libraries that adopt online systems, automation can be highly idiosyncratic and widely varied in sophistication. Each system retrieves and displays records in a different way, making it difficult to write standards based upon a common set of bibliographic principles. Because it is technologically feasible to store larger records does not mean that all libraries will be willing to commit the necessary resources to do so, nor is it advisable for all catalogs to offer this additional information.

While there are increased opportunities in the computer age for expanding our access to catalog records, there are also constraints that make a universal code of cataloging rules at best an uncertain proposition. The potential for automated catalogs provides the technological, and in some cases economic, rationale to encourage expanding the size of records to increase access, but differing degrees of development within libraries suggest that less sophisticated computer and manual catalogs will persist in the age of automation. Catalog records must take account both of the potentials of automation and the persistence of the past to guarantee that bibliographic records can fit comfortably into any expected environment.

Scope of the Catalog Code

In defining a catalog for the age of automation, it is appropriate to recall the opening statement of the second edition to the *Anglo-American Cataloguing Rules*: that these "rules are designed for use in the construction of catalogues and other lists in *general* libraries of *all* sizes" (AACR2, 1978, p. 1; emphasis added). It is a considerably broader statement than the first edition, which was designed "primarily to respond to the needs of general *research* libraries" (AACR1, 1967, p. 1; emphasis added). The distinction is crucial.

AACR2 was planned as a hierarchical code with three levels of description. This design has been advantageous to American cataloging, permitting the economical sharing of records and the integration of records of differing levels of fullness into one catalog. It is essential that one cataloging code be able to support different cataloging systems because libraries will continue to depend upon the Library of Congress as the single most important source for cataloging and the presence of the bibliographic utilities will continue to foster shared cataloging among libraries. The idea of a code of rules existing solely to support a generic computer catalog is untenable. We cannot predict the variety of automated environments in which the code will operate, nor can we safely assume that all catalogs will be automated. We must also be mindful of the tremendous investment already made in machine-readable records and make certain that the past can coexist with the future.

What we must strive for is a fundamental agreement on the objectives the catalog is to serve and the design of records that can be smoothly integrated into any environment. There is a danger the computer will heighten the disparity in types of catalogs among libraries, further dividing the bibliographic world into the technological haves and have-nots. The focus in designing future catalog records should be on the common bibliographic principles that can unify all catalogs. The code must be built upon the commonality of catalog structure, not necessarily upon any specific formal implementation.

Before we look at these common bibliographic principles, I will examine how the computer has changed our perception of the bibliographic record itself.

Transformation of the Record: Linear Versus Transparent Access

Until the online catalog arrived in libraries, access to catalog records was linear. Short of reading the entire catalog, the only way to find a bibliographic description was to use one of the headings assigned as a window to it.

It is apparent that there is a separation between bibliographic access and subject access, but the model of a bibliographic record with descriptive headings or access points that are decidedly distinct from subject headings has never been strictly true. There has always been a hazy boundary between what is considered subject access and what is descriptive or bibliographic access to a title. For example, a time-honored technique for providing access to a title when there is not a legitimate subject heading has been to find a suitable keyword in the title and make an inverted or truncated title-added entry. Although this is no longer a formal part of our rules, many libraries continue to make added title entries for such specialized works as highly technical doctoral dissertations for which no appropriate subject heading is available. Older codes legitimized the practice by entering categories of titles under a memorable catchword as a rudimentary means of subject access. A similar back-door method has been used to invert portions of conference and corporate-body cross references to emphasize a significant term when the actual entry elements were considered too generic or the file too large to permit ready and convenient access.

In a curious reversal of history, the nineteenth century catalogers who argued in favor of catchword entry have been vindicated by our current technology. What was a primitive and inherently limited means of subject access to titles through the descriptive portion of the record is now ripe with possibilities because the computer can search any word in a record. Although standard bibliographic headings will continue to play an important role in retrieving records and organizing bibliographic descriptions into logical displays and relationships, the former definitions of what is considered an entry point no longer apply. Instead of the heading being a window to the record, the entire record is transparent, able to be viewed from many different perspectives. Theoretically, access to the bibliographic description may be sought through any part of the record, although obviously some limitations should prevail. It is hard to imagine, for example, a fruitful search for the pagination of a bibliography or a series number without the series title.

Several examples spring readily to mind in which the boundary between subject access and descriptive access is at best ambiguous in an online catalog. Summary notes, written as unbiased descriptions of works, have generally been restricted in current practice to juvenile literature, audiovisual material, and books cataloged by some public libraries. In the future, summary notes may be included in bibliographic records for a much wider range of literature. Through keyword searching, summary notes may be used to retrieve documents that have been defined in the user's mind as the functional equivalent of a subject search. In composing summary notes, the descriptive cataloger will have to be aware of its retrieval *and* its descriptive value. Catalogers will have to think more like indexers of online search services, who routinely add abstracts that are searchable fields in records.

An embedded table of contents or index in a catalog record also displays characteristics of both subject and bibliographic access. A table of contents or index can provide a subject approach to a work through term searching, but recording these parts of the book is also an act of transcription, or descriptive analysis, of the parts of the work. More important, a table of contents and an index are stable and objective elements in a catalog record, whereas traditional subject analysis and classification take their notation from external sources.

The content of a book index is often made up, at least partially, of names within the work. The normalization of names, even when assigning subject headings to a work, is governed by the rules of descriptive cataloging. The descriptive catalog code has already sanctioned table of contents information in formal contents notes, though the Library of Congress has narrowly restricted the practice [*Cataloging Service Bulletin* (Summer) 1985 **25**:40]. Contents notes up to now have been used to characterize the scope of certain types of works, but not to provide analytical access to a work contained within another unless one takes the additional step of making explicit added entries.

The blurring of the boundary between description and access has implications for the catalog code. Free-text searching and its variants, such as truncated word matching, weighted searching based on frequency analysis and proximity searching, will become more important in catalogs. Records must be prepared that will use these techniques to the best advantage. The computer removes many of the retrieval decisions from the user. Whether a search is bibliographic or subject based, or whether the record is retrieved by a formal access point or by an element in the description, can be transparent to the user. However, to achieve consistently structured descriptions, certain categories of enriched access points need to be defined as the province of descriptive cataloging.

Tripartite Structure of the Record

Given that automation permits opportunities for increasing access to catalog records and that the code will be required to serve different manifestations of automated and manual catalogs, how, then, do we structure a catalog record flexible enough to serve our various needs? Catalog codes traditionally divide the structure of a descriptive catalog record into two parts: descriptive data and elements that provide access to these data. However, as we have seen, the distinction between description and access is fading, just as is the distinction between subject and bibliographic access. For the sake of analysis I would like to describe another, tripartite structure to a record as it might exist in an automated environment. The tripartite structure can help us to visualize how a future catalog might operate and how a code for constructing records for that catalog might function. The three structural tiers to a record are (1) the document surrogate, (2) the document guide, and (3) the document text.

A design objective for the proposed record structure is that it must be able to function in both automated and manual environments. This does not mean that the record must exist in the same form in each environment. However, there must not be a conflict or structural incompatibility between the two.

Document Surrogates   The first tier in the structure of the future catalog record is the most familiar. It is called the *document surrogate* because this portion of the record represents characteristics of the document, as a substitute for the entire text, by an abbreviated, highly formalized citation structure. The descriptive surrogate includes most of the important elements of bibliographic description called for in AACR2, as well as bibliographic access points (personal and corporate names, titles, uniform titles, and so forth).

Rules governing the document surrogate tier should be completely operational in both a manual catalog and an online catalog without any potential for conflict. For example, because of its literalism, the computer requires that headings intending to represent the same person or body always be in the same form, unless a large set of rule-handling exceptions is programmed. On the other hand, in a card catalog a person would be able to interfile records in which one uses an abbreviation in a heading and one does not. Here, the code must be tailored to the computer rather than the manual catalog so that compatibility may exist. Another example: a strictly machine-based code could dispense with rules for alternative title entry because a free-text search would automatically index it. Such a rule would not make operational sense for a manual catalog because access to the record is still linear.

The document surrogate is the structural tier that up to now has been the focus of catalog codes. My conception of this portion of the record would make changes in both the data it includes and how it is accessed. For example, formal contents and summary notes would not appear in this portion of the record. Sometimes it would be irrelevant to speak of added entries when they do not serve any collocating function. An added entry is a string that is attached to a bibliographic record to provide a window or point of access to it. If that string is already present in the description and if the catalog can search that string, then an added entry is redundant. It would be better for the code to define minimal requirements for *necessary and sufficient* access to a record, with the local institution or system determining the appropriate technique to guarantee that access.

Document Guides   The second tier of the record is the *document guides,* which are substantive parts of the bibliographic item or synopses of the content. Document guides have existed for some time in catalog codes, but these guides can be developed to take advantage of computer technology. There are two purposes behind including document guides in the catalog record: first, to provide what has been termed *enriched access* in the catalog, that is, access to nontraditional bibliographical aspects of the book; and second, to help fulfill Cutter's often ignored third object— "to assist in the choice of a book" (Cutter, 1904, p. 10) by providing the user a preview of its nature and contents before retrieving it from the shelf. Access by computer to these guides will of necessity be through secondary or uncontrolled terms, a theme to which I will return in a moment.

Contents notes are a type of document guide that have been included on records only infrequently. They are not structured in either the code or the machine-readable cataloging (MARC) format to provide efficient access by computer because they are devised to be read, not searched. As long as the contents note was meant merely to characterize the nature or scope of a text, there was no need to include in it anything but the last name and initials of the author and as little of the title as made it intelligible. However, if the contents note is also a point of analytical access to the record, transcribing the names of authors and complete titles as they appear on the publication would enhance the potential for retrieval. This has implications for the design of the MARC format. As long as the contents note was used only in a display as a block paragraph on the catalog record, there was no need to precisely delineate its elements; however, to assist the computer in manipulating contents information in retrieval a formal structure of tags and subfields is necessary.

Another document guide that will grow in importance is the summary note. To date, it has been applied very restrictively. However, the increasing importance and familiarity of our public with online database search services, as well as the growth of linked systems and remote storage facilities, will increase pressures to add summary notes to all bibliographic records. By adding summaries to the descriptive record, we open the door to sophisticated retrieval of records.

The document guides I have discussed thus far are extrapolations and expansions of elements that are now already present (if only infrequently) in our catalog records. Future codes may greatly expand points of access through additional document guides. Indexes and chapter summaries, or abstracts, are candidates to be included in future records. Precise descriptive rules for recording data like these and new MARC structures to communicate them and make them amenable to computer searching will be needed.

One reason we have been frugal with our document guides in the past (apart from the obvious economic restraints) is because they have been viewed as an element of description intended for display, not access. By recognizing that in an automated catalog description *is* access, we can further tap the power of the computer.

Document Texts   The last tier in the record structure is the most ambitious and the farthest from reach. It is the availability of the book's complete text online. The introduction of the *textual tier* of the record would symbolize the realization of the electronic library. At this stage the catalog would be transformed from an instrument for retrieving document surrogates into one for retrieving facts and for armchair browsing of a bibliographc collection, which may not even be physically contained within one building. The third tier of the record may be carried out gradually (for instance by encoding only the first and last paragraphs of each chapter), which would allow some online browsing, but not overload our human or computer resources.

As exciting as a catalog is that incorporates full texts, the prospects for achieving it anytime soon remain slight, except perhaps in experimental form, in small, specialized libraries, and as subsets of larger collections. There are tremendous logistical problems to designing such a catalog, not the least of which is the ability to capture textual data in machine-readable form either through direct communication with the publisher or through complete conversion of the printed page at the source of cataloging by some sort of electronic transfer technology. Other significant problems include the issue of copyright, affordable graphics terminals capable of presenting a page in its entirety with illustrations, and the question of computer power and storage devices capable of manipulating such tremendous volumes of data. Perhaps the most intriguing problem system designers will encounter is what to do with records for the nonbook media we have now collectively decided should be integrated into our catalogs.

Although the tripartite record I have presented as a model may be several generations away, I believe that it does contain some important ramifications for designing a catalog code. What is required is a conception of the catalog as capable of managing multiple tiers of access to information. In particular, it has implications for the design of the MARC format. We must begin to think about revising the MARC format to allow a single bibliographic record to be viewed structurally in ways other than allowed for in, say, component parts records. Thus one level might be those elements defined as the document surrogate, a second level as the document guides, and the third level the document text. Control fields in the records could link each level to the others.

There are several advantages to a tripartite record structure. First, it would allow systems at different stages of development the flexibility of handling records according to local requirements. One system may only need the document surrogate, while another would be capable of processing document guides as well. The scheme would also allow administrative mechanisms whereby libraries would pay for only those parts of the record that they are capable of using, and publishers could recoup royalty costs for full text transfers. Another advantage to the scheme is that system efficiency could be improved because computers can read and process smaller records more quickly than larger records. Processing tasks could be differentiated according to the different types of subrecords. For example, in one task a system may operate on only document surrogates, bringing them into the central memory as commanded. Since a brief record can satisfy most library and patron use of the catalog (Seal,

1983), the computer would not need to devote resources to the document guide or text portions of the record for every transaction.

The idea that the rules for cataloging should be enunciated with the results of a catalog in mind rather than the specific means of attaining them is a recognition that the linear dictionary catalog is no longer the only catalog for which rules are needed. This leads us to a more critical examination of system software, which has a great effect on the success of retrieval and the display of bibliographic relationships within the automated catalog. The profession exerts little control over vendor-supplied software. Each developer of a system carries out retrieval and display mechanisms in a different fashion. Although it would be short-sighted to limit software innovations unduly, there is also a danger that the development of catalogs is moving out of librarians' hands and into those of vendors, who are not necessarily concerned with the finer points of bibliographic principles. We now have so-called online *catalogs* operating in some libraries that subarrange the entries of an author according to the order the records entered the system which, if not cause for criminal prosecution, at least is an affront to bibliographic decency. What is needed in a code is a set of principles for organizing a catalog, for providing minimal standards of access, and for properly displaying relationships among works and authors. Any vendor that does not incorporate at least the option for those standards in its software would be said to be in noncompliance with the code. One can even envision a professional association that would review vendor software and certify it for the profession as meeting certain minimally accepted standards.

Uncontrolled Headings in the Automated Catalog

Dividing the catalog record into a three-tiered structure gives us a way to focus on the problem of access in an automated age and to reexamine the catalog's traditional objectives. The first objective of the catalog, which is to locate a particular publication in the library, does not suffer in the automated catalog. It is, in fact, the great virtue of the computer to be able to locate discrete units of information rapidly. An imprecisely rememberd title that would be lost in a sea of cards is suddenly revealed in the automated catalog because of the computer's ability to index many more terms of entry and to combine terms to narrow the scope of the request.

The second objective of the catalog, which is to collocate authors and works, is much more difficult to realize in the automated age, however. It is the very nature of the computer, its ability to handle and process vast quantities of information, that encourages us to retrieve separate, unrelated bits of data. The catalog must use controlled access points if it is to achieve efficiently the second objective of showing the editions of a particular work and all the works the library has of a particular author.

Controlled access will remain a fundamental characteristic of the code of the future. Controlled access points, whether personal or corporate names, conference headings, or uniform titles, are characterized by the cataloger's normalization of the name or title using rules to formulate one standard heading that represents all variants and manifestations. Although it is possible to avoid normalization in a computerized catalog through an authority control mechanism that simply accounts for all variants (Burger, 1984), it would probably not be effective. Controlled, normalized headings will remain a part of cataloging rules even in advanced online systems because of the efficiency they guarantee the user in being able to locate works and authors and because of their role in displaying bibliographic relationships logically.

There is another sort of access in an automated catalog, however, beyond controlled access. This is access which is based upon secondary or enriched access points. Parts of the record that are candidates for secondary access are contained in what I have called the second tier of document guides, such as contents notes, indexes, and abstracts. Although uncontrolled headings have been used in other types of databases, there has been a reluctance to allow them into the library's catalog, and rightly so. In the catalogs we have been building, and the technological base upon which we have been working, we would have had chaos had we not exercised rigid control over the headings entering the catalog. The unprecedented interest in authority control issues for the last 10 years attests to the vigor of the theory of controlled access points.

Economic constraints, however, impede expanding the concept of authority control to secondary access points. On the one hand, the pressure to add search and descriptive vocabulary to catalog records is compelling. Technology makes it feasible and attractive to expand the size and retrieval characteristics of catalog records. This technological power is coupled with rising expectations of users who are becoming familiar with the sophisticated search programs of the online databases and of librarians who are demanding quicker and more effective access to records. On the other hand, providing controlled headings much beyond what we are providing now is likely to prove economically impossible. Adding normalized headings to a record remains the single most expensive part of cataloging: it is normalizing the form of the heading rather than choosing a correct main entry that is the real culprit in the battle to control costs. If it were even economically possible to add the type of enriched data that we have been discussing, attempting to control the added headings would prove to be beyond the resources of even our largest libraries.[2] We would have to rely upon the Library of Congress to lead us in applying controlled secondary headings, but a national library that is in a period of economic retrenchment is an unlikely candidate for such a role.

The ability of the computer to process large amounts of data and extract the desired item rapidly creates the very seeds, therefore, of the demise of universal authority control where every heading in the catalog is normalized. Authority control has always been an intellectual exercise that is based upon the human ability to link disparate information from a wide variety of sources into a recognizable pattern and to make inferences and decisions about that information. It is the process of cataloging that is least compliant to rule making and mechanization, which is why it has always been the most expensive part of the process. The application of artificial intelligence or expert systems to establish names in a traditional authority control process is unlikely to be operationally widespread for decades, if ever.

Because universal authority control is not an economically sound option, librarians will have to compromise in making certain entries, testing the principle of collocation that has been the hallmark of the Anglo-American cataloging tradition. Particularly for tables of contents and indexes, names will be entered in the fullest form available to increase the possibility of machine retrieval. The purpose of these fields would be for online browsing, to preview the content of texts, to search titles by keyword to improve analytical access, and to do secondary author searches.

Such an open-door policy to headings in the catalog would have its largest effect on analytical entries, for the prospect is that authors may be entered in the catalog in several forms besides the controlled form at the document surrogate level. Only in those instances in which the analytical name was not already the surrogate entry would there be no collision. For example, a collection of short stories or essays by one author would present no name variants because the name will have already been established for the monograph. However, the identity of the analytical *work* in such an instance could suffer. Those names and titles that the cataloger deems important enough to collocate into author and literary units may still be normalized through traditional added entries or as complete component parts records; that is, in certain limited instances the secondary access points in the document guides may migrate to the status of controlled access points in the document surrogate.

The thought of giving up controlled access does not come easily, but there are reasons beyond economic expediency for permitting uncontrolled access to second-tier information. Document guides are by definition secondary to the primary bibliographic keys users employ when approaching the catalog. Users are less likely to be interested in collocating names originating in second-tier areas because often they will be approaching it from a free-text subject perspective. In second-tier areas there is less likely to be a need for collocating literary units because proportionately the literary and the bibliographic unit are more likely to be the same than with the monographic literature: there will be no literary unit to gather either because the unit is unique or because the unit is reprinted with exactly the same title. Finally, if controlled and uncontrolled files are clearly segregated, as suggested earlier, we will have a way to maintain the two forms of catalogs, manual and automated, and to build them from the same record core. We can then require that vendor software distinguish the retrieval commands for each so that patrons of the catalog are not misled when a search does not retrieve complete author and literary units. If a library does discover that there is a need to collocate names or assemble literary units, it can be done through traditional added entries.

Summary

Automated catalogs have been functioning in libraries a few scant years. The new catalogs have been driven by a technology that is encouraging the development of larger enriched records with many more access points. Since the argument against authority-controlled secondary access points is primarily one of economics, it is possible that at some future date economic, technological, or political conditions may change to bring these secondary access points within the scope of the traditional catalog. Expert systems with large factual databases able to find patterns and draw inferences from existing bibliographic records may eventually make universal authority control a practicable option. In the meantime, however, our choice is not whether we will have controlled or uncontrolled headings in the catalog. The present generation of online systems has already presented us with a *fait accompli*. Our only clear course is to begin to develop records and retrieval techniques to manage these uncontrolled headings without unduly compromising the objectives of the catalog.

Notes

1. Many of the proposals for adding information to catalog records are summarized in Mandel (1985).

2. One study, for example, found that adding the names from tables of contents as access points would easily triple the number of name entries in the catalog (Svenonius, Baughman, and Molto, 1986).

VI

Bibliographic Structure

In its most general sense *structure* refers to an aggregate of elements related, or arranged with respect, to each other. The conceptual power provided by looking at entities in terms of their structure has proved itself in many disciplines. It seems appropriate, therefore, in a consideration of the conceptual foundations of descriptive cataloging, to take a systematic look at the various bibliographic entities that lend themselves to structural analysis. These include bibliographic descriptions, catalogs, and the bibliographic universe itself.

The structure of bibliographic descriptions consists of data elements arranged and presented in a given order. Thus, card catalog formats and MARC formats represent different but related bibliographic structures, the former intended for display and the latter for communication.

The structure of a catalog or catalog database consists of bibliographic, authority, and holdings records arranged in a given order and referencing one another through a variety of syndetic relationships. Thus, filing rules, together with ordering devices, such as the main entry and *see* and *see also* references, define a catalog structure.

The structure of the bibliographic universe is defined by taking as fundamental elements those bibliographic materials to be described in the process of descriptive cataloging and then characterizing them in terms of their properties, the aggregates to which they belong, and the relationships they bear one to another. A given bibliographic item may have the property of being a monograph by a certain author, published at a certain date in a certain place; it may be classified as a subedition of a certain edition of a given work; and it may exhibit the relationship of being a sequel to another work.

So pervasive is the concept of structure in theoretical analyses that it is addressed in some form or other by most contributors to this volume. Pat Wilson discusses the relationships among bibliographic entities such as item, text, and work; Michael Carpenter explores the function of the main entry as an ordering device; Tom Delsey characterizes "the third wave of standardization" as one in which entity-attribute relationships are formalized; John Duke proposes a three-level structure for access; and Sara Shatford Layne introduces structural concepts in her discussion of integration in relation to the objectives of the catalog.

In Part VI, three chapters are devoted to examining aspects of bibliographic structure. The first, entitled "Descriptive Cataloging Rules and Machine-Readable Record Structures: Some Directions for Parallel Development," is by John Attig, an Associate Librarian/Cataloger in the Bibliographic Services Department of the Library at Pennsylvania State University and a longtime contributor to MARBI and CCDS. Attig's topic is structures for communicating bibliographic information and, in particular, structures for communicating information about bibliographic relationships. He begins with a discussion of MARC, in which he compares it with AACR2 and reviews recent format developments. The idea that there could be a combined AACR2–MARC, i.e., a single standard governing both the content and tagging of bibliographic data, he dismisses as deceptively simple.

Recent activity surrounding MARC has been singularly creative and has resulted in a statement of principles, the development of several new formats, and attempts at the integration of and the removal of bias in formats. It is significant as well for two lacunae it has revealed in present structures for bibliographical control: Attig identifies these as (1) the inability of present format techniques to deal satisfactorily with bibliographic relationships, and (2) the inability of present descriptive cataloging techniques to (a) delineate clearly what items constitute the bibliographic universe, in the sense of being the objects of description, and (b) distinguish satisfactorily generic and copy-specific descriptive information. A discussion of these two lacunae forms the remainder of Attig's chapter.

Bibliographic relationships are central to the objectives of the catalog; without them the catalog's collocating functions could not be met. However, Attig points out, it is difficult to accommodate the MARC formats, which were designed primarily to communicate records, to the task of communicating bibliographic relationships among records. Part of the problem is that the communicating of a given bibliographic relationship between institutions presupposes that the receiving institution has each of the two records participating in the relationship. Another part of the problem is the mechanics of communication: should one record containing all related records as subrecords be communicated, or should each of the records participating in a relationship be sent separately along with sufficient information to establish the relationship? Either approach meets with difficulties.

The development of the USMARC Format for Holdings and Locations, together with the ever-increasing trend toward union databases, has made it increasingly apparent that AACR2 does not deal adequately with the question of what constitutes a unitary object of bibliographic description. Present guidelines, expressed for instance in LCRI 1.0 and the OCLC Input Standards (OCLC, 1986), are ad hoc in that they are not based on principle; besides, they are expensive to implement. Attig argues that prior to deciding at what levels we should exercise bibliographical control we must develop some reasoned answers to fundamental questions such as what constitutes significant variation among bibliographic items, what constitutes generic and copy-specific bibliographic information, and what constitutes holdings as opposed to bibliographic information.

From his vantage in the forefront of standards development, Attig contributes importantly to cataloging theory by identifying serious problems in present structures for bibliographic control. They are problems that cannot be addressed at a technician's level or in an ad hoc manner; rather they require for their solution a conceptual analysis of the bibliographical universe.

Barbara Tillett, Head of the Catalog Department at the Central University Library at the University of California, San Diego, is the author of the second chapter on bibliographic structure. Entitled "Bibliographic Structures: The Evolution of Catalog Entries, References, and Tracings," it deals with bibliographic structures in terms of bibliographic records and relationships among them. Tillett's theme is that bibliographic relationships are essential to the effective clustering and identification of bibliographic records in retrieval. She develops her theme in a historical examination of structures that have been evolved to embody bibliographic relationships, beginning with the structure underlying Panizzi's system of cross references, which includes (1) name-to-name, (2) name-to-work, and (3) work-to-work references. This structure was appropriate for the nineteenth-century catalogs of Panizzi and, later, Cutter. However, at the beginning of the century when the technology of mass production permitted distribution of printed cards by the Library of Congress, it became economically advantageous to substitute added entries for some cross references. At that time it was not clear and, as

Tillett observes, unfortunately even today it is not clear, when bibliographic relationships should be expressed by cross references and when by added entries.

In the 1960s technological change again stimulated structural change in the representation of bibliographic relationships. With computer-based catalogs has come a shift in the locus for name variants from the bibliographic record to the authority record. And again Tillett points out the shift was and still remains somewhat muddied, since a conceptual distinction between bibliographic records and authority records is not always observed. Tillett concludes her historical overview of the effect of technology on the design of bibliographic structure by reaffirming the verity of the bibliographic relationships postulated by Panizzi and asking for a clearer delineation between structures used to link bibliographic records and those used to link name variants.

When a catalog code incorporates several different methods for achieving a desired end and no rationale is given for when one is used and when another, there is a failure of theory. Tillett's chapter is a valuable contribution to this collection of papers on the foundations of descriptive cataloging, not only for its depiction of how technology has affected bibliographic structure but also for revealing conceptual discrepancies in need of theoretical attention.

The third chapter on bibliographic structure is by Edward T. O'Neill and Diane Vizine-Goetz, research scientists in the Office of Research at OCLC. Their chapter, "Bibliographic Relationships: Implications for the Function of the Catalog," looks at computer technology in relation to bibliographic structures: the problems it has raised and the potentialities it has to offer. A consequence of the creation of catalog records in machine-readable form and the widespread use of online shared cataloging has been the emergence of global catalogs. Various problems attend such catalogs, including complex bibliographic structures not immediately apparent to catalog users, the presence of multiple records for a given item, and the occurrence of large sets of items representing a single work. It is this last problem that O'Neill and Vizine-Goetz focus upon. An example of the problem is *The Expedition of Humphry Clinker,* by Tobias Smollett, which in the OCLC database is represented by over 100 records. The frequency in global catalogs of multiply manifested works such as this is clear evidence that bibliographic structures appropriate for pinpointing a particular item in a local environment do not suffice in a global one.

A first step in addressing the *Humphry Clinker* problem is to define a bibliographic structure which can organize bibliographic records for multiply manifested works. O'Neill and Vizine-Goetz propose a structure that is hierarchically defined in terms of works, texts, editions, printings, and books. Works, texts, editions, and printings represent sets of bibliographic items derived by successive subdivision. The definition of entities such as these is fundamental to organizing the bibliographic universe, yet the literature of librarianship and bibliography, including the cataloging codes themselves, exhibits considerable confusion and disagreement in this respect. The definitions proposed by O'Neill and Vizine-Goetz are based on a premise defended earlier by Wajenberg in relation to his definition of authorship, *viz.,* that bibliographic distinctions must be grounded in a bibliographic reality. Extrabibliographic considerations, such as whether spirits can indeed be authors or whether a translation really adheres enough to the original to be deemed the same work, are not admissible. In the determining of the workship of a particular item, as in determining its authorship, primary consideration must be given to what is stated in the work itself. Another feature of the definitions of bibliographic entities provided by O'Neill and Vizine-Goetz is that they are accompanied by guidelines for application; this feature contributes toward their operationalization and, ultimately, toward their eventual consistent application.

Are new organizing structures needed for online catalogs? This chapter by O'Neill and Vizine-Goetz demonstrates that the computerization of cataloging does in fact exacerbate certain problems; in particular, it reveals cracks in traditional bibliographic structures. But this is not the only reason to look at alternative structures. Another reason is that online catalogs can support data structures more complex than could ever be possible in card catalogs and, thus, unlike traditional structures, they should be able simultaneously to meet both the first and second objectives of the catalog.

Like other authors in this section, O'Neill and Vizine-Goetz have identified a structural problem in present methods for representing bibliographic relationships. But they are constructive as well, proposing a hierarchical model to address the problem and, in so doing, providing a point of departure for future research in the ordering and display of bibliographic records.

Descriptive Cataloging Rules and Machine-Readable Record Structures: Some Directions for Parallel Development

John C. Attig

There has always been a close relationship between the descriptive cataloging rules and the emerging formats for machine-readable cataloging (MARC) records. That relationship has become so close that periodically we hear suggestions that the cataloging rules be rewritten in MARC tags or that a single standard should govern both the coding and the content of MARC records.[1]

Unfortunately, the situation is not that simple. I would like to explore selected aspects of the relationship between descriptive cataloging rules and MARC formats: first, historically, in terms of the developments of recent years; and then, speculatively, in terms of some issues for future development.

USMARC: Background and Recent Developments

Background The first MARC format was developed at the Library of Congress in 1966, for the purpose of distributing LC cataloging in machine-readable form to a small group of subscribers. A revised version, MARC II, went into use in 1968 and has been working and evolving ever since.[2]

There are now seven USMARC formats for various kinds of bibliographic data, plus separate formats for authority records and for holdings and locations.[3]

MARC is a *communications* format, developed to promote the exchange of bibliographic and authority records between systems.

A MARC record involves three elements:

1. A *record structure,* which provides a mechanism for organizing and labeling the data in the record.

2. *Content designation,* which consists of machine-readable labels that enable a system to locate and isolate for manipulation the individual pieces of data which make up a MARC record.
   Three types of content designation are provided: *tags* identify fields or groups of elements; *subfields* identify individual data elements, the smallest units of data; and *indicators* provide further information about the field.

3. The *content* of the fields and subfields. Generally speaking, content is *not* part of the MARC standard. MARC provides a data structure for content prescribed by external standards, such as descriptive cataloging rules and conventions; subject cataloging rules, lists, and conventions (including classification systems); identifying numbers such as ISBN and ISSN; and coded data elements. These last are defined as part of the format specifications, since there are no relevant external standards. With this single exception, MARC does not prescribe the content of data elements. Neither does it, with a very few exceptions, prescribe whether individual data elements must be present in any particular record. Such prescriptions are contained in standards such as those just listed, or in special content standards such as the National Level Bibliographic Record documents[4] or OCLC's *Bibliographic Input Standards* (OCLC, 1985).

Some Comparisons with AACR2 In many ways, AACR2 is similar to MARC. Like MARC, the descriptive cataloging rules deal with communication and with the construction of standard records for shared use. AACR2 provides a structure for bibliographic records by organizing the description into areas and elements which roughly correspond to MARC data elements. AACR2 also provides a means of identifying the elements, viz, the ISBD system of prescribed punctuation. The ISBD and MARC systems of content designation work on similar principles and are generally compatible—with a few unfortunate exceptions.[5]

Unlike MARC, AACR2 does prescribe the content of elements, in terms of data to be transcribed from prescribed sources. It also defines mandatory and optional elements for various levels of cataloging.

Both AACR2 and MARC are international, but in different ways. AACR2 is maintained by an international body, the Joint Steering Committee, and all changes must receive approval by this body after thorough review by the national cataloging committees and national libraries. The MARC structure is a formal American National Standard (ANSI Z39.2-1985) and an international standard (ISO 2709-1981). There are many implementations of this structure, each of which defines content designation more or less independently of the others. USMARC is one of these; there are other national formats in other countries. In addition, there are extensions of USMARC defined by almost every system which supports it. For example, OCLC has extensions for call numbers and holdings; RLIN has extensions for local data and for acquisitions. Thus, there are a variety of MARC formats with varying degrees of compatibility.

Both AACR2 and USMARC are maintained cooperatively. The Library of Congress and committees of the American Library Association have significant roles in both.

Finally, both AACR2 and USMARC have just ended a period of unusually intense activity and both for much the same reasons, such as the emergence of new types of bibliographic material. In the case of USMARC, however, the changes have been more profound.

Recent Developments in USMARC *Statement of Principles.* In 1983, LC published a document entitled "The USMARC Formats: Underlying Principles."[6] This was an attempt to set down the conceptual basis of what USMARC is all about. It tried to describe the historical principles which account for the formats as they presently exist and to identify "a provisional set of working principles for further format development" (p. 148). Prominent among the principles are the following:

Consistency The various MARC formats developed separately, usually in response to the needs of special users. Consistency across formats was not felt to be a decisive factor and therefore was not achieved. Now most MARC users must support more than one format and, in a multiformat environment, each inconsistent piece of content designation for essentially the same type of data exacts a penalty. It has been suggested that the ideal situation would be a single format for bibliographic records of all types. There would be a common set of data elements applicable to all types of bibliographic records and sets of specific elements applicable to special types of material. Any field or subfield could be used in any record if there were relevant information to record. This concept has been called *format integration* and is the subject of a proposal currently being considered by the USMARC Advisory Group. However, it is not clear that all inconsistencies among the formats can in fact be eliminated without requiring the costly revision of vast numbers of existing records. Therefore, while there is a commitment in principle to consistency in the formats, it is not yet clear to what extent existing inconsistencies can be removed.[7]

Bias Likewise, there has been an attempt to remove some of the biases from the formats. MARC was originally developed by and for the Library of Congress and contained many examples of special treatment for LC data and cataloging practices. The transformation of LCMARC into USMARC is an achievement of the last six years, as these features have been removed from the formats and elements have been redefined for general use. For example, field 050 may now be used for LC classification numbers assigned by any institution and the values of the Encoding Level codes have been given general definitions not tied to the workflow at the Library of Congress.

Other biases have also been noted in the formats, including one that may come as a surprise in this context: a bias toward the Anglo-American cataloging rules. It comes as a shock to some of us to find that there are MARC users out there who do not use AACR2, even some whose attitude toward our code is less than reverent. Yet the last six years have served primarily to expand USMARC beyond the scope of the cataloging rules and to enable it to serve communities of users who do not necessarily follow AACR2. Let me summarize these format developments and the user needs that prompted them.[8]

> *Technical reports* (1981). New data elements for technical reports were added to the Books format at the request of a group of government librarians. These elements support control of report literature through the identifying numbers assigned to reports at various stages of their existence, through the various funding/contracting/investigating agencies responsible for reports,

and through subject access techniques other than the precoordinated subject terms familiar to libraries.

Rare books (1981). Rare-book librarians need to describe and provide access to features which are particular to individual copies of a title rather than to an edition as a whole. The provisional techniques added to the formats to support the exchange of copy-specific information marked the first venture of USMARC into the area of local data.

Analytics (1982). Analytics are items which are physically and bibliographically part of a larger entity which must be described as part of the description of the analytic. Although the cataloging rules have always included rules for analysis, the technique has been primarily the province of the abstracting and indexing services. The need to describe and define relationships among different bibliographic levels proved an almost insoluble problem for the MARC formats. The solution finally adopted was a limited one, allowing descriptive data for both levels to be carried in a single record, but also providing data elements which might be used to link data stored in separate records.

Computer files (1982). The MARC formats had to deal with computer files in advance of changes in the cataloging rules because of the increasing significance of such material both in special data archives and in general library collections. The particular needs were for the description of a type of material which has no permanent physical characteristics and for the control of the various hardware, software, and documentation necessary for use of the material.

Archives (1983). The revision of the manuscripts format, indeed its transformation into a format for archival control, represents the widest departure from traditional library cataloging. Archival control records are not primarily bibliographic descriptions; rather, they are processing control records. Archival collections, unlike most library material, are not self-describing or self-defining. They must be created and given an identity by the archivist, who must keep careful track of the process by which this is accomplished.

Two- and three-dimensional material (1983, 1987). Most recently, the Films format has been transformed into a format for Visual materials by adding elements applicable to two-dimensional graphics and to three-dimensional artifacts and naturally occurring objects. Much of the motivation for these changes has come from curators of archival and museum collections, who, like the archivists, do not think in terms of bibliographic description and control, but in terms of inventory control and classification.

Authorities (1981). At the same time that all these changes were being made to the bibliographic formats, the Authorities format was revised in light of the developing needs of the Linked Systems Project and was expanded to include data elements for series.[9]

Holdings and locations (1984). Finally, a new format for holdings and locations has been developed. At the moment, it exists primarily to support ANSI Z39.44-1985, the standard for serial holdings statements. Elements for nonserial holdings statements will be added as that ANSI standard is finalized. Beyond its present application, moreover, the very existence of this format opens new possibilities. Already, elements for recording physical condition of, and preservation decisions about, individual copies have been added. Other data which are confined to a particular institution or copy now have a potential place within the USMARC formats.

Summary   Most of the developments just described are leading us beyond the descriptive cataloging rules in one way or another. We have been forced to acknowledge that while USMARC has a special relationship to AACR2, it cannot be restricted to any single set of rules. Rather, as stated in "The USMARC Formats: Underlying Principles" (sec. 2.4), it must "serve as a vehicle for bibliographic and authority data of all types, from all agencies," including those who do not use the Anglo-American cataloging rules.

In the course of these developments, we have faced some tough problems and learned some things about what works and what doesn't. We also initiated some developments fraught with significance for the future. However, this long period of intense creativity is now over. For the past several years, there has been a conservative tendency, similar to the reaction following the publication of AACR2. There is a feeling that too much change is ipso facto a bad thing, and that we need to spend more effort investigating the costs and benefits of proposed changes.

Issues for Future Development

In spite of this conservative trend, it is inevitable that both AACR2 and USMARC will continue to develop. In particular, the implications of some new format techniques need to be explored. In this exploration, concepts of descriptive cataloging have a role to play. Conversely, new format techniques may encourage us to reexamine some of those concepts.

In the remainder of this chapter, I would like to raise two issues. One of these takes a particularly significant descriptive cataloging concept and shows the difficulties of dealing with it in the MARC formats. The other takes a relatively neglected area of descriptive cataloging and shows how recent format developments offer interesting possibilities for enhanced bibliographic control.

Relationships In a recent lecture, Michael Gorman noted "the MARC record is a complex record that has no connection with any other record. What we need are simple records with complex connections" (Lewis, 1986). The concept of connections or relationships is a crucial one for descriptive cataloging, lying at the heart of the collocating function of the catalog. Yet it is a very difficult concept for the MARC formats to cope with.

MARC is a communications format. Although it is used by some systems as a processing format, its primary function is to allow records to be exchanged between systems.

It is simple to communicate *records*. It is very difficult to communicate *relationships*.

Take the simple case of a serial title change. Each of the two records involved will include a field called a linking field, which contains the earlier or later title. Although the data in these fields can be displayed as a note, this is not their primary function. Nor do these fields exist principally to provide an access point to the record in which they appear, although this too can be done. Their primary function is to define a relationship between the record in which they appear and the record for the related title. There are various ways in which a system can indicate this relationship: it can display the note and let the user search for the related title; it can index the linking fields so that the related records are always retrieved together under either title; or it can establish some type of machine linkage between the two records which will allow a user to move easily from one record to the next. But all this cannot be communicated simply. When one record is sent to another system, there is no guarantee that the related record is also sent *or* that the receiving system has the record *or* that a link will be established even if it has the record, since, for example, a different decision might have been made concerning choice of entry or title proper.

There are all kinds of relationships that are significant in descriptive cataloging: bibliographic relationships such as analytics, translations, and revisions; authority relationships; holdings relationships. All involve establishing and maintaining links between logically independent records.

The most certain technique for communicating such relationships is the creation, at least for purposes of communication, of a single self-contained record with all related records treated as subrecords. The possibility of a superrecord with subrecords was thoroughly explored by the USMARC advisory group during its struggle with the problem of analytics. The idea was that the description of the larger, or "host," item would be included in a subrecord on the record for the analytic. It was a nice idea, but it turned out not to be feasible. There are too many kinds of relationships that could apply; the records could become too extensive; there would be too much duplication of subrecords. For instance, in analyzing a festschrift, the subrecord representing the book as "host item" would be duplicated in each of the analytic records. The final straw, however, was purely technical: the technique would have meant that one of the most important structural constants of USMARC, the length of the directory entry, would have become a variable, thus requiring revision of all existing processing programs.[10]

The alternative to subrecords is to communicate separate records with sufficient information so that the links can be (re)established by the system receiving the record. The problem is how to guarantee that related records are communicated or that they already exist in the receiving system and how to provide the linking information. The former is a database management problem that won't go away, but the discussion here will concentrate on the linking technique itself.

The traditional technique used to link records is to rely on the data in the records to establish the relationships. In virtually all access points, the content of the heading field may be used to establish the relationship of the record to other records with an identical heading.[11] In certain special cases, the formats include fields (760–787) specifically designed to carry linking information, such as author and title, which serve to identify the related record. In current systems, data from linking fields are rarely used to establish a direct link between records. Instead, the searcher is expected to use the information about related items as the basis for further searching. However, the format does support more direct linkage, and the possibilities deserve exploration.

It must be noted that all record-linking techniques that rely on content matching are uncertain, particularly outside the system in which the records were created. I may create an authority record with the heading "Smith, Thomas." In my system, there may be a relationship between that authority record and all bibliographic records with that heading; in other systems, that heading might represent an entirely different entity. The possibility of false matching cannot be eliminated unless the entire decision-making process is reconstructed in the new context.[12]

Another technique for linking records involves the use of some particularly well-behaved piece of data to establish the relationship. The most likely candidates are the various numeric identifiers such as the LCCN, ISBN, ISSN, etc. Unfortunately, few "standard" numbers turn out to be sufficiently well behaved because they do not always uniquely identify a single bibliographic entity. The most reliable element to use in establishing a link is the record control number of the related record in the receiving system. Such a control number is recommended for linking holdings records to bibliographic records in the MARC holdings format, which contains a field that says in effect, "These are my holdings for RLIN record no. xxxxxxx." The problem with this is that it constitutes a barrier to record sharing because each system tends to use different record control numbers. What is needed is a reliable identifier that is common to all parts of the national network. An encouraging example of such a common identifier is the record control number used in the LC/NACO Name Authority File. With the advent of the Linked Systems Project and the wide distribution of this file, these control numbers should provide reliable and consistent identification of authority records for users of most processing systems. Expansion of this model of shared cataloging might provide equally reliable identifiers for bibliographic records. This seems a fruitful model to develop.

These are some of the ways in which the USMARC formats support linkages among records. However, there is an inevitable tension here. As noted above, bibliographic relationships are primarily defined within the context of a particular set of records; they do not translate automatically to other systems containing different sets of records. Yet the MARC formats were not designed to support the maintenance of relationships within a system, but rather to promote communication of records between systems. Given this tension between maintaining relationships and communicating records, Mr. Gorman's "simple record with complex connections" is unlikely to be all that simple and the connections may not necessarily mean all that much when communicated beyond the system in which they were first established.

Local Data and Union Databases   The Anglo-American cataloging rules have never come to grips with local data. Or rather, the problem may be the other way around. The rules assume that catalogers are always describing a particular copy of the item in hand. What they do not seem to have recognized in sufficient detail is the widespread existence of union databases of shared cataloging, in which each record supposedly represents no one particular copy but rather what is common to all copies.

But all copies of what? AACR2 does not deal with the question of what should be the target of the description and what is information about an individual library's copy. The Library of Congress has an interpretation of rule 1.0 which deals with the decision whether to treat a new item as "edition" or "copy." OCLC's *Bibliographic Input Standards* includes an appendix on "when to input a new record" (OCLC, 1985, p. 117–128). All of these are based on the definition of "edition" in AACR2, but all of them reflect the need to go beyond what is provided in the rules themselves.

One tendency of cataloging rules and conventions is to treat quite minor physical variations as requiring separate descriptions. This practice has been recognized as expensive and highly redundant in the many cases where the variations do not conceal the essentially similar nature of the different versions (Schmierer, 1985, p. 1). Such is the case, for example, of different types of microform produced from a single original or master negative; they are all bibliographically equivalent. However, the differences are very important to a user who needs to find the right machine to use. The problem is one of bibliographic control. We need to know what works are represented in our collections; we also need to know all the relevant physical characteristics of particular copies.

In the past, the only way to achieve control over both works and the physical characteristics of their various manifestations was to describe each manifestation in a separate bibliographic record. This was because both the cataloging rules and the MARC formats had allowed little opportunity for recording local data in any kind of organized way.

The existence and implementation of the USMARC Format for Holdings and Locations changes this. The format already provides for a structure of multiple holdings records linked to a single bibliographic record. The holdings records include elements for the description by each institution of the item's location, call number, and piece holdings, its physical characteristics, and reproduction information. In theory, the format could include specifications for *any* information about local copies which differs from the general description. It could even include access points applicable only to an individual copy or copies. The holdings record provides a location for individualized description of local variations without loss of control over those variations.

The existence of a holdings format provides the opportunity to think conceptually about which aspects of a biliographic entity should be described in a bibliographic record and which should be treated as local variations.

American libraries have already begun to treat certain differences in physical format as local variations. A widely followed LC policy for cataloging microform reproductions calls for separate description of each type of microform, but the description is to be formulated in terms of variations on the original [*Cataloging Service Bulletin,* **14** (Fall) 1981: 56–58]. Many institutions, including the Library of Congress, simply treat microform reproductions as copies of the original, at least in some cases. Since such copy information is not usually shared outside the library owning the item, the fact that it is held in microform may not be known. However, if the note describing the microform were included in a holdings record, along with all the coded data that seems to be necessary for controlling microforms, then it could be attached to a single bibliographic description for the original.

Other choices need to be made about different versions in essentially the same medium. Is it really necessary to have three separate bibliographic records just because a micropublisher issues an item on film, fiche, and opaque? Is it necessary to create separate bibliographic descriptions of each type of sound recording of a single performance issued by the same publisher? At least some of these details could be treated as local variations and recorded in holdings records. The problem is deciding where to draw the line and then designing data structures that can keep track of, and intelligibly display, the information required in the appropriate context.

Before decisions can be made or data structures designed, however, there must be some solid conceptual analysis of the bibliographic universe: of the forms in which bibliographic material is manifested as text or performance, of the ways in which texts and performances are captured and master versions created, of the physical formats in which these masters are reproduced for use. There need to be some concepts of what constitute significant variants at each of these levels. The resulting categories need to be organized. Only then can we intelligently decide at what level(s) bibliographic control should be exercised. Then these decisions can be embodied in descriptive cataloging rules for describing items at the level determined and for describing local variations. And finally, system designers will be able to exercise their creativity in designing data structures that will link related bibliographic and holdings records so that records are properly retrieved and clustered and so that information in holdings records can be effectively displayed.

The conceptual analysis has already begun, under the auspices of the Library of Congress, which commissioned Helen Schmierer to look into the problem of multiple versions of the same work. Her analysis and a proposal from the Serial Record Division, which deals primarily with the problem of multiple versions of a serial, are being considered by the Library.[13] One of her strongest recommendations is that we must "reach some relatively firm conclusions about what is bibliographic data, what is holdings data, and what is both" (Schmierer, 1985, p. 14). This is one of the most important tasks we face in the field of descriptive cataloging and one that calls for us to reconsider some fundamental concepts of biliographic control.

Conclusion

I noted earlier that the pace of change in both descriptive cataloging rules and in machine-readable cataloging formats has slowed. Nevertheless, I think it is clear that major challenges remain in both areas. The particular issues I raised are, I hope, ones that emphasize the interaction of fundamental concepts. The concepts underlying the MARC formats include the function of MARC as a vehicle for the exchange of records and the techniques provided for organizing information within bibliographic, authority, and holdings records. The concepts underlying the cataloging rules include the basic functions of bibliographic control: why we need bibliographic descriptions, what it is we need to describe, what elements constitute the description, and how these elements interrelate. As we face particular issues, it is necessary that both descriptive catalogers and MARC format designers understand the fundamental concepts in both areas and that they work together to refine and develop these concepts in the light of new challenges.

Notes

1. The call for an integrated cataloging standard is often voiced, and I must admit a certain sympathy. However, there are some very real difficulties with the concept, both practical and theoretical. The practical problem is that, while there is a single set of descriptive cataloging rules for the Anglo-American community, achieved with considerable effort in the course of preparing AACR2, there is no comparable unity in the formats for machine-readable records. Within the Anglo-American community alone there are four national formats, an international exchange format (UNIMARC), and numerous format extensions, such as those of OCLC and RLIN. While there is a great deal in common among these formats, there are also some striking differences. *Which* MARC format should be integrated with the cataloging rules? Or do we take a giant step backward and perpetrate a "UKMARC edition," a "USMARC edition," etc.?

From a theoretical perspective, it is necessary to remember that cataloging rules and MARC formats have quite distinct functions. The cataloging rules prescribe the content of bibliographic descriptions; the MARC formats provide a structure and a set of machine-readable labels for all kinds of bibliographic data. There is a grave danger that integrating the two standards would reduce AACR2 to a set of instructions for filling in the blank space after the MARC tags, or it would reduce the MARC formats to a set of instructions for coding AACR2 records. If these dangers can be avoided, if the functions of the two standards can be kept distinct, then it might be possible to draft a document which would *illustrate* the integrated *application* of both standards, probably in a particular context, such as an OCLC-based system.

2. Henriette D. Avram, the principal creator of the MARC formats, has written their official history (Avram, 1975). Walt Crawford's book on the MARC formats includes an excellent summary of their history, brought up to 1984 (Crawford, 1984, p. 115–133). This work also provides the best available background on all aspects of the USMARC formats.

3. The bibliographic formats, for *books* (originally published in 1968), *serials* (1970), *maps* (1970), *films* (1971; now called *visual materials*), *manuscripts* (1973; now called *archives and manuscripts control*), *music* (1973), and *machine-readable data files* (1982), have been published together in *USMARC Format for Bibliographic Data* (USMARC Bibliographic Format, 1988). Also available are the *authorities* format (USMARC Authorities Format, 1987) and a "final draft" of the *holdings* format (USMARC Holdings Format, 1984).

4. The Library of Congress has prepared National Level Bibliographic Record (NLBR) standards for books (1980), films, maps, music, and serials (1981) and a National Level Authority Record (1982). The NLBR specifications have been integrated into the USMARC documents cited in the previous footnote.

5. The most glaring exception is the title and statement of responsibility area (USMARC, field 245). The extremely complex structure provided in the rules, particularly in the provisions concerning parallel titles and works without collective titles, is not fully supported by USMARC. It is interesting that the UNIMARC format (International Federation of Library Associations and Institutions, 1980, p. 41) makes an explicit connection between the two systems of content designation. In the Descriptive Information Block, which corresponds to ISBD areas 1–6, the ISBD punctuation is not carried at the subfield boundaries. However, the problem of parallel information proved to be too complex to deal with in this manner, and a UNIMARC subgroup recently affirmed that the equals sign would need to be carried in addition to the subfield codes (Bourne and Rather, 1986).

6. The statement was published in the *Library of Congress Information Bulletin* (May 9, 1983; p. 148–152) and in *Information Technology and Libraries* 2 (1983, p. 309–315). An annotated version appears in Crawford, 1984, appendix A, p. 183–193. The substance of the statement has been incorporated into the USMARC specifications for record structure (USMARC Specifications for Record Structure, 1987, p. 1–10).

7. I originally proposed this idea in 1981, in a USMARC advisory group discussion paper entitled "The Definition of a MARC Format." A revised version of this paper was later published (Attig, 1983a). In 1983, formal discussions by the USMARC advisory group began on another discussion paper, "Integration of USMARC Bibliographic Formats." These discussions established the principle that consistency across formats was a significant goal, but that it was unclear that existing inconsistencies could be removed without prohibitive costs. During the next several years, the Library of Congress canvassed the bibliographic networks concerning the extent of integration they could support. There was general (if grudging, in some cases) support for format integration in general. There was also agreement that the most urgent need was for a technique which would allow full coding of records for nonprint serials. (This is a problem because all bibliographic records must fit under the umbrella of a single USMARC format. The serial aspects can be fully coded in the Serials format or the nonprint aspects can be fully coded in the Visual Materials format, but there is no way to code both aspects.) With this mandate, LC in June 1987 presented a set of proposals which would (1) allow coded-data fields for more than one type of material in the same record, thus resolving the problem of nonprint serials; (2) add all content designators to all formats for which they had not yet been defined or (what amounts to the same thing) remove all format restrictions on the use of content designators; (3) remove all inconsistencies in the definitions of content designators; and (4) simplify the formats by removing unused or unnecessary content designators. In July 1988 all the proposals were accepted and

only implementation and documentation questions remain to be settled. Thus after almost 10 years of effort, a new USMARC format for bibliographic records will soon be issued. Along with the drafting of the statement of principles and the significant expansion of the formats (to be discussed later), this represents the crowning achievement of a decade of remarkable progress for the MARC formats.

8. Walt Crawford (1984, chapters 5–8) provides detailed discussions of the changes.

9. The series treatment fields (p. 640–646) are particularly interesting, because their structure underlines the fact that authority control is a matter of making and implementing decisions and that these decisions are specific to the particular system in which they are made. Thus it was necessary for series authority records not only to include the decisions (analysis, classification, tracing, numbering) but also to indicate *whose* decisions they were.

10. The history of the struggle with analytics is described by Walt Crawford (1984, p. 105–107). The technique eventually adopted is described in McCallum, 1982. Incidentally, a combined-record technique has been used in USMARC. In the holdings format, the holdings fields either may be given alone in a separate record or may be included in a biliographic record. This was possible because the holdings relationship is such a simple one and did not require the sort of complex techniques required for other kinds of record linking.

11. There is a problem in deciding what "identical" means; it is not always possible for there to be an exact match which includes both full data and content designation. For example, some subfield coding will be missing from the linking fields 760–787. Even in terms of content alone, one has to decide whether differences in punctuation, capitalization, and/or diacritics are significant.

12. It is important to remember that there are limits to the powers of automation. Shared cataloging can only go so far in providing economies, because it is still necessary to integrate records into the local catalog. Until such time as we all contribute to the same authority files and catalog against the same file of bibliographic records, it will be necessary to redo locally the work required to define all the many relationships among records within the context of the local catalog.

13. In July 1988 the Library of Congress presented to the USMARC Advisory Group a discussion paper on "*Communication of Records for Multiple Versions.*" At this early stage in the discussion, the approach taken calls for separate records for each version with a generalized linking technique for communicating information about the relationships among records.

Bibliographic Structures: The Evolution of Catalog Entries, References, and Tracings

Barbara B. Tillett

A title suggested to me for this chapter was "A Funny Thing Happened on the Way to the User-Friendly Catalog,"which I rather like. However, upon reflection, the things that happened on the way are more curious than funny, so I've taken the Darwinian approach. As my title states, this is an examination of the evolution of entries, references, and tracings. The evolution itself both demonstrates the importance of linking devices in catalogs and reveals a parallelism between changes in technology used to produce the catalog and changes in the structure of the catalog.

Since the introduction in the late 1960s of the MARC format, the design of online catalogs has depended on the MARC structure for bibliographic records. MARC was built with card production requirements in mind and hence reflected the needs of the card technology. A decade after the introduction of the MARC format, when the nature and future of the catalog and authority control received considerable attention, several authors presented futuristic projections for online catalog structures. Most of these authors noted that it was time to look beyond cards, time to take advantage of computer capabilities. Yet nearly another

149

10 years have passed, and we are still relying on the card-based MARC formats for our bibliographic and authority record structure.

As we shall see, record structures are changeable and inevitably reflect the technology available for producing the catalog. The underlying conceptual structure of the catalog, on the other hand, can and should remain fairly constant. What is meant by conceptual structure is the framework for records and links among records that a user must visualize in order to optimally use the catalog. As long as we clarify the basic conceptual structure of the catalog, we provide a serviceable underlying rationale to guide the use of the catalog, regardless of the catalog's form.

Our present-day views of the catalog's conceptual structure can be traced at least as far back as the mid-nineteenth century when Panizzi strongly defended the library catalog as a vital tool to access a library's holdings. His rules reflect a conceptual structure based on entries, that is, single, full records for each cataloged item, and three classes of cross references to link the user's choice of entry with the catalog entry (Rules, 1841). The conceptual structure of the catalog then consists of *records,* composed of *data elements,* and *connections* among the records. Connected records form *clusters,* which share a particular type of relationship. Records are made to describe bibliographic entities and to control subjects and names used as access points, where names include personal, corporate, conference, and geographic names, as well as names given library materials, that is, titles, and particularly titles of works or parts of works.

A catalog user expects to find materials by author, title, or subject. When asking for an author, the user expects to find all the works with which that author is associated and all the editions of each work. We know that such expectations were first stated by Cutter as his *Objects* (Cutter, 1876, p. 10) and later reworded by Lubetzky (Lubetzky, 1969, p. 14). Unfortunately, such expectations have been limited by cataloging rules which, in order to manage the ever-increasing size of the catalog, call for a maximum of three authors and often fewer than three subjects. Such rules may be unnecessarily restrictive in the computerized environment, particularly as storage costs continue to decline. But as catalogs become larger and greater numbers of records are associated with individual access points, there is a greater need for more distinctive paths to help us arrive at our destination: the target bibliographic item. At present the mixture of entries and references all too often combines all paths into traffic-jammed highways with no road signs. How did we get into this traffic jam? And more to the point, how can we get out of it?

One approach to effective retrieval is to provide displays of related bibliographic records, clustered and identified according to distinctive bibliographic relationships. For example, if we specify the function of names associated with bibliographic items, retrieval and displays of retrieved results can be refined to better respond to user queries. Similarly, if we clarify the relationships among items, we provide better-defined paths and road signs for searching the catalog. In current computer jargon, we need to specify the conceptual structure of the catalog in terms of entities, their attributes, and relationships.

One interpretation of the entity-relationship model is to consider entities as records, attributes as data elements, and relationships as the connections which link both records and data elements.[1] In libraries, we heretofore have called entities by various names depending on the evolutionary stage of the catalog: registries, entries, or records, including all of the various kinds of entries and records, such as main entry, added entry, and cross references. These entities in turn are made of attributes or data elements which compose a record. For example, attributes include main-entry headings, title statements, author statements, imprints, and notes. Some attributes may serve as access points to the record. Relationships, on the other hand, are connections among entities, between entities and their attributes, and among attributes. Typically, relationships are represented in the catalog by devices, such as cross references and access points, that connect and provide access to bibliographic records. Research indicates that although the relationships inherent to a catalog have not changed over time, the methods or devices used to represent relationships have changed (Tillett, 1987). Likewise, the forms of entities and their attributes used in the library catalog have evolved through various cataloging rules.

The Evolution of Catalog Entries

It is probably not surprising that the evolution of catalog entries directly corresponds to the evolution of the physical form of the library catalog. Just as catalogs emerged from inventory lists on clay tablets and progressed through handwritten card catalogs, typeset book catalogs, and printed or typed card catalogs to arrive at computerized, COM, and online catalogs, so catalog entries have evolved from single, brief entries on a chronological list and progressed through single-author entries, and cross references in book catalogs, and more complex added entries in card catalogs to arrive at the present MARC-formatted records in machine-readable form.

A chronological reading of the cataloging rules from Panizzi in 1841 (Rules, 1841) to the present second edition of the *Anglo-American Cataloguing Rules* (AACR2, 1978) reveals a shift in the use of entries corresponding to the type of catalog in vogue. For example, Panizzi's rules suited the predominant book and handwritten card catalogs of the mid-nineteenth century. As a result of the economic restrictions on the size of book catalogs and the extensive time involved in writing cards for the handwritten card catalogs, Panizzi's rules called for a bibliographic item to be described in full only once, by means of an "entry." To provide more complete access to the entries and to make the catalog more than a mere finding list or inventory of the collection, cross references were to be included. Panizzi's three classes of cross references were

1. name to name,

2. name to work, and

3. work to work.

The first class of cross references referred the catalog user from a variant form of name to the form chosen for an entry. The second class of cross references directed the user to a catalog entry for a work from headings which might be considered equally as important as the main entry in accessing the entry. Such headings included personal, corporate, conference, and geographic names, as well as the names of works, i.e., titles. The third class directed the user from one work to another work, most commonly from parts of a work to the whole work.

Entries and cross references continued to be the basic elements of the catalog through the turn of the century, even after the card catalog first made its appearance. The use of handwritten cards and the effort to economize on the number of entries perpetuated single full entries and brief additional entries.[2]

In early cataloging rules there were special instances, however, that called for multiple entries, usually double or dual entries. By double entry is meant two full records for the same item, each record being given a different main-entry heading. Double entry was particularly useful when it was not clear which of two authors should be acknowledged as the primary author for the record. This practice, first used in Jewett's cataloging rules, dates from 1852 (Jewett, 1852). For example, his rule XXII for publications of corporate bodies called for recording the book twice, once under the heading for the general title and again under the name of the individual personal author.[3] Following Jewett, Cutter had several rules prescribing conditions for double entry, such as: for both author of the text and designer, when the illustrations were important (Cutter 1876, Rule 6; 1889, Rule 7; 1891, Rule 7; 1904, Rule 8), for the composer of music, as well as for important authors of the words to the music (Cutter 1876, Rule 7; 1889, Rule 9; 1891, Rule 9; 1904, Rule 11), and for both the author of a concordance and the author concorded (Cutter

1876, Rule 11; 1889, Rule 17; 1891, Rule 17; 1904, Rule 20, with the author being concorded considered a subject entry). Beyond double entry, Cutter recommended multiple entry for the various contracting parties to a treaty (Cutter 1876, Rule 34; 1889, Rule 50; 1891, Rule 50; 1904, Rule 58). This use of multiple entries was later expanded using unit cards to provide full entries under each access point.

Another version of a multiple entry is the analytical entry, which evolved from an analytical reference; it provides additional records for individual items or groups of items in a collection or set. Panizzi's rules included such references, but the term "analysis" did not appear in cataloging rules until 1867 when the Library of Congress rules mentioned cases to be "analyzed" in rule 22 (Rules for Catalogueing, 1867). By 1876 Cutter's rules included an entire section on "Analysis" and analytical references were included in his definitions. While today several techniques are available in AACR2's Chapter 13 for analysis, ranging from separate entries to multilevel description, analytical references are no longer included as an option.

Similar to the analytical reference in linking two related works is the "see also" reference. The practice of using "see also" references from one valid heading to another dates from Cutters' first edition in 1876. In the section of Cutter's rules on style, under references (Cutter 1876, Rule 159; 1889, Rule 203; 1891, Rule 203; 1904, Rule 286), we find two types of references presented: "see" when there is no entry under the first term and "see also" when there is one. Cutter's example of a "see also" reference is for two subject headings, but in his fourth edition, rule 303, the "see also" is used also for name references to provide a general reference for spelling variations of surnames. By the 1908 *Catalog Rules* for works by individuals who also wrote as heads of departments, we are asked to see also the name of the department (Rule 58), or for works by a pope (Rule 12) to see also his name under his official entry.

The most common type of reference is the "see" reference, which refers the user from a heading not used to one that is used. But Cutter also used "see" references with elaborated wording, to provide connections between works or parts of works. For example, his rules prescribed the following phrases to connect periodicals that changed names:

"For a continuation, see" or

"For the previous volumes, see ..." (Cutter 1876, Rule 54; 1889, Rule 73; 1891, Rule 73; 1904, Rule 133)

Such phrases might appear either as referential notes on entries or as separate cross-reference entries.

Thus, Panizzi and Cutter were influential in establishing the basic structure of the catalog as a set of records with links among those records. Their records included entries and cross references; their links were references to names and references to works. But, their particular rendering of the catalog structure was altered at the turn of the century when a new technology for catalog production was introduced.

The Arrival of the Added Entry

In 1901 a most monumental occurrence changed the look of catalogs. In January of that year the Library of Congress (LC) began selling its printed catalog cards to libraries. In the introduction to the 1902 *ALA Rules— Advance Edition* the spirit of cooperative cataloging and the introduction of greater uniformity through LC's printed cards were cited as reasons for reviewing the cataloging rules and producing an "advance edition" (ALA Rules, 1902, p. 2–3). With the printed card catalog came a new concept, that of an added entry. With printed cards additional entries could economically be produced using the basic main-entry card, later known as the unit card, with a secondary heading typed at the top. So rather than a brief cross reference to provide additional access, librarians made a full added entry, similar in concept to the dual entry, but at comparatively less expense of time and effort. The *ALA Advance Edition* rules of 1902 were the first to mention added entries. Yet no definition of "added entry" was provided until Cutter's rules in their fourth edition in 1904. The early rules had not distinguished when to use an added entry and when to use a cross reference. Before the advent of added entries, references had to both provide secondary access to bibliographic records and link headings for related names or works. As for which to use when providing access to a bibliographic record, an added entry or a reference, there were nearly as many rules in the codes from 1902 through 1949 requiring cross references as there were requiring added entries. When to use references and when to use added entries continues to be unclear, even in the current rules.

It was in the preface to the fourth edition of his rules published in 1904 that Cutter acknowledged the advent of printed cards and provided the first definition for "added entries."

> *Added entry,* a secondary entry, i.e., any other than a main entry. (Cutter, 1904, p. 13)

Cutter also added an annotation to his definition of "reference" to point out the phenomenon brought about by printed cards.

> In a printed-card catalog added entries often take the place of references, because one thereby gives more information with less work. (Cutter, 1904, p. 21)

What Cutter was referring to was the fact that card catalogs based on a printed unit-card system could include the full bibliographic description of an item under each heading for the item. Cards with typed headings at the top could then be filed in the appropriate alphabetical position in the catalog. In Cutter's rules, entries were full registries of books in the catalog, whereas references, lacking imprints, were partial registries. The term *cross reference* was used exclusively, at least in the first through third editions of his rules, to describe a reference from one subject to another. But on just what occasion added entries were to take the place of references or even whether references were still appropriate at all in a printed card catalog he did not make clear. His examples, however, showed that he continued to advocate the use of references, particularly references for name variations. In any case, whether to use references or added entries to access bibliographic records remained an unspecified either-or in Cutter's rules as well as in the 1902 *ALA Rules—Advance Edition*. In each of the three catalog codes from 1902 through 1904 one rule would prescribe an added entry for an access point while another rule, for apparently the same sort of access point, would prescribe a cross reference. For example, looking at the access point for judges, the 1902 *Advance Edition* Rule 40 prescribes the use of a *cross reference* from a judge to the court where he presided. However, in the same set of rules, for users seeking the digests of opinions rendered, Rule 11 prescribes an *added entry* for the judge.

To add to the lack of clarity, from the 1902 catalog code onward there were rules calling for a "reference *or* an added entry." Such rules persist even through our current AACR2, e.g., Rule 26.5 and Rule 21.29G. In the 1908 code there were 14 rules requiring a choice between a cross reference or an added entry; with two exceptions, all were rules for headings rather than links. The first exception was Rule 19, which called for links between editions of works by using either an added entry with the referential note, "For a second edition of this work see . . . ," or a cross reference. The second exception was Rule 124, which dealt with newspapers that appear in several editions, such as Evening, Morning, Sunday. The examples given for the rule indicate the use of a cross reference to link a newspaper's title and its place of publication and the use of an added entry to link the main title and the title of the specific edition. The remaining 12 rules in the 1908 code, giving the cataloger a choice between making a cross reference or an added entry, were curious in that only added entries were shown in the examples. It may be that

libraries preferring to use cross references, in the cases described by
these rules, were those without printed card catalogs, that is, libraries that
could not easily create an added entry, or found it uneconomical to do so.

One of the economies cited by Cutter in 1904, Rule 114, promotes
further confusion by describing an added entry but calling it a reference:

> In printed-card catalogs a reference for a particular book is made
> by inserting the whole card with suitable heading and with
> underlining of such parts of the title or notes as will show why the
> reference is made.

It would appear, thus, that the term *reference* was used to indicate both
the referential instruction, e.g., "A see also B," as well as the device
containing that instruction, i.e., the cross reference entry. From Panizzi's
rules through Cutter's third edition (1891), the only device for access to
bibliographical entries beyond the main-entry heading was the cross
reference. But once added entries were introduced, the rules from 1902
onward provided for a wide variety of additional entries under headings
once managed by cross references. This naturally contributed to the
ambiguity over which device to prefer in a given situation, the cross
reference or the added entry.

As time progressed, indications of when to use added entries
and when to use cross references became clearer: added entries were
consistently used for added access to a bibliographic record, while cross
references, called simply references, were used for name variations. Yet
there were still many rules in each of the catalog codes through AACR2,
which called for using cross references instead of multiple added entries
or added entries instead of multiple cross references. Basically, added
entries replaced cross references and vice versa when the replacement
resulted in a reduction of catalog cards. This economy to reduce the
number of cross references or added entries was suggested at least as
early as Aug. 6, 1901 in Rule 19 of the LC *Supplementary Rules* (Library
of Congress, 1905).

As the added entry, introduced with the advent of printed catalog
cards in 1901, gradually supplanted the reference and became a device to
provide supplementary access to bibliographic records from names, titles,
and subjects closely associated with the bibliographic items being described, the cross reference slowly evolved into a device to link variant
name headings. The cross reference directed the user from unused forms
of names used as headings to preferred forms of names (i.e., names of
persons, corporate bodies, bibliographic items, topical subjects, etc.).

Tracings and Other Record Keeping

Just as an evolution in the catalog and catalog entries took place, another evolution took place in the method by which cross references and added entries were recorded. As printed cards were introduced, a device began to be used to document the additional cards created for added entries and cross references. This device was a "tracing" or annotation on a main-entry bibliographic record that traced the path used to reach it from its added access points. The primary purpose of a tracing is to help the cataloger locate the respective added-entry record whenever it needs updating or correcting.

The way in which tracings for added entries are displayed on the main entry card or unit card has varied over time. The Library of Congress *Supplementary Rules on Cataloging* numbers 4, 5, and 6, all dated Jan. 7, 1904, provided specific instructions for printing tracings (not called so then) on catalog cards. Rule 6 required that tracings for added entries be printed on the front of the card from thereafter and follow the tracings for subject entries, which were numbered in Arabic numerals. The tracings for added entries were to be numbered in Roman numerals in the order of their importance. The rule also set up standard abbreviations to be used in tracings and added entries (e.g., jt. auth., ed., etc.). Rule 5 on "Recataloging" referred to a then-outdated practice of underscoring authors' surnames in contents notes to trace which analyticals were made. Rule 4 on "Annotation" characterized the ideal entry as a single printed card with added entries," i.e., tracings for added entries, on the front, compared to old entries taking as many as two or three manuscript cards with "added entries" on the back.

The first of the rules examined that used the word *traced* for tracings on main-entry cards was the *Library of Congress Rules on Cards* rule for "Added Entries" dated Dec. 16, 1907 (Library of Congress, 1899–1940),[4] which prescribed writing a note on the back of the main-entry card for all added-entry cards, for cross-reference cards which referred only to that particular work, and for analytical cards. When analytical entries were too numerous to easily include on the back of the main-entry card, the rule prescribed writing "work analyzed" instead. While this 1907 rule contradicts the 1904 rule to record tracings on the front of the card, it can be seen as illustrating the difference between the internal practices at the Library of Congress for its official catalog, reflected in the *Rules on Cards,* and the practices for its printed card program, reflected in the LC *Supplementary Rules on Cataloging.*

The 1941 *ALA Catalog Rules* followed the practice described in the 1904 *Supplementary Rules* above. On the main-entry card for a work were traced all of the added entries made for it. The 1941 rule went on to elaborate.

> The main entry, used as a master card, may bear in addition the tracing of related references and a record of other pertinent official data concerning the work. (ALA Catalog Rules, 1941, p. xxvi)

These other pertinent data included the full name of the author, when the full name was not the form chosen for the heading, and transliterated or translated titles and names. Thus, until 1969, there were tracings for both added entries and references appearing on the main-entry card.

Problems arose with the early rules for tracings. The problem can be seen on old cards in LC's official catalog, where the "see from" tracings for "see" references can be found typically handwritten with blue x's or red x's on the unit card.[5] The tracing of a reference on a bibliographic record usually meant that the reference applied only to a heading used on that bibliographic record. However, as the catalog grew, references which applied to headings used on earlier bibliographic records might well apply to headings used on later bibliographic records. Thus, there was the problem of creating repeated references on many main-entry cards; for instance, the tracing Twain, Mark, had to be written on each of the main-entry cards for his works, which were entered under Clemens, Samuel Langhorne, 1835–1910. The solution at that time was to trace the reference on several bibliographic records, but to make only one cross-reference card in LC's official catalog. When there were numerous name variations it became cumbersome to repeat the multiple variations as traced references on each main-entry card to which the references applied.

Approximately two-thirds of personal names occur in a library catalog only once,[6] but for variations of name on the remaining one-third the task of correcting tracings can become quite difficult and time consuming. The task could be accomplished more efficiently through a single separate record recording the variations represented in the reference, thereby avoiding the repetitious recording of the reference on each bibliographic record to which it applied. Some inconvenience of correcting tracings remains for the card environment, but for the online environment it disappears. Changes made to a single separate authority or "control" record could automatically generate a correction in the corresponding bibliographic records. One application of this procedure is the global update feature of some current online catalogs.

There is evidence that as far back as 1899 the Library of Congress had a supplementary rule on "authority cards" for creating just such a separate record to contain all variants of the name used as a heading for the first time in the catalog.[7] Among other things, the authority card was to contain the full name and an itemization of references made from varying forms of the name. In both the first and second editions of the *Anglo-American Cataloguing Rules* the requirement remains to "make a record of every reference under the name heading or uniform title to which it refers in order to make possible a correction or deletion of that reference" (AACR2, 1978, p. 492), but these later rules do not specify where such a record is to be kept: in the card catalog or in a separate file, for the public or for the catalogers? As we have seen, through 1941 the catalog rules specified tracing references on main-entry cards.

As can be seen on cards entered into the official catalog at the Library of Congress after 1969, the Library of Congress discontinued making variant-name "see from" references on main-entry cards. From that point onward only tracings for secondary entries (subject and added entries) were traced on authority records. This shift from the bibliographic record as the locus for variants of the main and added entry headings to the authority record is not documented in any of the rules nor in the current descriptive cataloging manual used by LC. The move possibly was influenced by changes resulting from LC's use of the MARC format in 1968 and LC's division of its official catalog into a name-title and a subject catalog in 1969 (Library of Congress, Processing Department, 1969).

Regardless of the historical reasons, the simple logic of tracing subjects and added entries on bibliographic records and tracing references on authority records makes sense. The bibliographic record should document all headings used for its access and all links to related bibliographic records, while the authority record, which I prefer to call a control record, should document all of the variations of names used as headings and links to related names.

This distinction between the bibliographic record and the authority record, while logical and potentially useful, is not reflected in current practice. For example, in current cataloging, series treatment is documented in an authority file; the authority or control record indicates whether the items in a series are classed together or separately and whether a series added entry should be made for individual titles in the series or not. However, series authority records are actually pseudo-bibliographic records in that they also include details about the numbering, publication information, and bibliographic history of the series. These are the kind of descriptive elements we expect to find in a bibliographic record. In fact, when a series is treated as a serial, the same elements may be repeated in both an authority record and a bibliographic record.

Another instance of the confused boundary between bibliographic and authority-control records can be seen in the handling of a name variation for a title of a bibliographic item. While names of works that have more than one manifestation often are included on authority records as uniform titles with their title variations, the practice persists of including title variations for a bibliographic item in bibliographic records. Logically, they are name variations for the work and belong in an authority record. Possibly one reason they remain in the bibliographic record is because redundancy is much less likely for names of bibliographic items than for personal or corporate names.

Future Structures

To further elaborate on my interpretation of the conceptual structure of the catalog, one structure might embody entities, i.e., two types of records; their attributes, i.e., the data elements which make up the records, many of which act as access points to the record; and relationships which link records. The two types of records would be:

1. bibliographic records, and
2. control records.[8]

There would be two kinds of control records, name and subject, which provide control over names (i.e., personal names, corporate names, conference names, names of works and series) and subjects used as access points to bibliographic records. Name control records would include a default citation form of name with name variations and links to related names. Subject control records would include subject terms with their synonyms and broader, narrower, and related terms. Bibliographic records would give us descriptions of items together with identified access points to that description.

Directly connected to the bibliographic records would be what we might call subrecords for holdings; these would provide information concerning call number, copies, volumes, specific location, and other local identifiers of a particular item, such as barcodes.

Relationships are links to and among the entities. In my view there are bibliographic relationships, name relationships, subject relationships, and access-point relationships. As you might have guessed, Panizzi's three classes of references have provided us with the conceptual structure of relationships, our links being names to names (name and subject relationships), names to works (access-point relationships), and works to works (bibliographic relationships).

Devices indicating a bibliographic relationship would appear in the bibliographic records where the citation forms, or possibly numerical identifiers, for related or associated works would be given as parts of linking notes or as qualifiers to a title or edition statements, with appropriate coding to specify the type of bibliographic relationship. Name relationships would appear in name control records where the reference tracing would be the device to link all variant forms, and the citation form or numerical identifier would be the device to link associated names. Each of the devices would include coding, which would describe the specific association or relationship.

As is often suggested, bibliographic records would be derived from basic information drawn from the title pages and preliminaries of bibliographic items. There would be no redundant tracings of headings used either as access points or links to other bibliographic records, because such access points and links would simply be coded as such within the bibliographic description. A move in this direction was made in the MARC serials format, which has tagged citation forms of titles to link earlier and later titles associated with the serial in question, rather than repeating this information in separate notes. Through the tag and its indicators, a note can be generated for online displays or for printed products, such as catalog cards, for those libraries that will continue to rely on cards. The online link to the related bibliographic records can be made from that same nonredundant information.

Futhermore, the data elements, that is, the attributes of records, would consist of the following.

1. Blocked and tagged title-page information. We can envision a day when the title page is machine readable or is scanned to become machine readable, similar to today's Optiram or Kurzweil scanning. The identification of attributes may be assisted through knowledge-based computer systems to provide preliminary blocks and tags for human editing.

2. Notes added to the bibliographic record as needed, tagged to reflect the type of relationship when one is represented, avoiding the need for a redundant tracing. We would need to slightly modify some of the MARC tags and indicators for notes which incorporate links to another bibliographic record.

3. Subject access terms, that is classification and authorized forms of subject headings would be added. Present MARC tags seem adequate for this purpose.

4. Identification numbers, such as ISBN, ISSN, and LCCN in their own fields, as now done in the MARC formats.

5. Links made to associated subrecords for holdings information, that is, volume, copy, barcode, and specific location and call number of the associated physical items held by the library.

6. Links to the control records for names and subjects provided through the inclusion of control numbers and/or the citation form of name (personal, corporate, conference, titles, series) found in the description. The incorporation of such links would eliminate the need for separate tracings for the citation forms. If the citation form immediately followed the title-page form, it would be clear exactly what is being linked. One reason to prefer a citation form over a numerical link is that not all libraries can contribute yet to an international bibliographic and access control database to provide a standard number for every name, so instead, the form of the name prescribed by cataloging rules is a more convenient and universal link. A future global telecommunications network may make numerical links universal. For example, the authority control record number now included in machine-readable authority records distributed by the Library of Congress could be used as a numerical identifier.

Now that we have reached the next technological step in the evolution of the catalog, the cataloging rules and mechanics of recording need to progress accordingly to take advantage of the new technology. What have we learned from all of this that will help the future structure of the library catalog? What I have tried to show through the review of the evolution of references, in particular, is that we should clearly identify the purpose of, and differentiate between, devices we use to link *records* versus devices we use to link *name variations*. Through the evolution of tracings we learn that we should also differentiate between bibliographic records and control records and use control records to avoid the redundancy of tracing name variations in bibliographic records. We can also see it is essential to specify the type of relationship or link that is being made, particularly, in large catalogs and computerized catalogs, so that users have clear road maps to follow and can expect to travel with ease on whichever path they choose.

Obviously, the reason all of this is so interesting now is that online catalogs and computer systems provide us with the opportunity of linking records and tagging information to facilitate construction of displays and printed products. Just as Panizzi intended to make the catalog of optimum utility to his library users within the bounds of time and money constraints, we should be thinking of ways to optimize the computer's capabilities. Needs of users and economic constraints are continuing themes that affect all catalogs and their corresponding catalog rules. We have reached another milestone in technology, just as we did at the turn of the century with the advent of printed cards. And just as the sharing of printed catalog cards changed cataloging rules and the structure of catalog entries, the computer-based catalog will certainly make its impact on the evolution of the catalog entry and bibliographic structure.

Acknowledgments

I would like to acknowledge the helpful comments received from Dr. Elaine Svenonius and Dr. Michael Carpenter, and the editorial assistance provided by Robert Ruffin, Ph.D. candidate, University of California, San Diego, through the numerous drafts of this chapter.

Chronological List of Cataloging Codes Examined

1841 "Rules for the Compilation of the Catalogue." In British Museum. *The Catalogue of the Printed Books in the British Museum,* V. 1, p. v–ix. London: British Museum, 1841. [Often referred to as "Panizzi's 91 Rules."]

1852 Jewett, Charles Coffin. *On the Construction of Catalogues of Libraries, and Their Publication by Means of Separate Stereotyped Titles. With rules and examples.* Washington, D.C.: Smithsonian Institution, 1852.

1853 Jewett, Charles Coffin. *On the Construction of Catalogues of Libraries, and Their Publication by Means of Separate Stereotyped Titles. With Rules and Examples.* 2nd Ed. Washington, D.C.: Smithsonian Institution, 1853.

1867 *Rules for Catalogueing* [sic] *in Congressional Library,* May 1867 [unpublished manuscript].

1876 Cutter, Charles Ammi. *Rules for a Printed Dictionary Catalogue.* Washington, D.C.: Government Printing Office, 1876.

1883 Cooperation Committee of the American Library Association. "Condensed Rules for an Author and Title Catalog." *Library Journal,* **8** (1883): 251–254.

1889 Cutter, Charles Ammi. *Rules for a Dictionary Catalogue.* 2nd Ed. Washington, D.C.: Government Printing Office, 1889.

1891 Cutter, Charles Ammi. *Rules for a Dictionary Catalogue.* 3rd Ed. Washington, D.C.: Government Printing Office, 1891.

1899–1940 (approx.) [*Library of Congress Rules on Cards*] including supplementary rules, preliminary rules, etc. [The incomplete set examined was dated from 1902–1940 with reference to rules from 1899.]

1902 Cooperation Committee of the American Library Association (1883). *ALA Rules—Advance Edition. Condensed Rules for an Author and Title Catalog.* Revised by the Advisory Catalog Committee. Washington, D.C.: Government Printing Office, Library Division, 1902.

1904 Cooperation Committee of the American Library Association (1883). *ALA*

Rules—Advance Edition. Condensed Rules for an Author and Title Catalog. Revised by the Advisory Catalog Committee, 1902, issued by the Library of Congress. Washington, D.C.: Government Printing Office, Library Division, 1904.

1904 Cutter, Charles Ammi. *Rules for a Dictionary Catalog.* 4th Ed., rewritten. Washington, D.C.: Government Printing Office, 1904. (U.S. Bureau of Education. Special Report on Public Libraries, Part II)

1905 Library of Congress. *Supplementary Rules on Cataloging, 1–11. [March 1905].*

1906 Library of Congress. Special Rules on Cataloging, 1–21: to Supplement ALA Rules—Advance Edition. Washington, D.C.: Government Printing Office, Library Division, 1906.

1908 Committees of the American Library Association and the (British) Library Association, comps. *Catalog Rules: Author and Title Entries.* American Ed. Chicago: American Library Association Publishing Board, 1908.

1931 *Guide to the Cataloging of the Serials Publications of Societies and Institutions.* 2nd Ed. Compiled and edited by Harriet Wheeler Pierson. Washington, D.C.: U.S. Government Printing Office, 1931.

1941 Catalog Code Revision Committee of the American Library Association, with the collaboration of a Committee of the (British) Library Association. *ALA Catalog Rules: Author and Title Entries.* Preliminary American 2nd Ed. Chicago: American Library Association, 1941.

1949 Division of Cataloging and Classification of the American Library Association. *ALA Cataloging Rules for Author and Title Entries.* 2nd Ed. edited by Clara Beetle. Chicago: American Library Association, 1949.

1949 *Rules for Descriptive Cataloging in the Library of Congress.* Washington, D.C.: Library of Congress, Descriptive Cataloging Division, 1949.

1959 *Cataloging Rules of the American Library Association and the Library of Congress: Additions and Changes, 1949–1958.* Washington, [D.C.]: Library of Congress, 1959.

1961 International Conference on Cataloguing Principles. *Statement of Principles Adopted at the International Conference on Cataloguing Principles, Paris, October, 1961.* Annotated Ed., with commentary and examples by Eva Verona, assisted by Franz Georg Kaltwasser, P. R. Lewis, Roger Pierrot. London: IFLA Committee on Cataloguing, 1971.

1967 The American Library Association, The Library of Congress, The Library Association, and The Canadian Library Association. *Anglo-American Cataloging Rules.* North American Text. Chicago: American Library Association, 1967.

1974 The American Library Association, The Library of Congress, The Library Association, and The Canadian Library Association. *Anglo-American Cataloging Rules, Chapter 6: Separately Published Monographs.* North American Text. Chicago: American Library Association, 1974.

1975 *Anglo-American Cataloging Rules, Chapter 12, Revised: Audiovisual Media and Special Instructional Materials.* North American Text. Chicago: American Library Association, 1975.

1978 The American Library Association, The British Library, The Canadian Committee on Cataloguing, The Library Association, The Library of Congress. *Anglo-Amerian Cataloguing Rules.* 2nd Ed., edited by Michael Gorman and Paul W. Winkler. Chicago: American Library Association, 1978.

Notes

1. There are, of course, other interpretations of the entity-relationship model with respect to catalogs, such as looking beyond the catalog's conceptual structure to view entities as items being described in the catalog.

2. At the time of the first three editions of Cutter's rules, 1876–1891, catalogs were constructed of two types of "registries:" (1) full registries with title and imprint, which were called entries, and (2) partial registries, called references, that omitted the imprint and referred to the full entry. Cutter preferred the term *reference* over *cross reference,* with cross references being exclusively used for subject references. The plain *reference* had several functions: (1) it served as a directional device for name variations, as in Panizzi's first class of cross references; (2) it provided added access to works, as in Panizzi's second class; and (3) it linked works, as in Panizzi's third class.

3. Similarly Jewett's rule XXI required the cataloger to create a "second entry" for a book with a double title, such as was commonly the case with German books of entire treatises of several authors. One entry would be made under the general title and the second entry under a special title, when such double titles were given on the book.

4. This rule replaced a rule of Oct. 2, 1902, that I was not able to obtain.

5. Blue x's were for the public catalog, red x's were for the official catalog.

6. This was found by both Potter (1980, p. 15–16) and McCallum and Godwin (1981, p. 198).

7. The LC *Rules on Cards* entitled "Authority cards" revised on May 5, Aug. 8, Nov. 19, 1902 and Dec. 16, 1907 and amended Feb. 7, 1919 lists 1899 as the first date of the card. Unfortunately, I have not been able to locate copies of any of the rules on cards before 1902, and lack some of the rules on cards after 1902.

8. This structure is somewhat similar to one suggested by Michael Gorman in his talk at the 1977 and 1978 Canadian workshops on automated authority files (Gorman, 1978). In Gorman's view, the catalog would consist of bibliographic records, subject records, and name records with links. Records would fall into clusters and the links connecting those clusters would be coded through a general linking field. The field would be repeatable indefinitely and would show the type of record and the relationship to the work being connected to. New links could be added at any time.

Bibliographic Relationships: Implications for the Function of the Catalog

Edward T. O'Neill
Diane Vizine-Goetz

Introduction

The distinction between a book and a work and their respective relationship to bibliographic records in the catalog has long been an important cataloging concept. The significance of each was discussed at some length by Lubetzky (1961, 1969) and Verona (1959, 1963). Lubetzky (1969, p. 11) identified the problem:

> The book, it should be noted, comes into being as a dichotomic product—as a *material* object or medium used to convey the *intellectual* work of an author. Because the material *book* embodies and represents the intellectual *work,* the two have come to be confused, and the terms are synonymously used not only by the layman but also by the cataloger himself.

Lubetzky and Verona generally agree on the objectives of the catalog, which according to Verona (1959, p. 79) are:

1. The rapid location of a particular book;

2. the provision of information concerning all editions, translations, etc., of a given work as far as they exist in the library;

3. the provision of information concerning all works by a given author as far as they exist in the library.

Furthermore, they are in general agreement on the advantages and disadvantages of using either the book or the work as the basis for the main entry. Verona states, "A catalogue designed for the first objective and neglecting the other two will have as its basic element the individual book . . ." (1959, p. 79). However, a catalog designed for the second objective will concentrate on only works. "Hence particular books will not be considered as single items but as representatives of a whole group of similar items, all belonging to the same [work]" (Verona, 1959, p. 80). The third objective is not significantly affected by the selection of either the book or the work as the main entry.

In addition to the points on which Lubetzky and Verona explicitly agree, they also appear to share many common assumptions, including:

1. The first two objectives are in many cases conflicting so that it is not possible for any catalog to weight them equally;

2. The book should be the primary bibliographic entity for cataloging purposes;

3. The main entry will be selected to represent the book if the emphasis is on the first objective or the work if the emphasis is on the second.

However, they differ on the importance of the first two objectives. Verona (1959, p. 95) argues that since the number of users approaching the catalog with requests concerning particular books will be much higher than the number of those looking for works, main entries should focus on the location of books, and works should be identified through added entries. Lubetzky (1961, p. 141) argues in favor of the work since (1) "a person looking in a catalogue under a name and title is interested not merely in the particular publication issued under that name and title but rather in the work represented by it," and (2) "the entry of editions and translations under their own titles as issued, with added entries to relate them, will encumber the catalogue with many useless entries, impair the systematic character of the structure of the catalogue and often confuse its users."

Changes Affecting Catalogs

Since the Verona–Lubetzky debates of the 1950s and 1960s, major changes have occurred which affect the use and creation of library catalogs. The most significant are:

1. The creation, dissemination, and use of catalog records in machine-readable form;
2. the widespread use of online shared cataloging; and
3. the globalization of catalogs.

The creation and dissemination of machine-readable catalog records has resulted in new ways of storing and accessing bibliographic data. Computer-based catalogs can support far more complex data structures than book or card catalogs. Unlike the card catalog, whose structure is evident, the physical organization of the online catalog is hidden from the user. Entries which would burden the card catalog pose no similar problem in computer-based catalogs. Kilgour (1979, p. 34) was one of the first to recognize that users need not be directly exposed to the physical structure of computer catalogs:

> The online computerized library catalog is a wholly new type of catalog having a drastically different design from the seventeenth-century bookform catalog and the nineteenth-century card catalog. The bookform catalog and the card catalog are linear arrangements of bibliographic entries, sometimes of enormous length. Online catalogs consist of a large series of miniature catalogs. . . .

These "miniature catalogs" can be organized very differently from the underlying database from which they are extracted and can even be customized to meet the particular needs of an individual user.

The widespread use of online shared cataloging systems has changed the ways most libraries obtain and create catalog records and, consequently, has increased their need to follow cataloging rules and standards. Previously, a library would obtain much of its cataloging on cards distributed by the Library of Congress or by a commercial processing service. When a card or other source of cataloging was unavailable for an item, a catalog record was created locally and typically not shared with other libraries. Deviations from cataloging rules and standards within a given library were usually unimportant. This is not the case in an online shared cataloging system, where a cataloging record is produced by using a record in the system's database which describes the item being cataloged or, if no existing record can be found, an original record is created online. Since in such a system many libraries are contributing to a common database, adherence to cataloging rules is paramount when creating original cataloging. Differing interpretations of cataloging rules and local cataloging adaptations have significant adverse consequences such as the creation of multiple bibliographic records for a single bibliographic item or the creation of incomplete bibliographic records.

The third factor influencing catalogs and their use is the globalization of catalogs. The catalogs of bibliographic utilities as well as regional online networks are expanding beyond regional or national boundaries to become global in scope. This is an ongoing process which should be further accelerated by the Linked Systems Project (McCoy, 1986). Increasingly, online union catalogs are being expected to provide information about bibliographic items regardless of where the items are located throughout the world. Now when we come to the catalog seeking information about a particular item or "all editions, translations, etc., of a given work," we no longer accept information that is limited to their existence in the local library. The local collection is but a small subset of this global collection.

One consequence of the foregoing changes, and especially that of the advent of globalization, is that ever greater numbers of items become associated with a given work. Previously, the number of different manifestations of a work was generally limited within a given library. Verona (1959, p. 91) points out that, prior to the twentieth century, library acquisition policy focused exclusively on collecting works and that "different editions of the same work were usually considered as duplicates and discarded from the library." In 1985 there was an average of 1.31 records per work in the OCLC database and that number appears to be increasing. More important, the average number of records per work increased to 5.0 when only works with multiple records were considered. Both of these figures exclude translations.

As an example, *The Expedition of Humphry Clinker,* whose publishing history is shown in Table I, is typical of a work that has a large number of records associated with it. This work was one of several that was included in a random sample of 100 bibliographic records taken from the OCLC database to ascertain the characteristics of works. For this work, there are 110 records representing publications by 53 different publishers over a 200-year time period. Among these 110 records are records for unique bibliographic items as well as suspected duplicate records. In a case like this a cataloger, when attempting to determine whether an existing record describes an item in hand being cataloged or

Table I
Publishing History for *The Expedition of Humphry Clinker* by Tobias George Smollett

Publisher	Number of OCLC records	Publisher	Number of OCLC records
G. Bell	2	Hurst	2
Bernhard Tauchnitz	1	Hutchinson	2
Bigelow Brown	1	International Pub. Co.	1
Bigelow Smith	2	G.W. Jacobs	2
Blackwell	7	Jenson Society	2
Century		Johnston and Collins	8
W. Clarke	1	Leathley, Exshaw . . .	1
Cochrane and Pickersgill	2	Leypoldt & Holt	1
C. Cooke	3	J. Limbird	1
J. Cumberland	1	Longman and Robinson	3
Davies, Smith . . .	1	Modern Library	5
Dean and Munday	1	Navarre Society	1
Dent	3	T. Nelson	2
Derby and Jackson	1	New American Library	1
Doubleday	1	Norton	1
J. F. Dove	1	Nottingham Society	1
Folio Society	1	Oxford University Press	13
Gibbings	3	Penquin Books	2
Harper	1	Rinehart	1
Harrison	1	Rivington	2
Haswell, Barrington and Haswell	1	G. Routledge	7
Hearst's International Library	1	J. Sibbald	2
Heron Books	1	G. D. Sproul	1
Holt, Rinehart and Winston	2	Three Sirens Press	2
Houghton Mifflin	3	University of Delaware Press	1
		J. Walker	1
		Watson & Banks	1
		J. J. Woodward	1

whether a new record should be created, is faced with a nearly impossible task. We do not believe that catalogers or patrons can be expected to select a record confidently from a set such as this one. The information that was sufficient to identify particular items and bibliographic relationships within a local collection is inadequate in this new environment.

Bibliographic Entities

The changing expectations and demands placed upon library catalogs lead us to suggest a new conceptual structure for organizing information about books and works. The concepts discussed in this section should be applicable to all bibliographic materials including films, videotapes, sound recordings, manuscripts, etc. However, for this presentation we will limit our discussion to monographs. Even within this limited context, the terminology typically used to define bibliographic entities is neither well defined nor consistent. Therefore, before developing the concepts, it is necessary to define our terminology. The following terms will be used to describe bibliographic entities.

Work A set of related texts with a common origin and content.

Text A set of editions with the same content.

Edition A set of printings produced from substantially the same type image.

Printing A set of books printed at one time or printed at different times containing no more than slight variations.

Book An individual physical manifestation of a bibliographic entity.

These definitions reflect a hierarchical relationship between the levels of bibliographic entities. The hierarchy results from a one-to-many association between the entities at the various levels. That is, every entity will be associated with one and only one higher-level entity but may have multiple lower-level entities associated with it. For example, every edition will be associated with only one text but may have several different printings associated with it. If these relationships are to be reflected in a catalog, the current unidimensional bibliographic structure must be replaced by one with five levels of bibliographic entities: the book, the printing, the edition, the text, and the work. A discussion of the entities follows.

Book A book, as defined here, is the bibliographic entity at the lowest level of the hierarchy and is the only one which corresponds to a physical object. All of the other bibliographic entities are abstract concepts. Various terms are used synonymously with *book,* and the term *book* is often used in ways incompatible with our definition. For instance, *item, bibliographic item, copy, volume,* and *document* as well as other similar terms have been used interchangeably with the term *book.*

It is the individual book that is used to derive the information necessary for cataloging since, for cataloging purposes at least, all of the books constituting a particular printing are assumed to be bibliographically identical. Therefore, any book can be used to determine the bibliographic properties of the printing.

Printing A printing is a set of books by the same publisher which are either printed at one time or printed at different times using the original type image with no more than slight but well-defined variations. As a general rule, the variations permitted within a printing are limited to the correction of minor typographical errors. The books themselves may or may not contain printing information. Commercial publishers commonly display printing information on the verso of the title page. The printing information usually includes the printing number and may also include the printing date.

Edition An edition is a set of printings that, at the time of publication, were bibliographically identical. An edition is usually associated with a text. Therefore, if the text changes, so does the edition. However, there are some changes which create a new edition without resulting in a new text. For example, a new edition will be created when a text is republished by a different publisher or with significant changes in type image, or both.

Text A text is a set of editions with similar content. The term *text* was introduced by Wilson (1968, p. 6) to describe the content of a book as independent from its physical form. A text is "a sequence of words and auxiliary symbols" which has "no weight and occupies no space" (Wilson, 1968, p. 7). For example, as Hagler and Simmons (1982, p. 74) point out, "the Bantam edition of *Bleak House*, or the 1923 edition, or the Limited edition, may all be identical, word for word, in their textual content, their differences being only in paper, typography, binding, price, and perhaps publisher's name." Thus, a single text comprises three editions. Any edition that has been revised or updated will form a new text. New texts formed by revisions are often identified by numbered edition statements or edition statements such as "New Edition" or "Revised Edition." A new text may also occur as the result of an adaptation or translation. Felix Sutton's abridgement and adaptation of *Ben Hur* for children is a new text. Similarly, *Moby Dick: La Ballena Blanca*, the Spanish translation of *Moby Dick: The White Whale*, is a new text.

Work   We define a work as a set of related texts with a common source. The term *work* is frequently used inconsistently and, as a result, the distinction between an edition, a printing, and work is often unclear. The term *literary unit* has also been used as a synonym for work. Carpenter found that the words *book* and *work* are used loosely in various definitions and that "sometimes they are even used interchangeably, with a corresponding confusion" (Carpenter, 1981, p. 118).

Using our definition, a work may be composed of substantially different texts. The texts, however, must have been derived either directly or indirectly from a common source. As the text undergoes successive revisions or reexpressions over time, the words and symbols forming later texts may be very different from the original but still represent the same work. In our discussion of text we identified *Moby Dick: La Ballena Blanca* and *Moby Dick: The White Whale* as separate texts, yet we consider them to be the same work. The translation is closely related to the original and was derived directly from it.

Identifying Bibliographic Relationships

The cataloging process can be viewed in a variety of different ways. For our purposes, we will treat it as a two-step process: first identifying the relationship of the book being cataloged to the existing collection represented by the catalog, and then determining the values of the attributes on which to base the cataloging record. It is the first step, positioning books into the bibliographic structure, that is the primary focus of this discussion.

When a book is acquired, it is generally a straightforward process to establish the relationship between the book and the collection. If the book is a new work it can be cataloged independently of the other works already acquired. However, if the book is a manifestation of a work already in the collection, it is necessary to determine if it is a new text, a new edition, or a new printing, thus positioning the book into a hierarchical bibliographic structure.

Traditionally, in Anglo-American cataloging, much attention has been focused on the edition. Therefore, in practice, it is usually only necessary to determine if the book represents a new edition. However, a more precise hierarchical positioning can improve the cataloging process, at least conceptually.

In the majority of cases, it is relatively easy to determine if a book is a manifestation of an existing work. Commonly, all manifestations of a work will have the same author or authors and the same title. There are, however, cases where different manifestations of a work will have different titles, different authors, as well as differences in content. One such example is shown in Table II. The *Guide to Reference Books* has had different titles and authors. It has been published over almost a century by different publishers and the content of the latest edition bears little resemblance to that of the original edition. Yet, most would consider all of these editions to represent the same work.

The crucial question then is how different can a new manifestation be without becoming a new work? When the title or the authorship or both change, what are the guidelines? Can we find a practical measure of similarity between bibliographic items? We could count the number of different characters, words, or sentences, but what would it mean? How do we clarify the notion of a work? Jolley (1963, p. 160) offers a promising approach to identifying a work. He states:

> The cataloguer is not a literary historian. He is only concerned with a work when it has been embodied in a publication. It is not his task to decide, on internal evidence, when a new publication of a law treatise becomes a new work or when a translation ceases to be a translation. . . . At the most the cataloguer must restrict himself to the task of relating works with exactly the same content but which have different titles, or works which have varying contents but same title, or which, although varying both in content and title, carry in themselves indications of their relationship.

The idea that a work carries an indication of its relationship to other books is particularly significant in that it introduces two new elements: the intent of the author or publisher and the requirement that this intent be obvious upon examination of the book. By this guideline, we accept a translation as being the same work if it purports to be a translation. No

Table II
Publishing History for *Guide to Reference Books*

Edition	Date	Authors	Publisher	Title
	1902	Kroeger	Houghton, Mifflin & Company	Guide to the study and use of reference books; a manual for librarians, teachers, and students
Title edition	1904	Kroeger	American Library Association Publishing Board	Guide to the study and use of reference books; a manual for librarians, teachers, and students
2d ed., rev. and enl.	1908	Kroeger, Mudge	American Library Association	Guide to the study and use of reference books
3d ed., rev. throughout and much enlarged	1917	Kroeger, Mudge	American Library Association	Guide to the study and use of reference books
[4th ed.]	1923	Mudge	American Library Association	New guide to reference books
5th ed.	1929	Mudge, Kroeger	American Library Association	Guide to reference books
6th ed.	1936	Mudge, Winchell	American Library Association	Guide to reference books
7th ed.	1951	Winchell, Mudge	American Library Association	Guide to reference books
8th ed.	1967	Winchell, Mudge, Sheehy	American Library Association	Guide to reference books
9th ed.	1976	Sheehy, Keckeissen, McIlvaine, Winchell	American Library Association	Guide to reference books
10th ed.	1986	Sheehy	American Library Association	Guide to reference books

judgment is required regarding the quality of the translation, nor its adherence to the original. Thus the cataloger need not attempt literary criticism.

It seems appropriate also to add the guideline that all texts associated with a work share a common origin. This implies that for every work there is a common source from which all texts are derived either directly or indirectly. This guideline is implicit in much of the discussion regarding works. For this purpose, *derived* is intended to imply a stronger relationship than just influence. Most works are influenced by other works. This distinction can be observed in citation patterns, particularly for scholarly publications. In new manifestations of a work, authors rarely cite earlier manifestations. However, since the influence of different works is generally acknowledged through citations, the existence of a citation is a strong indication that the cited item is not another manifestation of the citing work. By extending Jolley's approach (Jolley, 1963, p. 160) to identifying a work it is possible to formulate practical guidelines for determining when a book should be treated as a manifestation of a work:

1. The book has the same author(s) and title as at least one other manifestation of the work, or

2. the book has the same title and content as at least one other manifestation of the work, or

3. the book has the same author(s) and content as at least one other manifestation of the work, or

4. the book carries some indication that it was derived either directly or indirectly from another manifestation of the work.

Although these guidelines are not expected to eliminate all practical problems encountered when applying the definition of a work, they should reduce them significantly.

The guidelines for identifying works can be extended to texts. A book, then, should be treated as a manifestation of a text when the book is the same work and its content is composed of essentially the same sequence of words and auxiliary symbols as at least one other manifestation of the text. This definition relaxes Wilson's by adding the word "essentially" (Wilson, 1983, p. 5). It seems desirable to permit insignificant changes to occur within a text. These changes should generally be limited to minor editorial changes or correction of typographical errors which do not significantly alter the content of the work. For example, changing the British spelling of "colour" to "color" would not result in a new text.

A large body of literature exists which deals with the definition of an edition and the guidelines for applying the definition. We will not attempt to detail the various cataloging rules, guidelines, and rule interpretations which have been formulated to address this problem. A significant portion of AACR2 is devoted to this topic. Additional information can be found in the *Cataloging Service Bulletin* and the standards published by the bibliographic utilities. Basically, using this larger body of literature for additional guidance, a printing should be treated as a manifestation of an edition when it has the same text and was produced from substantially the same type image as at least one other manifestation of the edition.

A book should be treated as a manifestation of a printing when it has no more than slight variations from other manifestations of the printing. It has been difficult to determine consistently if the variations between two different printings are sufficient enough to create a new edition. Both Wanninger (1982, p. 359) and Jones and Kastner (1983, p. 212) have identified that a major problem for catalogers is the inability to determine consistently if the differences between two books are significant enough to justify treating them as different editions. A detailed review of the printing versus edition question is given by Jones and Kastner (1983).

Jolley's reliance on author or publisher intent can assist in making the required distinction right down to printings. There will always be some cases where it will be difficult or impossible to interpret consistently terms like *slight, substantially,* or *essentially.* However, frequently either the author or the publisher will provide clues regarding intent. When a publisher views the corrections made to a text as significant, it will frequently add a statement that this book is a "Revised version" or "Corrected edition" to the title page or verso of the title page.

A recent example in which the publisher's intent was clear is in the reissuing of *First Love: A Young People's Guide to Sexual Intercourse,* by Ruth Westheimer (*American Libraries* **17**; February 1986: 115). The original edition contained the statement regarding the prevention of conception: "The safe times are the week before and the week of ovulation." A corrected edition was issued with the word *safe* changed to *unsafe.* In terms of either the number of words changed or the number of characters changed, this would have to be considered a slight or minor change. It is certainly not a change that a cataloger would be expected to identify routinely. It is only when one considers the context of the statement and the intended audience that the error becomes major. In this instance, the book had to be recalled and a corrected edition issued. Even the color of the cover was changed from white to red to distinguish between the editions.

Conclusions

The widespread use and acceptance of online catalogs presents us with an opportunity to make major enhancements to computer-based catalogs by improving their underlying data structure. Computers can support complex data structures which would be impossible to use in card catalogs. However, this underlying complexity can be transparent to the user since display mechanisms can create display records customized to meet the needs of individual users. Users accustomed to traditional catalogs may continue to view displays similar to those currently used in online catalogs; however, others may prefer to view displays based only on works. With a well-designed data structure, online catalogs can meet both the first and the second objectives of the catalog without compromise.

VII

Integration

Integration is the final concept to be dealt with in this volume. It is one of the more abstract concepts to be considered and as will be seen is capable of various interpretations. One interpretation of particular significance for the conceptual foundations of descriptive cataloging is integration as it relates to a descriptive cataloging code. An integrated code is one that formulates a theory and practice of bibliographic description that is equally applicable to all types of material. Another relevant interpretation is integration as it relates to a catalog. An integrated catalog is one in which records for different types of materials are interfiled; an integrated catalog is usually but not necessarily the product of an integrated code.

Most recent literature on the subject of code integration has posited it as an unqualified good. Gorman, for instance, praises AACR2 by saying that in the respect of integration it represents a major breakthrough (Gorman, 1980, p. 42). However, there has been relatively little theoretical examination of the concept of an integrated code in the sense of asking questions about its desirability or feasibility. Also relatively unexplored are theoretical design questions such as: Under what conditions are general rules possible? And when does the presence of material-specific properties warrant specialized rules?

Two writers address the concept of integration and appropriately both begin by looking at the various meanings *integration* assumes in the literature of libraries and bibliographical control. Both give special attention to the concept in relation to integrated catalogs and integrated codes of rules.

Sara Shatford Layne, a librarian in the Physical Sciences and Technology Library at UCLA, writes on "Integration and the Objectives of the Catalog'' with a view to explicating the meaning of *integration* and showing its pertinence to the conceptual foundations of cataloging. She looks at four senses of integration: (1) shelf integration, in which materials on the same subject but of different media are placed at the same physical locations on library shelves; (2) functional integration, in which are unified the library operations of acquisition, cataloging, and providing reference service; (3) catalog integration; and (4) code integration. The major part of her chapter is devoted to a discussion of the last two types of integration.

Layne postulates two goals for integrated catalogs. These are to provide access to bibliographic information for two kinds of users: those who know what they want and those who do not know exactly what they want. As was noted above, in an integrated catalog, records for materials of different types are interfiled. An example Layne gives is of *Mutiny on the Bounty,* which might be represented in the catalog as a manuscript, a printed monograph, a screenplay, and as a sound, film, or video recording. The user who knows what he wants will identify one of these, i.e., a particular known item, as meeting his purpose. The user who does not know what he wants, being uncertain of purpose, might be willing to be instructed. For example, in searching for the book *Mutiny on the Bounty* he might find to his delight a video, which suits his needs even better. It is the second class of user that integrated catalogs can help the most. Layne speculates that the number of such users will increase in the future, as the number of different sources of information increases.

Layne turns next to the functions of descriptive cataloging. These are to provide access to bibliographic information for the two classes of users depicted above: to arrange bibliographic citations in a helpful order and to describe bibliographic entities in a way that will enable users to decide on their potential relevance. It is in the realization of the first of these functions, to arrange bibliographic citations in a helpful order, that Layne sees one of the most intellectually exciting frontiers of descriptive cataloging. She has several design considerations to offer. One is to use the concepts of author and work in formatting displays. Another is to collect bibliographic records into group-level and item-level displays.

As noted above, an integrated code is one that is equally effective in describing all kinds of library materials. Layne observes that it will always be necessary to use different terms to describe the physical characteristics of different materials. One implication of this is that an integrated code will have to contain not identical rules for describing and providing access to different materials, but compatible rules. Compatible rules are defined as those that contribute to meeting the goals of the catalog, no matter what kind of material is being described. In the design of a code of compatible rules the objective of consistency must be balanced against that of accurate representation.

What are the needs of a user in consulting a catalog? Probably no question is of greater consequence in addressing issues of catalog design. Layne postulates a conceptual model of the user who has unrealized needs and shows how an integrated catalog can meet such needs. In proposing design criteria for an integrated catalog, particularly for the display of bibliographic records, she contributes to the literature on conceptual foundations ideas having both theoretical and practical import.

The second author to write on integration is Ronald Hagler, Professor at the School of Library, Archival and Information Science at the University of British Columbia and, from 1964 through the publication of AACR2, Coordinator of the Canadian effort in catalog code development. His chapter is entitled "The Consequences of Integration." Shortly after the publication of AACR2 Hagler questioned whether an integrated code, in the sense of a set of applicable rules for all media, was desirable. Now, nine years later, he looks again at the desirability of integration; this time around, however, he looks at integration writ large. He identifies no less than nine different kinds of integration.

1. Integration of large-scale enumerative listings, such as national bibliographies. A twentiety-century phenomena, the widespread attempt to integrate files by merging them has created a number of problems. Chief among them is the need, for purposes of "deduping," to create unique identifiers for bibliographic entities.

2. Integration in methods of access to bibliographic information. In such an integration, a single terminal screen would serve as a window to many different databases. Particularly desirable would be the integration of A & I services with library catalog databases.

3. Integration of systems, in the sense that a single bibliographic record can be manipulated to serve a variety of purposes, e.g., cataloging, reference, acquisitions.

4. Integration of bibliographic records. By this is meant establishing item–work relationships as well as maintaining various links between and within records.

5. Integration of formats, such as the ISBDs and the MARC formats.

6. Integration of standards for descriptive cataloging, e.g., MARC and AACR2. This sort of integration is difficult to achieve politically because normally different professional committees oversee different standards.

7. Integration of cataloging rules which, according to Hagler, means not creating a special rule if a general one will suffice. With respect to integrated codes of rules, Hagler has several points to make. He warns that there may be a limit to how all-encompassing a rule can get and still be operational. He argues that making sound judgments on the basis of principle is far preferable to creating new rules, and he singles out the beginner and the perfectionist as the chief offenders in seeking a new rule for every new circumstance. He admonishes us to not confuse identification and description; heretofore we have been too anxious about uniformity in catalog descriptions, assuming this was needed to uniquely identify bibliographic entities when other, less expensive devices such as standard numbers might serve this purpose just as well. Finally he observes that output formats have gone somewhat adrift of the code and a truly integrated set of rules would incorporate, in addition to rules for description and access, also rules for the ordering and display of bibliographic records.

8. Integration of vocabulary. This Hagler sees as particularly needed in the transition from manual to automated cataloging environments.

9. Integration in the teaching of bibliographic control in a way that unifies cataloging, reference, and online searching.

Throughout his discussion of the various types of integration Hagler provides historical vignettes illustrating progress as well as setbacks and barriers yet to be overcome. His conclusion is that while an integration–specialization cycle is to some extent inevitable, the present integration revolution in the area of bibliographical control is desirable and shows great strength. Hagler's analysis of the concept of integration shows it to be rich in implication and central to a study of the conceptual foundations of descriptive cataloging. Indeed his analysis of the senses of integration could be regarded as an elegant overview of the major issues introduced in this volume.

Integration and the Objectives of the Catalog

Sara Shatford Layne

What do we, as librarians, mean by integration, and what does it have to do with the conceptual foundations of descriptive cataloging? My chapter is an attempt to suggest some answers to these questions.

The term *integration* has several specific meanings in our field, and I will start out by enumerating these meanings. Next, I will summarize my own perception of the basic goals for the catalog and functions of descriptive cataloging. Finally, I will concentrate on the kinds of integration that have the closest relationship to descriptive cataloging and describe the most important of these relationships.

Integration

Integration is, according to the first definition in the Oxford English Dictionary, "the making up or composition of a whole by adding together or combining the separate parts or elements; combination into an integral whole; a making whole or entire" (*The Compact Edition of the Oxford English Dictionary*, s.v. "integration"). Integration has come to have certain specialized meanings: in mathematics it is the operation used to solve a differential equation; in psychology it is the "coordination and correlation of the total processes of perception, interpretation, and reaction ensuring a normal effective life . . ." (*Webster's 3rd New International Dictionary of the English Language*, s.v. "integration");

in everyday conversation it is apt to refer to the "incorporation into society or an organization . . . on the basis of common and equal membership of individuals differing in some group characteristic (as race) . . ." (*Webster's 3rd New International Dictionary of the English Language,* s.v. "integration").

In my reading, I have identified four different meanings for *integration* as we librarians use it, four contexts in which we talk about combining separate parts or elements to make a whole.

First is a concrete meaning of integration: integrated shelving, or the placing of disparate library materials in the same physical location, arranging them on shelves according to whatever classification scheme the library uses without considering whether the item is a microfilm or a videocassette or a book or a periodical. The elements to be integrated are the actual items, the whole they form is the library collection. Jean Weihs has written persuasively on this subject (Weihs, 1984).

Even though disparate materials are *not* integrated on shelves, the records that describe them may nevertheless be integrated. In this, the second type of integration that I have identified, the elements to be integrated are records that describe library resources, and the whole that they combine to form is the library catalog. Let me emphasize here that I wish to use the broadest possible meaning for *library resources,* as well as for *library catalog.* I might include in *library resources,* for example, not only resources that libraries traditionally own, such as books, maps, manuscripts, and sound recordings, but also resources that libraries have access to, such as commercial databases and even organizations that possess information that they are willing to share with library users. *Library catalog,* similarly, includes but is not limited to a card file in an individual building: I would define a library catalog as any group of records that describes library resources and that tries to meet users' needs. I will try to define users' needs a little later, but first let me continue with enumerating the meanings of integration.

The third meaning I have identified for integration is integration of rules and standards for coping with the records that describe library materials. In this case the elements to be integrated are individual rules or standards, and the whole they form is a code of rules or a body of standards. *Anglo-American Cataloguing Rules,* second edition (AACR2) is a classic example of an integrated code of rules.

In the fourth and final meaning of integration, the elements that are combined are the various functions performed by libraries, such as acquisitions, cataloging, and public service. Integration of functions can be the result of the organizational structure of a library: for example, at the University of Illinois, holistic librarians perform cataloging, collection development, and public service (Gorman, 1983). I understand that the

University of Wisconsin–Madison is in the process of reorganizing its library system into clusters based on subject disciplines, with the intention that each cluster be as autonomous as possible, responsible for its own technical services, public services, and administration, and that each librarian be capable of performing several functions (speech given by D. Kaye Gapen at California Library Association, Los Angeles, CA, November 18, 1986).

Integration of functions can also occur in an automated system, independent of integration of functions in the organization of a library. ORION at UCLA is an example of an integrated system with which I have had personal experience: it is used for acquisitions, cataloging, and as an online public access catalog.

Although all the kinds of integration in libraries that I have defined here—integration of materials, integration of records, integration of rules or standards, integration of functions—have some sort of relationship to the foundations of descriptive cataloging, it seems to me that integration of records and integration of rules or standards have an especially close relationship. Before explaining in more detail the implications of this close relationship, I would like to take a little time to talk about my view of the basic goals of descriptive cataloging and the basic functions that are used to meet these goals.

Basic Goals for the Catalog

Twenty years ago, when I was in college and taking studio art classes, I had a teacher who from time to time would have us do a drawing using whichever hand we didn't normally use: in my case, since I am right handed, I would draw with my left hand. The purpose of this assignment was to force us to think again about what we were doing: it deprived us of the facile and almost automatic strokes that our normally used hand would make on the paper in response to our eyes seeing an arm, a leaf, or a fold of cloth. We had to struggle, deprived of our old visual vocabulary, to develop a fresh, if somewhat rough, new vocabulary to delineate that arm, leaf, or fold of cloth. I found it to be a valuable exercise, making me reexamine old assumptions and develop fresh approaches to drawing, even when I returned to using my comfortable and familiar right hand. Do not be alarmed: this does not mean that I am going to spend the rest of this chapter developing an entirely new vocabulary for descriptive cataloging. However, in preparing this chapter I did try to describe for myself, in words that seemed fresh to me, what we are trying to accomplish, through the use of descriptive cataloging, with the catalogs that we create.

I see two goals for the catalog. First of all, the catalog should help a person find a particular object that he knows exists, whether because he has previously seen it himself or because it has been described to him by others. Second, the catalog should help a person find an object of whose particular existence he was previously unaware, but that would be useful to him. Usually, such a person may have heard of a particular author and want something written by her, as, say, murder mysteries by P. D. James; or he may have heard of a work, such as Shakespeare's *Hamlet,* without knowing which edition would be most appropriate for him; or he might *think* he wanted a specific object, such as *Fundamentals of Physics* by Halliday and Resnick, published by Wiley in 1974, without realizing that a later and more appropriate edition exists. Unfortunately, we do not have a good idea of how many users fall into each of these two categories: catalog-use studies have not made this particular distinction (Yee, 1989).

Pending further research, I would like to postulate that the whole purpose of integrated catalogs is to help the user who doesn't know what he wants. In a recent issue of *Library Journal,* two sections in two articles not obviously on integration caught my attention. One article, on the creation of an automated union catalog in Idaho, said that the planning group wanted to put nonbibliographic information into the bibliographic database: the example given was that a patron searching for Thornton Wilder's *Our Town* would find a record for a current local civic theater production of the play as well as a record for the published script of the play (Oberg, 1986). The other article was about videocassettes in the library and mentioned how desirable it is that people looking for a book be made aware that there is also a video version, when such a version exists (Avalonne and Fox, 1986). These writers are, perhaps unconsciously, supporting the existence of integrated catalogs.

Liz Bischoff, when she was with the Pasadena Public Library, was working on a plan to include in the online catalog records that describe local organizations, so that people looking for, say, books on how to play bridge, would be made aware of the local bridge club. Although this last example is, strictly speaking, a matter of subject rather than descriptive access, the creation of a record for an organization would involve descriptive principles. Furthermore, the desire to provide access to the bridge club through the library catalog is based on the premise that people need information that exists in nonbook packages but frequently have not even considered that such packages might exist. The impulse to provide integrated shelving, which I did not and do not intend to discuss in depth, and which is also primarily a matter of subject access, is yet another example of acting on the assumption that people don't know what they want until they see it in front of them. One last example: map collections have reported substantial increases in use when records for their holdings are integrated into the general catalog (Buckallew, 1986). The user who knows what he wants, whether it is videos, or pictures, or maps, or information on local theater productions, can go to the appropriate separate catalog or collection. It is the user who isn't aware that he needs something in another medium who benefits from an integrated catalog.

Functions of Descriptive Cataloging

How do we meet, or try to meet, the goals for the catalog—helping a person to find what he knows exists, and also what he doesn't know exists? What are the basic functions of descriptive cataloging?

First, we try to provide access. We try to provide access to the record for an object so that the record may be found by someone who can describe that object, either completely or incompletely, thus serving the person who needs a known, particular object. But what about the person who doesn't know what particular object he wants?

I would like to suggest that it might be more useful to this second person if we take the view that we as catalogers provide access to the *catalog,* that we can limit our thinking dangerously by concentrating on providing access to particular *records.* The computer has led us to think of the catalog as a giant jumble of bibliographic records from which we try to retrieve or pull out certain records through the use of access points. Access points should be points at which the user gains access to the *catalog,* not merely access to a particular *record* in that catalog. Perhaps the frustration of some users with online systems stems from the fact that they had been able to use access points to enter the card catalog. Once there they had discovered records arranged in a helpful way, so that they were able to find both the specific objects they were looking for and related useful objects that they hadn't known about. This ability to use access points to enter the *catalog* is nonexistent or underdeveloped in many online systems. For example, as Anne Piternick points out it is still comparatively rare for online catalogs to have authority records, especially authority records that generate truly useful messages, integrated into the bibliographic file (Piternick, 1989, p. 30). Perhaps if we thought about providing access to the catalog instead of providing access to bibliographic records we would place more emphasis on constructing the kinds of authority records that Piternick calls for. Thinking of ourselves as providing access to the catalog might also influence how we create displays and select default displays.

The possibility for using access points to enter the catalog is there with computers, and if properly developed can result in online catalogs that improve on the card catalog. A card catalog presents records in one, fixed order; records in the computer catalog can be rearranged, almost instantaneously, to form a catalog tailored to the needs of a particular user or user group. However, unless we emphasize the importance of access to the *catalog,* this potential the computer has for creating tailor-made catalogs will not be fully explored.

The second function of descriptive cataloging is to provide a helpful arrangement of records. Once the person who doesn't know what he wants, including the person who thinks he knows but is wrong, gets to the catalog, he should find, or be shown, records arranged in such a way that he will be likely to find records for useful items. Perhaps because this provision of a helpful arrangement is the most difficult aspect of descriptive cataloging it seems to be frequently ignored. Providing a helpful arrangement may be one of the most important as well as intellectually exciting aspects of descriptive cataloging, and therefore we should not ignore, but rather emphasize it. Traditionally, we have arranged our catalogs on three principles: the first is the principle of alphabetic sequence, which has the advantage of being both predictable and almost universally understood. Beyond this principle, usually taken as a given, at least in this country, we have arranged or organized our catalogs based on the two closely related principles of authorship and work, as exemplified by Seymour Lubetzky's objectives and the *Paris Principles.* It is my belief that Lubetzky's second objective[1] and Paris Principle 2.2[2] are often misperceived as having to do with the access function of descriptive cataloging and with no other. At times, cataloging students have said to me, "no one wants *all* the editions of a work or *all* the works of an author." Probably no one, or very few people, does, or do, want *all* editions of a work and *all* the works of an author. But many people need to see options, displayed in a helpful way, and it is my perception that Lubetzky's second objective and Paris Principle 2.2 address, or begin to address, this need.

Finally, after we have provided description and arrangement, the third function of descriptive cataloging is to describe an object, describe it so that the user of the catalog can identify it either as the object he is seeking *or* as a potentially useful, although previously unknown, object.

Relationship of Functions of Descriptive Cataloging and Integration

Now we come to the relationships between the functions of descriptive cataloging and the two kinds of integration that are most important to these functions: the integration of records and the integration of rules and standards. Although the first function of descriptive cataloging, access, is related to integration of records and to the integration of rules and standards, I would like to focus on the relationship of the arrangement function to the integration of records and then on the relationship of the describing function to the integration of rules and standards, as well as to the integration of records.

Arrangement and the Integration of Records   It is my belief that author and work are still valuable as principles on which to base the arrangement of the catalog, valuable in that the resulting organization helps people find things that are useful to them, but of whose existence they were previously unaware, and that this is especially true in an integrated catalog. For example, the reader interested in P. D. James' murder mysteries might be delighted to learn that the library has a video of the Masterpiece Theatre version of one of her works; the actor looking for an edition of Shakespeare's *Hamlet* might be happy to find a sound recording of the play that he could listen to while reading it; the student looking for Halliday and Resnick's *Fundamentals of Physics,* second edition, might be pleased to discover computer software designed to help students work through the problems at the end of each chapter.

Let me remind you of two examples I cited earlier when talking about the purpose of integrated catalogs: the person who might be interested in the video version of a book and the person looking for Thornton Wilder's *Our Town* who might be interested in knowing about performances of that play. Not only do these examples argue for the creation of integrated catalogs, they also support the use of the principles of authorship and work as a basis for organizing and arranging the integrated catalog.

We, as descriptive catalogers, should come to be able to define *work* in such a way that it can encompass pictures, maps, films, archives, and computer files, as well as books; then we should keep this definition firmly in mind when we devise new rules or revise old ones. The definition of *work* should be linked to a definition of *authorship,* a definition of *authorship,* moreover, that encompasses the conditions under which all works, in whatever media, are brought into existence.[3]

The arrangement of an integrated catalog is important because a good arrangement helps the user of the catalog find items that he wants or needs; arrangement is critically important because of the potential scale of an integrated catalog. We may have the technology to combine every single catalog record in the country into a single database, creating an electronically integrated catalog, but without a great deal of thought given to arrangement such a catalog could become useless, except to those people who know exactly what they want and can describe that object accurately and completely.

O'Neill and Vizine-Goetz describe the problems of coping with multiple manifestations of a particular literary work (O'Neill and Vizine-Goetz, 1989). Their problem was limited to book manifestations: imagine how such a problem could multiply if records for pictures, films, sound recordings, and so forth were added to the catalog. Imagine, for example, a work that has been made into one or more movies, as, say, Charles Nordhoff's *Mutiny on the Bounty*. An integrated catalog might contain records representing manuscripts of the book; various editions of the book; a classic comics version; two film versions; the screen plays, costume designs, and publicity stills for the film versions; and sound recordings of the book being read. It is hard to imagine a catalog user who would want to sort through records for every single publicity shot, costume design, manuscript, and edition, one by one. Or imagine someone doing a search that is partly a subject search, for items by or about Abraham Lincoln. Let us suppose that records for every item in every library in the country were put into one database. I mean *every* item: every Lincoln letter in the Huntington Library, every photograph and every ephemeral political pamphlet from the Chicago Historical Society, every book in every elementary school library. No user, except perhaps a compulsive bibliographer, would want to see, as the result of an initial search, a description of every Lincoln letter, every picture of Lincoln, every children's book about Lincoln, and every scholarly text.

Can we, as descriptive catalogers, help solve this problem? I believe we can try to do so, in two ways. One way is to try to arrange records in a helpful way. Another way is to try to reduce the number of records to be arranged. I know this sounds silly, even facetious, like someone saying "We eliminated our cataloging backlog by cutting the library book budget." But my intention is not to reduce the number of records to be arranged by eliminating altogether some of these records, but rather by combining records for *individual* items into records for groups of items. Collection-level records are already made for archives and for graphic materials (Betz, 1982; Hensen, 1983). Historically, catalogers of archival films have tended to create single records to represent multiple manifestations of a film. The collection-level records made for archives are based on the principle of provenance, a principle that bears a close resemblance to the concept of corporate authorship; the records that archival film catalogers create seem to have been based on the principle that the concept of work is a valid basis for organizing the catalog. Wendy White-Hensen's cataloging manual for Archival Moving Image Materials, currently in use at the Motion Picture, Broadcasting, and Recorded Sound Division of the Library of Congress, calls for combining certain categories of manifestations of a film into a single record (White-Hensen, 1984). The chief problem with the resulting record appears to be that it is difficult to tell which elements of the resulting description apply to which of the manifestations being described in the record.[4] The impulse to group multiple manifestations of a work together is, I believe, a good one, but it should not obscure the need to distinguish and identify individual manifestations.

My point here is that descriptive catalogers should think about composing guidelines or establishing standards for *identifying* a group of items that could be described using a single record, and guidelines or standards for *describing* such a group of items once it has been identified. I am not suggesting that we stop making item-level records and make only group-level records, but that for many users a hierarchical search from group-level records to item-level records would help bring order to the bibliographic universe. Further, these guidelines and rules might best be devised by people who keep in mind the organizing principles of authorship and work.

The concept of contributing records for *groups* of items to an integrated catalog has advantages beyond the creation of a helpful arrangement for the catalog user. Much as archivists create finding lists for individual archives, so too could catalogers create finding lists for the individual items represented by a group record. Since group records would form their own separate minicatalog, it might be possible to have more flexibility in their creation than would have been possible if the same records were to be contributed to a national database. In a future, but not impossibly distant, world it should be possible for the person using the larger integrated catalog to explore electronically, and as desired, the finding lists or minicatalogs connected to collection-level or group records. The user would survey group-level records and decide for which groups he would like to look at item-level catalogs; he would then be led into the item-level catalog for that collection. Libraries could maintain their own distinct catalogs with the attendant control and flexibility, but the user would have the power to gain access to any catalog through a linked system. I suggest that, as we move toward larger, integrated catalogs, as we have more and more packages of information and a greater and greater technological ability to store large numbers of records describing these packages, that group-level records offer a solution to the problems of scale that will inevitably arise.

Description and the Integration of Rules   So far, I have been concentrating on integrated catalogs—now I would like to take a little time to talk about integrated *codes,* that is, about the integration of rules or standards. Our rules tell us how to provide access, how to organize the catalog, and how to describe items. Until quite recently we have had completely different sets of rules for cataloging different materials, just as we have had completely different catalogs. AACR2 comes close to representing the other extreme: identical rules for different materials.

It seems to me that a compromise is emerging and that a compromise is desirable. We need compatible rather than identical rules for different materials in order to have an effective integrated code. Initially, the rules for description in AACR2 were slightly different for different materials, as it was obvious that the physical description of a map could not usefully be done using the same terms one would employ to describe a film. The rules for access, on the other hand, were almost identical for all materials, with the notable exception of films, sound recordings, and video recordings, as it was less obvious that different conditions of authorship are inherent in different materials. Through revision and interpretation, as the years since the adoption of AACR2 have passed, both the rules for description and the rules for access have grown more different for different materials. Maps now have their own rule for entry under corporate author. Maps, graphic materials, archives, rare books, and archival moving images have had sanctioned, or semisanctioned, their own sets of AACR2-compatible rules for description.[5] This trend toward differentiating materials is mirrored in the development of the ISBD for Non-Book Materials: machine-readable data files were initially considered for inclusion in ISBD (NBM), but are soon to have their own ISBD (Bourne and Rather, 1986).

Compatible rules for descriptive cataloging are rules that help the cataloger meet the goals of the catalog, no matter what medium or material is involved. Do our rules help people find objects they know about as well as objects they don't know about but that would be useful? Can the user tell from a description that he has found what he was looking for or something that he would like to look at? We acknowledge that different terms are needed to describe the physical characteristics of different materials; we also acknowledge, as with the scale and coordinates of a map, that some materials have categories of characteristics that are unique to them, that have no corresponding category in other materials. Perhaps more changes are necessary; perhaps there should be even more differences than there now are in the description of different materials. We need to balance the need for consistency and predictability of a description with the need to identify and characterize an item as clearly and simply as possible, whatever material it may represent. More changes may also be necessary in the rules for access, if we are to provide a useful arrangement of records for users, an arrangement that tries to meet the goals, the objectives of the catalog.

Conclusion

Integrated catalogs are technologically possible now, on a grand scale, since we are able to take machine-readable records from a variety of sources and combine them, either into a single database or into a group of linked databases. I have tried to suggest ideas to keep in mind when we create integrated catalogs and integrated codes. I have also tried to emphasize the importance of keeping our basic goals or objectives for the catalog in mind as we make changes.

Integrated catalogs may also be more desirable, more necessary, now than they have been in the past. We are seeing an increase in interdisciplinary studies as well as an incredible increase in the quantity of information available: this means that the old model of research, when one could assume that one would know about all the important sources of information in one's field, is no longer universally valid. At the same time, the variety of materials that can record information is increasing, and our awareness as librarians of the importance of different materials as sources of information is increasing also. The result is a need for sophisticated intellectual access to a variety of materials in integrated catalogs—sophisticated because the users of these catalogs are less and less likely to come to the catalog knowing exactly what they want.

Notes

1. "The objectives which the catalog is to serve are two: . . . Second, to relate and display together the editions which a library has of a given work and the works which it has of a given author" (Lubetzky, 1960, p. ix).

2. "The catalogue should be an efficient instrument for ascertaining . . . 2.2 (a) which works by a particular author and (b) which editions of a particular work are in the library" (Paris Principles, 1961).

3. Martha Yee, responsible for cataloging at the UCLA Film and Television Archive, has started research that would help to create these definitions and also to measure their value in organizing the catalog.

4. I credit Martha Yee with pointing out this problem to me.

5. See for instance Anglo-American Cataloguing Committee for Cartographic Materials (1982), Betz (1982), Hensen (1983), BDRB (1981), and White-Hensen (1984).

The Consequences of Integration

Ronald Hagler

At a conference a few months after the publication of AACR2 I said, "I find it entirely conceivable that an investigation of the [nonbook] media . . . could result in a recommendation that the integration of cataloguing rules for all media is undesirable. The reasons why recent cataloguing history has seen an increasingly powerful current in favour of integrating the rules for all types of materials are diverse, but the trend is unlikely to be reversed" (Hagler, 1980). It is useful to inquire, nine years later, whether the trend toward integration continues or has been stalled or even reversed.

At the time, the observation was made only in the context of rules for the descriptive cataloguing of nonbook materials in library catalogues. I am now confident in broadening it to include all practices relating to the input, manipulation, and output of bibliographic records for all types of material, in all types of bibliographic agency, and in all kinds of bibliographic listing. In fact, during the past decade significant steps have been taken among society's other three public agencies which preserve documents as information, archives, museums, and galleries, toward recording their collections using practices and formats similar to those used in libraries.

In the face of barriers to integration early established by the history of separately developed, then entrenched, practices, the integration revolution is showing great strength. But it is too early to dismiss those barriers: they are still occasionally being renewed by administrative practices. Although it will probably never be secure against occasionally successful counterthreats, integration as a force is alive and healthy. The reasons, which once seemed "diverse" to me, have clearly coalesced into one: the computer.

If two decades of computerization had given us only bigger and more speedily assembled bibliographic files of the same kind as were in common use in 1965, without significantly affecting the processes of creating and using these files, the practice of information retrieval might well have suffered more than it benefited. Radical changes in those processes were, however, as inevitable as they seemed mysterious and difficult to control to a large number of those who became enmeshed in them in the early stages. The computer affected not only the technology of information handling, but its administration and ultimately the psychological reactions to bibliographic data and the process of locating it, of both its creators and its users.

The heart of these changes is integration: the computer is effectively enforcing respect for the integrity of all the functions which we now call by the single term *bibliographic control*. Full-scale integration of these functions is new enough still to hold some surprises. It is not long since we have come to realize that the catalogue and the circulation system of a library can share the same bibliographic record. It may yet be a while before we stop viewing the bibliographic function in a library institution as if it were essentially different from that in, say, an abstracting and indexing (A & I) service. In the limiting precomputer technology the lip service accorded the integrity of bibliographic operations could not be matched in practice. We even lacked a single term to cover both the creation and the use of bibliographic records, their storage and their physical display at the point of use, or the unified technical procedures as between, say, acquisitions and cataloguing functions. *Bibliographic control* is a term introduced by the integration revolution; the related term of the computer revolution is *networking*.

Speaking of Bibliographic Integration

The most distressing consequence of integration to me as a teacher has been the sweeping change it introduced to the vocabulary of bibliographic control. I must shy away from the term *cataloguing* with its single-function and institutional-library implications, and should perhaps even prefer *bibliographic file* to the old *catalogue* with all its single-purpose connotations. Unless I am specifically distinguishing it from other contexts in the creation and use of bibliographic data, I should probably even sidetrack *library* in favour of *bibliographic agency,* or just *agency,* albeit with severe discomfort. When we have once again reached subconscious agreement on the scope and context of our terms, we may be able to revert to more felicitous terminological shorthand, but until then the deliberate use of some new jargon is unfortunately necessary to remind us of the vanishing of old limitations and the imposition of new contexts.

First Principles: Standardization, Compatibility, Integration

The entire history of bibliographic control is that of the establishment of standards and their subsequent modification. Bibliographic standards embody and give force to the first principles of adequate identification and of consistency. These are first principles because if they are challenged, the whole bibliographic structure as we know it topples, whereas standards can and do vary and change within the same principles.

The Chicago Manual of Style (The University of Chicago, 1982) and AACR2 both aim at making a single bibliographic file internally consistent. In order to claim compliance with the consistency principle, is this sufficient or do different bibliographic lists also need to be consistent among themselves? AACR2 goes farther in securing compliance to a common rule because it is more prescriptive than the *Chicago Manual* but also because the latter does not set out to legislate for combined or shared files of bibliographic references.

Although sanctified by the strongest force of convention and therefore potentially the most integrating principle we have, consistency is thus easily shown not to be an all-or-nothing issue, but a relative one. It is still often required to cede precedence to such pragmatic forces as budgets, or the real or supposed differences among materials to be listed, or uses of the list. In the field of descriptive bibliography, as opposed to library cataloguing, where it is an axiom that there are hardly any fixed rules, the characteristics of the material being dealt with determine the descriptive practices adopted, and consistency implies only the ad hoc application of an experienced judgment. One who works in that field would not applaud the imposition of AACR2, or *any* particular set of rules, as a single standard required in the name of consistency.

We therefore invoke the practice of "Compatibility," the compromise available when the relativity of our First Principles and the multiplicity of our Standards give rise to variant practices. The typical untrained user, having, perhaps unconsciously, established a few search strategies which coax a card catalogue to give up some useful information, goes to other bibliographic tools which are not compiled according to exactly the same standards but whose presentations of bibliographic data are sufficiently compatible as not to cause serious delay or confusion in the shift from tool to tool. For that user, the requirement of consistency is minimal: a little integration goes a long way. After all, experienced searchers often do not even notice the inconsistencies rampant among current bibliographic tools. The administrative face of compatibility is called *cooperation*: it is invoked when institutions become deadlocked over what should constitute standardization.

The concept of integration cannot be entirely separated from these other concepts of first principles, standards, and compatibility, although it is not synonymous with them. It is, however, the newest of these concepts in practice, made visible separately from the others largely within the present generation and brought into prominence by computer applications. Integration is the making of two into one. In respect of cataloguing standards it is the creation of a single rule to deal with problems which had previously been the focus of two or more different rules; it is the discovery that a single type of solution will satisfy conditions which had previously resulted in two differing approaches. In the storage of bibliographic records it is the combining of two previously separate records, or parts thereof, into a single record. In the display of bibliographic information it is the combining of two previously separate lists into a single one. In online retrieval it is the abandonment of one command language and reprogramming the software to be responsive to another, existing command language; it is the collapsing of two separately applicable search strategies into a single unified strategy. The administrative face of integration is called *centralization*. The fewer different principles, standards, procedures, or operational units or agencies are involved, and the fewer detailed rules they embody or follow, the more integrated is the practice.

Integration and Specialization

The abstract philosopher can perhaps deal with integration as an absolute, treating everything in existence as a function of the one concept "being." In practice, however, integration, like consistency, is relative. I prefer the word *specialization* to characterize the opposite of integration, rather than its proper linguistic opposite. These two opposing forces, the centripetal and the centrifugal, do not act separately, but rather in dynamic and constantly shifting balance. Whether the thought or activity be political, scientific, philosophical, or bibliographic, a period in which integration has been in vogue is inevitably followed by one in which specialists once again spin out emerging details into separable categories for study or action. Conversely, once enough discrete elements of any situation have been identified, someone is bound to attempt their unification. Einstein's expression of the unity of matter and energy in his literally world-shaking equation $e=mc^2$ was such a step. But having isolated and mathematically described the four most basic forces of nature (gravity, electromagnetism, and the strong and weak forces within atoms), physicists are now seeking the "Grand Unified Theory," a mathematically expressible unification of the four.

History seems to look on most unifiers as geniuses and most specialists as drudges. To avoid making such a value judgment, one might merely observe that Platos, Newtons, Einsteins, and McLuhans come along infrequently enough to stand out more. The names of some recent figures in our field whose basic tendency has been toward integration are deservedly well known. Jewett hypothesized a practical method for capturing original cataloguing for an item only once, mechanically reproducing it for the catalogues of any number of subsequent agencies (Jewett, 1852). Cutter created a unified cataloguing rule incorporating description, name and subject access, and alphabeting (Cutter, 1876). Lubetzky asked, most cogently, "Is This Rule Necessary?" (Lubetzky, 1953, p. 14) and started on the path to AACR. Kilgour found a single name-title compression code to be an effective method of searching a file of over 10 million bibliographic records. Verona proposed the simplest solution yet to the corporate-name complex (Verona, 1975). Gorman launched the International Standard Bibliographic Description, coalescing the world's variant rules for item description; then when within five years it threatened to splinter he was tenacious enough to devise the outflanking action now known as ISBD(G) (1977).

Integration Appears on the Scene

That most of these should be names from the Anglo-American world of library practice does not represent this writer's ethnocentric selectivity. Integration was fostered in this environment long before the computer or the new concept and term *bibliographic control*. For centuries until the very recent past, there seemed to be a distinct and growing lack of control. Neither was any physical limit perceived to the number of separate bibliographic lists produced, nor was any notable alarm raised over the growing number of different rules and patterns for their compilation and their presentation to the so-called *end user* (another new term). The library community prided itself on a greater concern for bibliographic detail than others but did not share common rules on a significant scale until nearly the twentieth century. After all, who would ever search two different lists or catalogues simultaneously or have the temerity to try to combine the existing catalogues of two different agencies or the projects of two different bibliographers into a single file?

The Processing Department of the Library of Congress has been, ever since the Great Reorganization of 1898, the staunchest advocate and greatest practitioner of bibliographic integration, setting an example much imitated, and not only in North America. We have long taken the essential unity of its practices for granted, often not realizing that the degree of bibliographic integration which it made a common part of our unconscious was in fact quite extraordinary. Long before it sent the bibliographic world into the computer era and a new wave of integration, two of its projects fostered the integration of bibliographic lists, of the rules for their compilation, and of the technology for their presentation and maintenance. The dissemination of the LC catalogue card showed that integration could save money, not only because of sharing the data on it, but also through the standardization of equipment and supplies for its use. The start of a national union catalogue showed that integration pays off in improved service. As a tradeoff, both required adherence to a single continent-wide, later worldwide, set of cataloguing standards. Has *anything* changed?

The Integration of Enumerative Bibliographies

Four hundred years ago, the prospect of identifying and listing in a single compilation all the world's printed books was not a necessarily overwhelming one. Four hundred years before that, an attempt was made to prepare a union list of all the manuscripts in the English monasteries. Librarianship continues to value comprehensiveness: it was long commonplace in library catalogues to interfile bibliographic records for monographs, for journal articles, for items in anthologies and collected works of many types, and for many other kinds of document. That we have not generally done so recently only confirms that integration is not viewed as an absolute good and that its virtues are judged in relation to a very complex environment. In a long period before 1898, an environment characterized by strengthened single institutions, practical and economic difficulties of dealing with large manual files, and the fragmentation of the unified intellectual life of Europe became inimical to integrative bibliographic projects.

Perhaps under the inspiration of the American national union catalogue, the twentieth century saw renewed interest in the most tangible kind of bibliographic integration: truly large-scale enumerative listings, for example, national bibliographies, few of which outside of

Europe antedate the Second World War; union catalogues and union lists of serials holdings; and of course comprehensive indexing tools for journal material in hundreds of subject fields. This obvious kind of integration is now very fashionable, if rarely commercially profitable: it usually has to be subsidized. Unlike most of its pre-twentieth century predecessors, the modern comprehensive bibliography, in its print version, is almost certain to be serial in nature. But the terms *monographic* and *serial* are irrelevant to a file in machine-readable form, amendable and searchable online. (Now if we could just make *all* serial publication "irrelevant," we could get rid of many rules, lists, etc.) This merging of monograph and serial is the ultimate in chronological integration.

The most massive possible single lists, a *Répertoire Bibliographique Universale* and a companion *Répertoire Iconographique Universale*, were begun in all seriousness and with reasonable funding, both public and private, at the beginning of this century. No practical limit was foreseen to the number of 3 × 5 index cards which could be interfiled for journal and other documentary information on all nonscientific subjects. It was not an information explosion but an economic depression which stalled the plans of Messrs. Otlet and LaFontaine and perhaps laid to rest for our time the dream of an integrated universal bibliography. Although the computer has radically reduced both the storage and the manipulation cost of a large-scale integrated bibliography, it has also removed some of the need for ever larger *single* lists by making it possible to search several different lists simultaneously. What constitutes a separate bibliographic file becomes a moot point when the computer is programmed to create a joint index to many files. This index integration is potentially more useful than any simple expansion of particular bibliographic files.

The transfer of records from database to database by computer and the merging of whole retrospective files, or just the indices to these files, led to a need for automated methods of duplicate recognition, *deduping,* in the current jargon. The manual merging of entries into the American national union catalogue, both in its card form and later for print publication, showed how difficult this process could be even for experienced cataloguers. The variety of cataloguing practices and errors evident in every large file, and the variety of bibliographic circumstances which can confuse the identification of two different bibliographic items, make it impossible to automate the task using only the natural language of authors, titles, etc.

Coding systems therefore began to be developed even before the advent of the computer to provide a more positive identification for individual items and/or for their surrogate bibliographic records. These include the music plate number, the coden, the government issuing agency inventory number, the LC card number, the record label number, the serial numbering in the trade list or national bibliography. But no one of these, not even the newer more comprehensive standard numbering schemes, ISBN and ISSN, can be relied on to identify duplicates in a large file, particularly a retrospective one. A solution being explored is to create a new code from within the existing records to be merged or searched. Thus the Universal Standard Book Code (USBC) proposed at the University of Bradford creates a 15-character code from five specific areas of a MARC record (*The British Library Bibliographic Services Newsletter* **33** (April) 1984: 3–4). The Serials Industry Systems Advisory Committee (SISAC) code combines some existing coding into an alphanumeric string uniquely identifying a single issue of a journal or a single article within that issue (*Society for Scholarly Publishing Letter* **8** (1986): 1–2). In an attempt to generate a code which can establish the unique identity of an individual copy among the editions, issues, and states of early printed books, there is a proposal for a "fingerprint" system based entirely on elements from the physical item rather than from its bibliographic record (Institut de Recherche et d'Histoire des Textes and the National Library of Scotland, 1984).

Integration of Bibliographic Records

A similar, and equally difficult, problem of integration is that of linking certain records with each other within a bibliographic file. The underlying issues involved, both of them intractable, are (1) whether a physical item or the intellectual "work" it contains should constitute the basis for the bibliographic record, and (2) how comprehensively to define a "work." The division between library cataloguing and the work of the A & I services on the first of these two issues shows that it cannot be washed over by the simplistic observation that the description relates to the physical item while access points relate to the work. This may be true in theory, but it is simplistic when applied to the practice of creating machine-readable formats.

　　While all library cataloguing codes claim to base the entry on the physical object, some embody noticeable sympathies toward treating the work as the basic unit. In Anglo-American practice, dash entries once linked supplements to their base volumes on the same entry; anthologies of excerpts from a journal once took the same main-entry heading as the originating journal. AACR2 claims greater adherence to the physical-item basis, but the present controversy over how to treat a microform reproduction shows that the issue lives on. AACR2 also provides, in rules 1.5E and 1.9, for the integration of accompanying material with a basic entry either in its Area 7, supported if desired by an access point, or more briefly in its Area 5.

As for linking separate records, AACR2 practice is restricted to the provision of explanatory notes and at least one common access point for any closely related items. Individualized record-to-record links proved too fraught with practical difficulties when MARC was being developed and entries incorporating dashed-on items were quickly abandoned. Unfortunately, the community of MARC users has not pursued a general rationale either for the linking of separate records or for the provision of levels within a single record to cover a work and its part, a journal and an article within it, an item and its continuation, etc. Instead, it dealt with the most pressing practical part of the problem as an isolated issue, creating a separate holdings format to deal with the attachment of institution-specific and copy information to a basic record. This notable failure to look at a problem in an integrated way will not make it go away. The *Common Communication Format* (1988), which does provide for levels within records, may prove more attractive than MARC as a basis for the continuing development of computer formats.

Integrated Methods of Access to Bibliographic Information

As noted above, the computer's functional integration of the means of accessing bibliographic records, whether or not they happen to reside in the same list, is of far greater consequence than the integration of the lists themselves. This is a reversal of the long-standing trend of the manual period, which saw different rules and arrangements for different lists. For example, the distinction between the single-library, or single-branch, catalogue and the union catalogue is growing dimmer. What was once searchable only in several different sets of periodical indices is now accessible simultaneously via a single searching service and on a single terminal. The difference between a library's online public access catalogue and an external indexing service need not be noticeable to the patron, since a common command language is now entirely feasible. The terminal screen is the single window to many hitherto separate types of bibliographic databases and the variety of operations through which information is put there are largely "transparent" to the user. This integration of the searching function is today's most dramatic advance for the user of bibliographic services.

For the manager of bibliographic data, today's buzzword is *the integrated system*. A single master bibliographic record for an item, its elements tagged for separate manipulation, is created locally or copied from elsewhere, and stored. It can be used in whole or in part, locally or at a distance, permanently or temporarily, in many systems and sub-systems simultaneously, displayed online or in batch mode with its elements in any sequence, printed on card, paper, microfiche, or a printing plate.

Integration does not, however, necessarily mean instant simplification: the integrated bibliographic system is far from simple and establishing one to replace previously manual operations has often been traumatic for administrator, employee, and public alike. In larger institutions, up to 20 years have hardly sufficed to create and implement the necessary software, usually in parts, often changing direction or even backtracking en route, and with long pauses for regrouping as personnel are retrained, job descriptions changed, and unwelcome unexpected implications, usually budgetary, dealt with. Most smaller institutions waited until reliable package, or turnkey, systems became available, and even these have only recently achieved large-scale integration. The benefits of integration are never immediate. It is harder for the specialist mentality to assess them.

The Strains of Format Integration: ISBDs, MARCs

Essential to the success of the integrated bibliographic system was not the integration, but paradoxically the separation, of the bibliographic record into as many parts as anyone could conceive of being used independently for any purpose. To be on the safe side, it was probably chopped up a little more than absolutely necessary into fields and subfields, then coded and "indicated." This new formatting was expressed manually in the ISBDs and in a machine-readable version in MARC in the late 1960s. The ISBDs do not deal with access points and historically there is only a tenuous causal connection between them and MARC, but in concept and function they are complementary. If there had been an attempt at cooperation nearer their birth, some minor but jarring discrepancies might easily have been resolved. Their total integration would provide practical gains in the automatic production of ISBD punctuation from corresponding MARC tags, or vice-versa.

But each of these formats had enough early problems of its own staying integrated. As soon as the original ISBD was allowed to split into one version for monographs and another for serials, the tendency toward incompatible differences among the various ISBDs planned became a serious problem. Fortunately it was nipped in the bud by agreement on an ISBD(G). But the ISBD system is not yet complete and may never be. The recent effort of several years' duration to establish an ISBD(CP) for component parts as a standard to link the library cataloguing of monographs and whole serials with the citation of journal articles, conference papers, etc., by the A & I services reached an impasse and was unfortunately suspended.

ISBD started out on the international stage as an attempt to unify national differences. MARC did not, a fact which merely delayed its need to face exactly the same problems. When its first version was devised at the Library of Congress in 1965, MARC was overtly linked with the requirements not only of a dying cataloguing code little used outside the circle of North American academic and research libraries, but also of the catalogue card of which MARC was the designated assassin (Avram, Freitag, and Guiles, 1965). When the present basic structure was adopted after a trial period, it was adjusted to the requirements of the brand new AACR1, a code which promised much in the international library world but which was as yet unproven and not yet widely adopted. The A & I services, having long since departed from library practices in bibliographic description in the manual mode, saw no need to revert to them in the machine mode. Not surprisingly, then, while many machine-readable bibliographic formats were soon being modeled on the general structure of the original LC MARC format, there was a real threat of practical incompatibility. The pendulum was swinging toward specialization.

International meetings were soon held to find a technical compromise among the differences reasonably demanded by the varied users of machine-readable bibliographic formats. The resulting standard, ISO 2709-1981, known in the United States as ANSI Z39.2-1985, requires adhering formats to adopt a common label and record structure, ensuring translatability at an acceptable level. Within this standard three basic types of format have emerged: (1) the family of MARC formats used in the library community, with UNIMARC (1980) as the common denominator; (2) the UNISIST Reference Manual developed for A & I services (Dierickx, 1981), but little known in the United States or Canada; and (3) the newest and most widely applicable, the *Common Communication Format* (1988).

Except for the proprietary formats used in-house by the established Anglo-American A & I services, compatibility has thus been tenuously preserved, although not the integration which characterizes the ISBDs. Translation of bibliographic data from one format to another in its journey from creating agency to final user is certainly not economically desirable or indeed theoretically necessary, but at least it is possible. The major translation work involves national and international agencies and the largest bibliographic utilities. Perhaps they can best hide the cost of nonintegration.

Hardware and Software: Some Hard Facts of Nonintegration

A significant drawback of creating and using machine-readable bibliographic data on an integrated basis is the fact that software written for one hardware system will not necessarily operate on another. Fortunately, much thought went into the question of how to make the original MARC format compatible with the requirements of all the then-known hardware. However, if every bibliographic agency used the same, or completely compatible, hardware, we would surely by now have fewer and probably cheaper software packages for the input, manipulation, and output of records in any ISO 2709-based format, and therefore more trouble-free upgrading of local applications to the current state of the art, fewer homemade single-institution systems, and certainly greater interagency compatibility—in other words, more integration.

But that is not The American Way. Despite the belated attention given to format compatibility, neither hardware nor software is developed with interbrand compatibility in mind: rather the opposite. Although most of it was developed with public-sector funding, bibliographic software is now virtually all proprietary. Much good software was, alas, developed for hardware components either chosen by or imposed on particular agencies. Who can predict when the shakedown period will end, a few systems will emerge clear winners over the others, and a greater degree of integration will result? In the meantime, the battle for commercial supremacy rages.

Even those outside the United States must accept the consequences. In the richer countries and at more affluent times, incompatible duplication of software was known to occur even within the same funding agency, the one hand not knowing, or perhaps just not caring, what the other was doing. Alas, agencies in poorer parts of the world are usually perforce the recipients of gifts of hardware and software, not always of the current design. They pray for luck more than trying to make wise decisions on cooperation and integration.

Integrating the Rules

The integration of cataloguing rules is an intellectual occupation, not a physical interfiling of citations or the programming of a common search strategy. Yet descriptive cataloguing rules have always been affected by the physical fragmentation of bibliographic lists and by disparities in access methods; they probably played their own part in helping to preserve that fragmentation. An obvious example is the parallelism between common shelving arrangements for government publications according to the hierarchy of their issuing agencies, and cataloguing rules which still require more subordination in headings for governmental names than for nongovernmental ones. Similarly, the administration of the book, kit, motion picture, and sound-recording collections by different units in many institutions a generation ago meant that each type of material would have its own separate catalogue and it did not matter if the rules for their compilation varied significantly.

Integrating the rules means, quite simply, not to create a special rule if a general one will do. It involves a concentration on first principles. Specializing the rules means concentrating on ad hoc solutions to specific problems. Theoretically, perhaps there should be no conflict: every specific problem should be solvable within the framework of a limited number of general principles. Details should have more the character of examples than of additional rules. In practice, however, this has not been the case, and each cataloguing rule has found its own balance somewhere in the spectrum between the goal of total application of general principles and that of idiosyncratic solution to specific problems. The ALA author-title cataloguing code of 1949 (ALA Rules, 1949) leaned strongly toward the latter end of the spectrum; AACR2, in its original 1978 form, leaned toward the former.

The integration–specialization cycle seems inevitable. Before we start on another swing of it, we should investigate how integrated a cataloguing rule can get and still be operational. Certainly rules of the past were briefer than today's. But they did not have to cope with the cataloguing of computer files or videotapes. Perhaps Gorman's tongue was in his cheek, but I think not far in, when he published "The Most Concise AACR2" consisting of two rules (Gorman, 1981). Descriptions in several national bibliographies were prepared according to the original 1971 ISBD(M) of hardly 20 pages for a number of years before the first detailed cataloguing rule to incorporate and interpret its practices became available. The Library of Congress, under pressures both to apply and to reject ISBD(M), saw to its incorporation into AACR1 in much greater detail in mid-1974 before applying it (Chapter 6, 1974).

When a rule is introduced or significantly changed, something this generation has seen perhaps too frequently, the call goes out for more examples and for interpretive guidelines which usually only amount to yet more examples. The inevitable early inconsistencies in application can be laid to the fact that those applying the then-new standard are still thinking in an earlier context. This is essentially a temporary situation: the generation with the good fortune to have to learn, and teach, only one current code, not three as I have, should not see the ambiguities that I do, unless my generation of instructors is still perversely perpetuating them.

If changing rules cause uncertainty for a time in application, however, so do novel bibliographic situations, and we appear to be in the midst of an epidemic of these. Near-print items such as technical reports and many conference proceedings have long been notorious for uninformed presentation of often incomplete data. Then publishers of serials began playing with titles, logos, and fancy designs which obscure the intended organization of bibliographic data. Now title pages even of staid university-press monographs are afflicted with the artsy-designer craze; everyone down to the copy editor and jacket designer gets "prominently" named; publishers and distributors can hardly be told apart any longer. Reprinters find ever more ingenious ways of making their products look original. Those who create corporate names have abandoned familiar structures in the search for the memorable, or just the gimmicky, acronym. We are simply not dealing with the same kind of display of bibliographic information as before, and what we do see is much more idiosyncratic.

This may appear to provide a strong case for reintroducing more specialization to the cataloguing rules, but the same arguments eventually led to the sinking of the 1908 *Catalog Rules* in its North American usage under a weight of amendments that inevitably became internally contradictory. Making sound ad hoc judgments based on principle and experience is greatly to be preferred to creating a new rule. One who has assimilated the rule's principles and context at the most integrated level is satisfied by creative interpretation of them. People of two other types are unsatisfied by this method. The beginner, whose bibliographic experience is still limited and unconnected, finds it difficult to analyze the situation in hand. Seeking to substitute printed example for experience, this person can fail to recognize that the example is in the rule to illustrate an entirely different situation. The other unsatisfied cataloguer is the perfectionist, to whom the thought that one item in ten-thousand might be differently treated by two people is anathema. But *is* it? I was once a perfectionist. Now that I have experienced more of the infinite variety of bibliographic situations, I realize the impossibility of providing a recognizable rule to cover every circumstance. It is harsh, but I think true, to say that perfectionists are often the most able, but the most unwilling, to take responsibility for exercising judgment.

AACR2 is the first code to be maintained formally by the same autonomous body that wrote it. The experience of this body has demonstrated that code makers have little control over the proliferation of quasiofficial interpretations which can threaten the integrity of the rule as written. Would it make any difference if we all considered rule interpretations, whether from a national agency or any other source, simply as part of a teaching text on rule application rather than as de facto changes or additions to the rule? Probably not. Neither the beginner nor the perfectionist likes to admit that experience and judgment, ambiguous though they may be, are not evils to be tolerated but virtues to be encouraged.

The argument that given a common rule one should be able to achieve absolute uniformity in practice is given more credence in North America, where for almost a century we have been trained to think that the only right way is however the Library of Congress does it, or would do it, if it had gotten around to it. We find it hard to put ourselves into another frame of reference, one much more common outside this continent, which sees less need for uniform interpretation and therefore for specialized rules. Such a view does not hold that any old way will do; rather it sees that very occasionally there may exist more than one right way.

AACR2: One Standard or Many?

Total uniformity of description for a given item was long held to be desirable for adherence to the first principle of adequate identification. In fact, *identification* is not synonymous with *description*. Although the latter function has long been forced to serve the former purpose, the need for it to do so is much diminished. In respect of manual searching, there was once an overpowering concern that an entry might not be retrievable if it did not exactly match a complex norm governing the choice and form of a particular access point. The virtual abandonment of single-entry lists among major bibliographic tools means that concern is no longer relevant. In respect of computer searching, there no longer exists *any* practical limit to the number of access points available. We are after all in the era of full-text searching of huge databases. For purposes of positive identification, one or more of the many standardized numbering or coding schemes mentioned earlier is a much more satisfactory guide than any predictable uniformity of catalogue descriptions.

Relieved of the need uniquely to identify then, the cataloguing code can concentrate on useful description for specific purposes and listings. Cutter's short, medium, and full descriptions return via AACR2 to fulfill their originally intended roles. Most of the options embedded in Part I are not "either-or" options. They are "less-or-more" options which made adherence to the essential parts of the rule possible in a wide variety of practical situations. A great many of these are in fact nothing more than specific elaborations of the option most frequently misunderstood and overlooked in the code: rule 1.0D on fullness of the description, a rule whose purpose was to ensure that all agencies provide at least a minimum of data when they input to shared networks.

Because in the card technology what was typed onto an entry was exactly what the ultimate user saw, AACR2 is still written as if it were a code only for inputting data. Use of the computer, however, separates what is input from its output, or display, formats, allowing selection and reformatting decisions to intervene. Output formats have unfortunately gone somewhat adrift of the code and seem to be considered by many to be independent of cataloguing rules. Special attention is now required to reintegrate them with those rules, especially in the context of online catalogues, where as yet user expectations are not too fixed. The line-per-entry truncated author/title/date display which often appears on a terminal screen as an initial response to a search is acceptable as a preliminary step in selecting which records will be examined in fuller form. It is not, however, a bibliographic record. In itself it cannot adequately identify anything. Rule 1.0D should be invoked to govern whether the in-house display or the interagency communication of the records themselves will take place in short, medium, or fullest possible form. Instead, committee after committee has laboriously reinvented this wheel in deliberating what should be "mandatory," "required if present," and "optional" data elements, whether for in-house systems or for sharing in networks and utilities. Perhaps rule 1.0D needs fine tuning, but it is a sound basis for standardizing both record sharing and output displays.

ISBD, abetted by the computer, completed the separation of the function of describing an item from the function of formulating name access points for it. AACR2 governs both. The highest degree of uniformity of practice has always been expected of the latter function. Through times of plenty and of want, libraries have always spent heavily on careful work to ensure that the name of each different person, body, place, or work be established in a single standardized form with all necessary cross references. The cost of this, and a fear that a name heading might appear in different forms in two catalogues, has led at least North American libraries to rely in practice more on the name forms established by the Library of Congress than on the cataloguing rules which they and LC presumably use in common. Distribution by several national agencies of name authority records separated from bibliographic records has made the copying of standard forms easier.

Software and budget considerations continue to prevent many libraries from taking full advantage of automated authority control, but eventually every online catalogue will provide automatic linking of bibliographic descriptions with separate authority records containing a fuller cross-reference structure than is now common in manual searching. The user of such a system will be shown the appropriate bibliographic records regardless of which of the name forms held in the authority system is sought. The cataloguer's distinction between a cross reference and an added entry will be invisible to the user. The difference between the established form of a name access point and any cross reference to it is reduced to the technical matter of which form shall be the basis for the authority record.

As in the case of description, AACR2 deliberately allows some variation in the establishment of name forms and is subject to varying interpretation in occasional complex instances. Two "either-or" options exist in Part II (Rules 22.3C2 and 24.3A) in the intractible area of linguistic differences. When such options merely give rise to more cross references, invisibly to the user, bothersome issues like these and the treatment of pseudonyms will simply vanish.

This development is of major significance in potential database integration. Name authority work is the issue which most seriously divides the bibliographic style of libraries and that of the A & I services. The latter typically do no work to establish whether different name forms are used by a person or body; hence they cannot create cross references systematically. They rely in online searching on the techniques of browsing, keyword accessibility, and truncation in order to maximize hits on appropriate entries in response to name requests. These techniques are less perfect but also far less costly—or, rather, the cost of any time spent on linking name forms is shifted directly to the user at the time of searching. Library online systems will incorporate these techniques also; many already do. Integration notwithstanding, two systems are always better than one.

In any case, with the Linked Systems Project operational and the creation of name authority records now being shared in the library world, must we wait very long for the inevitable breakthrough: the linking or even the integration of the names occurring in an A & I bibliographic database with those in a library authority database? The technology exists. Sooner or later, the money will. Does the political will also exist more closely to integrate these two types of bibliographic service?

Descriptive Cataloguing: One Standard or Many?

Before the computer age, it was not too difficult to establish which matters should be codified among agencies and which could be left to the individual agency to decide for itself. Bibliographic description and the choice and formulation of name-title access points are functions which the twentieth-century consensus declares should adhere to common, and not single-situation, standards. On the other hand, classification, the use of subject indexing terms, the arrangement, i.e., filing, of entries, and once again the form of catalogue output are held to be open to local option. In these areas, competing rules exist, for example, Dewey's versus LC's classification; LC's versus Sears' subject headings versus PRECIS; ALA's versus LC's filing rules—to say nothing of the numerous subject-analysis vocabularies and other techniques designed for specialized collections.

Cutter's *Rules for a Dictionary Catalog* of a century ago was more integrated than our AACR2. The fewer than 200 pages of its 1904 edition governed description, name access points, subject headings, filing, and transliteration; also the physical form of the resulting card entry, its dictionary arrangement, and its housing (Cutter, 1904). In prescribing the latter elements of practice, Cutter and the later codes through AACR1 linked the information in the catalogue entry with the means of its communication and thus were very specific to the library community.

Today, the use of MARC and other ISO 2709-based formats has to a degree divorced the content of the entry from its communication. Why the departure from a long-existing integration? Why are not at least the MARC tags, indicators, and subfield codes a part of AACR2? One answer a decade ago was that not every library used, or was dependent on, automation in cataloguing. In fact, until quite recently very few in-house systems, as distinguished from bibliographic utilities, were capable of dealing with full MARC content designation. Another answer is that the detailed MARCs vary slightly from one another. But the code already embodies options whose use is specific to particular institutions, countries, or regions (only in rule 1.1C1 is the geography of the option openly acknowledged).

The real reason lies in the politics of standards adoption, which now acts as a strong force against integration. In the 1960s many cataloguers like myself, unfamiliar with automated techniques, naively felt that since making bibliographic records machine readable need have no direct effect on the rules, so technical a task could be left to others! As a result, different committees came to have control over AACR2 and MARC. The same tendencies have seen what Cutter once accomplished alone spread over dozens of committees. Even if today there is useful overlap in committee membership, but therefore wasteful redundancy in committee work, integration of the increasingly related aspects of catalogue creation and maintenance is now harder, not easier, to achieve. Each committee guards jealously the fragments of the empire which it governs. No committee can see the whole with the unifying eye of a wise individual.

Now that we have accepted computer-mandated changes in our filing rules, library filing is much more standardized and also more integrated with that of nonlibrary directories, indices, and other commercial tools familiar to our users. Troublesome complexities such as the location of name-title access points ensure that some libraries remain unable to adhere to the detail of any official library filing rule. There may therefore be some advantage in *not* immediately reintegrating filing rules with those for formulating name access points. An individual agency can still claim adherence to the cataloguing standard required by its network or consortium even if it ignores, for the time being, some aspects of the filing standard. A return to Cutter's ideal of a cataloguing code which presumes agreement on a filing rule might not be so difficult, given that there are few variations among the widely sanctioned computer filing rules which interact with AACR2; Rule 24.13, Type 6 is one which would have to be reassessed depending on which filing rule was adopted.

Teaching Descriptive Cataloguing

It has become fashionable, among cataloguing administrators at least, to deplore a tendency toward diminishing the amount of cataloguing instruction every student must endure in an MLS program. In partial response, ALA's Cataloging and Classification Section sponsored a survey in 1985 of the relevant courses offered at the ALA-accredited schools (*RTSD Newsletter* **11** (1986): 71–78). The uncertainty expressed by the surveyors concerning what is actually taught within those courses was no surprise, but it is clear that the intent to teach how to catalogue is being displaced, especially at the beginning level, by more general instruction in how to use bibliographic data.

   If there ever was a day when a knowledge of the current rules, of reference sources, and of typing formats sufficed for an entry-level cataloguing position, it is gone. MARC arrived with the computer. Hands-on experience of the operation of typical bibliographic utility software is highly desirable and many would say that to teach the detailed use of more than one software package is necessary. The number of words to be assimilated in various interpretation manuals, inputting guides, and network policy directives, merely for first-day effectiveness, now seems almost the cube of the number of words in the official cataloguing rules. A significant amount of information on the history of rules and techniques, at least as they have operated in North America since about 1960, will be required until almost everyone has "recon-ed" and "flipped." Now that the truly independent cataloguing department is virtually a thing of the past, a body of administrative-political background on the functioning of cooperation and networks is also essential. Finally, even the beginning cataloguer is now perforce a supervisor, if not an administrator.

   For the poor beleaguered student, this is not only integration, but very-large-scale integration indeed. To go back to one of the opening themes of this chapter, the success of integration in the teaching of the new bibliographic control is heavily dependent on the unambiguous use of a new agreed vocabulary of integration. The student finds it very confusing to have the separate vocabularies of the fragmented parts of the old manual cataloguing processes still embedded in the existing literature and too often perpetuated by sloppy thinking or merely the assumption of adequate communication among practitioners.

For both the individual teacher and for curriculum development within a whole program, it is difficult to bring the principle of integration to bear in this area. In the program in which I teach, what a descriptive cataloguer needs to know is spread out over a number of courses, some required, some not; some with the word "cataloguing" in their titles, some not. Can it at least be introduced within a coherent course sequence? I would like to think it could, but I admit that I have not yet found the way to do so without overly infringing on similar needs for integration as viewed to different effect by instructors in other areas of the curriculum.

I am a poor teacher. To date, I have been unsuccessful in convincing a significant number of my own colleagues of some aspects of my views on integration, but I shall not give up trying because ways must be found to fix the concept and practice of bibliographic control in the student mind as a single coherent concept and practice transcending the perceived job-related bounds of cataloguing, reference, online searching, etc. As its basis, the bibliographic record must be presented as essentially the same thing whether it be the item identifier in a transaction in the circulation system, an entry in an antiquarian bookseller's catalogue used by the book selector, the listing of an article in an A & I service, the entry in an individual or a union catalogue, or the footnote in a monograph. Teaching the means of building and searching machine-readable bibliographic records must not be too distantly separated in the student's mind or course notes from teaching its transformations in manual or print formats.

The Consequences of Integration

By way of conclusion, then, what are the consequences of integration in descriptive cataloguing? Ideally, they are (1) a simple cataloguing code for description and name access points, (2) which is uniformly applicable to all types of materials including parts of documents, (3) which can be uniformly interpreted by experienced persons, (4) of which a standard computer format is an inseparable part, (5) which is used consistently by all segments of the information community, certainly including both libraries and the A & I services, for bibliographic records, (6) these records being automatically linked to the body of name authority records which are established nationally and internationally according to the same rules.

Are these consequences economically and politically possible? One can only point to where we are in 1988 and to note how quickly we got here. On the political side, the tempest in the teapot in early 1973 over the imposition of ISBD is now a silly episode from a distant past. It is hardly eight years since a much simplified and integrated rule was inaugurated widely: the *de*superimposed AACR2 quickly supplanted not only its predecessors but also its competitors in audiovisual, cartographic, and other areas. In hardly 20 years, MARC in one of its reasonably compatible look-alikes has become an inseparable companion of every library-based cataloguing code. Meanwhile, another ISO 2709 offspring, the *Common Communication Format*, is showing signs of success at least in the developing world of integrating the library community with the A & I community.

On the technical side, MARC in its fullest form, once thought to be restricted to use in large mainframe-based systems, can now be the basis for processing in systems of every size. The number of different bibliographic records in single databases is now well into the 8-figure range, and increasingly these databases are being linked into coordinated systems searchable by common command languages. Computers are shunting bibliographic records among themselves automatically using international standards for Open Systems Interconnection (Library of Congress, 1986). Huge databases of name authority records are available both manually and in the prototype Linked Systems Project. The automatic cleaning up of old messy files, replacing "bad" bibliographic records with "good" ones, and attaching them to name and subject authority records is not only commercially feasible, it is a growth industry. Finally, the *Common Communication Format* is showing us the direction to pursue in dealing with the thorny issue of levels in, or nests of, bibliographic records.

It has always been in the nature of bibliographic control to be essentially integrative, and internationally so; yet there remain barriers to fuller integration. Perhaps hardware incompatibilities are being bypassed, but integrated software is now so complex that the problems of intersystem sharing increase rather than decrease. This creates an inhibiting resistance to needed changes in the MARC formats. Will it be necessary forever to retain in USMARC and CANMARC so many provisions for long-obsolete remnants of dead cataloguing codes?

Although the principal spur to integration was the computer, manual products will not disappear from use. These include print and COM outputs from machine-readable files as well as ancient lists compiled according to mysterious bygone practices. The degree of integration of principles and practices cited for online systems will simply never be applicable to either. Differences between the content of manual and online versions of databases are well known in the subject indexing field; there will inevitably be permanent differences also in the field of description and name access and continuing need for the trained user to be able to master more than one parallel system of bibliographic control.

Between the library community and the abstracting and indexing services there remains a gulf, perhaps more psychological and administrative than technical. In fact, if we are seriously interested in advancing integration a major step, we of the library-related institutions must invite representatives of the A & I services, most usefully in North America via the National Federation of Abstracting and Indexing Services, to discuss bibliographic description and name access with us. In North America, where the independence of the A & I services is most pronounced, commercial searching services have become the link not only among the various A & I databases, but also between them and library databases. In the developing countries where automation is just beginning, the fact that all services are usually in control of the public sector offers hope that the automated catalogue and the automated index will not begin on separate paths. Libraries are rediscovering, often by cooperative ventures, the benefits of incorporating into their main databases types of material once thought the preserve of the A & I services. They are also beginning to incorporate software designed for the other community into their computer systems.

The indicated trends are mostly in the direction of integration. They are already so well advanced that we now have a pretty good idea of where we are going. We may need more money and more political will, but integration is no longer a pig in a poke. We know its hazards as well as its benefits. We also know what will happen if we do not pursue the present trends: the opposite of integration is disintegration.

Abbreviations and Acronyms

AACR1	Anglo-American Cataloging Rules, edition 1
AACR2	Anglo-American Cataloguing Rules, edition 2
A & I	Abstracting and Indexing
ALA	American Library Association
ANSI	American National Standards Institute
BDRB	Bibliographic Description of Rare Books
CANMARC	Canadian Machine-Readable Cataloguing
CCDA	[ALA] Committee on Cataloging: Description and Access
COM	Computer Output Microform
CONSER	Cooperative Online Serials [Program]
COSATI	Committee on Scientific and Technical Information
DIALOG	[Lockheed's information retrieval service]
DIS	Description Independent System
DUCS	Description Unit Card System
DUS	Description Unit System
IFLA	International Federation of Library Associations and Institutions
ISBD	International Standard Bibliographic Description
ISBD(A)	International Standard Bibliographic Description (Antiquarian)
ISBD(CM)	International Standard Bibliographic Description (Cartographic Materials)
ISBD(G)	International Standard Bibliographic Description (General)
ISBD(M)	International Standard Bibliographic Description (Monographs)
ISBD(NMB)	International Standard Bibliographic Description (Non-book Materials)
ISBD(PM)	International Standard Bibliographic Description (Printed Music)
ISBD(S)	International Standard Bibliographic Description (Serials)
ISBN	International Standard Book Number
ISO	International Standards Organization
ISSN	International Standard Serial Number
JLA	Japan Library Association
JSC	Joint Steering Committee [for revision of AACR]
LC	Library of Congress
LCCN	Library of Congress Card Number
LC/NACO	Library of Congress/National Coordinated Cataloging Program
LCRIs	Library of Congress Rule Interpretations
MARBI	Machine-Readable Form of Bibliographic Information

MARC	Machine-Readable Cataloging
MEDLARS	Medical Literature Analysis and Retrieval Service
MEDLINE	MEDLARS Online
MeSH	Medical Subject Headings
MLS	Master of Library Science
NACO	National Coordinated Cataloging Operations
NCCP	National Coordinated Cataloging Program
NCR	Nippon Cataloging Rules
NHUCS	No Heading Unit Card System
NLBR	National Level Bibliographic Record
NUC	National Union Catalog
OCLC	Online Computer Library Center
OPACs	Online Public Access Catalogs
ORION	[UCLA's Online Catalog]
OSI	Open Systems Interconnection
RAK	Regeln für die alphabetische Katalogisierung
RLIN	Research Libraries Information Network
SISAC	Serials Industry Systems Advisory Committee Code
UBC	Universal Bibliographic Control
UBC/SDI	University of British Columbia, Selective Dissemination of Information
UCLA	University of California, Los Angeles
UDC	Universal Decimal Classification
UKMARC	United Kingdom Machine-Readable Cataloguing
UNIMARC	Universal Machine-Readable Cataloguing
USBC	Universal Standard Book Code
USMARC	United States Machine-Readable Cataloging
WLN	Western Library Network

Bibliography

Works cited are given in the reference list style of Turabian (Kate Turabian, *A Manual for Writers of Term Papers, Theses, and Dissertations*, 5th Ed. (Chicago: The University of Chicago Press, 1987). The main entry for each work is under author, personal or corporate. To facilitate ease of reference, well-known or frequently cited manuals, codes of rules and standards emanating from corporate bodies are cited in the text by a catch-word or phrase. Thus, a code like AACR2 is referred to in the text as (AACR2, 1978) rather than as (American Library Association and others, 1978). In the bibliography itself a *see* reference is made from the catch-word or phrase to the correct form of entry.

AACR1 (1967). *See* American Library Association, Library of Congress, The Library Association and Canadian Library Association. 1967.

AACR2 (1978). *See* American Library Association, The British Library, Canadian Committee on Cataloguing, The Library Association, Library of Congress. 1978.

Abbay, Olivia (1987). Pseudonyms: Changing the Rules. *Catalog. Aust.* **13 (March)**: 17–22.

ALA Catalog Rules (1941). *See* American Library Association. Catalog Code Revision Committee; and The Library Association. 1941.

ALA Cataloging Rules (1949). *See* American Library Association. Division of Cataloging and Classification. 1949.

ALA Glossary (1943). *See* American Library Association. Committee on Library Terminology. 1943.

ALA Rules (1902). *See* American Library Association. Cooperation Committee; and the Advisory Catalog Committee. 1902.

ALA Rules (1904). *See* American Library Association. Cooperation Committee and the Advisory Catalog Committee. 1904.

American Library Association and The Library Association (1908). *Catalog Rules: Author and Title Entries*, American Ed. Chicago: American Library Association Publishing Board.

American Library Association. Catalog Code Revision Committee; and The Library Association (1941). *A.L.A. Catalog Rules: Author and Title Entries*, Preliminary 2nd Ed. Chicago: American Library Association.

American Library Association. Committee on Library Terminology (1943).

A.L.A. Glossary of Library Terms: With a Selection of Terms in Related Fields, ed. Elizabeth H. Thompson. Chicago: American Library Association.

American Library Association. Cooperation Committee (1883). Condensed Rules for an Author and Title Catalog. *Libr. J.* **8**: 251–254.

American Library Association. Cooperation Committee and the Advisory Catalog Committee (1902). *A.L.A. Rules—Advance Edition. Condensed Rules for an Author and Title Catalog*. Washington, D.C.: Government Printing Office.

American Library Association. Cooperation Committee and the Advisory Catalog Committee (1904). *A.L.A. Rules—Advance Edition. Condensed Rules for an Author and Title Catalog*. Washington, D.C.: Government Printing Office.

American Library Association. Division of Cataloging and Classification (1949). *A.L.A. Cataloging Rules for Author and Title Entries*, ed. Clara Beetle. 2nd Ed. Chicago: American Library Association.

American Library Association, Library of Congress, The Library Association and Canadian Library Association (1967). *Anglo-American Cataloging Rules, North American Text, with Supplement of Additions and Changes*, ed. C. Sumner Spalding. Chicago: American Library Association.

American Library Association, Library of Congress, The Library Association and Canadian Library Association (1974). *Anglo-American Cataloging Rules. Chapter 6: Separately Published Monographs*, North American Text. Chicago: American Library Association.

American Library Association, The British Library, Canadian Committee on Cataloguing, The Library Association, and Library of Congress (1978). *Anglo-American Cataloguing Rules*, eds. Michael Gorman and Paul W. Winkler. 2nd Ed. Chicago: American Library Association.

American National Standards Institute (1985a). *American National Standard for Bibliographic Information Interchange: Z39.2-1985*. New York: American National Standards Institute.

American National Standards Institute (1985b). *American National Standard for Serial Holdings Statements: Z39.44-1985*. New York: American National Standards Institute.

Anglo-American Cataloguing Committee for Cartographic Materials (1982). *Cartographic Materials: A Manual of Interpretation for AACR2*, ed. Hugo L. P. Stibbe. Chicago: American Library Association.

ANSI Z39.2-1985. *See* American National Standards Institute, 1985a.

ANSI Z39.44-1985. *See* American National Standards Institute, 1985b.

Atherton, Pauline (1978). *Books are for Use: Final Report of the Subject Access Project to the Council on Library Resources*. Syracuse, New York: Syracuse University School of Information Studies. Text-fiche ED 156 131.

Attig, John (1981). The Definition of a MARC Format. In Library of Congress. Automation Planning and Liaison Office. *Discussion Paper No. 3*. Washington, D.C.: Library of Congress.

Attig, John (1983a). The Concept of a MARC Format. *Inf. Technol. Libr.* **2 (March)**: 7–17.

Attig, John (1983b). Integration of USMARC Bibliographic Formats. In Library of Congress. MARC Standards Office. *Discussion Paper No. 7*. Washington, D.C.: Library of Congress.

Avalonne, Susan and Bette-Lee Fox (1986). A Commitment to Cassettes. *Libr. J.* **111 (Nov. 15)**: 37.

Avram, Henriette D. (1975). *MARC: Its History and Implications*. Washington, D.C.: Library of Congress.

Avram, Henriette D., Ruth S. Freitag and Kay D. Guiles (1965). *A Proposed Format for a Standardized Machine-Readable Catalog Record: A Preliminary Draft.* ISS Planning Memorandum No. 3. Washington, D.C.: Library of Congress, Office of the Information Systems Specialist.

Bates, Marcia J. (1986). Subject Access in Online Catalogs: A Design Model. *J. Am. Soc. Inf. Sci.* **37 (Nov.)**: 357–376.

Baughman, Betty and Elaine Svenonius (1984). AACR2: Main Entry Free? *Catalog. Classif. Q.* **5 (Fall)**: 1–15.

BDRB (1981). *See* Library of Congress. Office for Descriptive Cataloging Policy. 1981a.

Bender, Todd K. (1976). Literary Texts in Electronic Storage: The Editorial Potential. *Comput. Humanities* **10 (July/Aug.)**: 193–199.

Beniger, James R. (1986). *The Control Revolution: Technological and Economic Origins of the Information Society.* Cambridge, Massachusetts: Harvard University Press.

Betz, Elisabeth W. (1982). *Graphic Materials: Rules for Describing Original Items and Historical Collections.* Washington, D.C.: Library of Congress.

Bourne, Ross and Lucia Rather (1986). Harmonization of the ISBD's. *Int. Catalog.* **15 (Oct./Dec.)**: 39–40.

Bouvier, Irmgard, ed. (1977). *Regeln für die alphabetische Katalogisierung: RAK.* Wiesbaden: Reichert.

Brault, Nancy (1972). *The Great Debate on Panizzi's Rules in 1847–1849: The Issues Discussed.* Los Angeles: The School of Library Service and The University Library.

British Museum (1841). Rules for the Compilation of the Catalogue. In *The Catalogue of Printed Books in the British Museum,* v.1: v–ix. London: British Museum.

Buckallew, Fritz A. (1986). The Online Catalog and Map Usage. *Map Online Users Group Newslett.* **21 (Aug.)**: 2–3.

Burger, Robert H. (1984). Artificial Intelligence and Authority Control. *Libr. Resources Tech. Serv.* **28 (Oct./Dec.)**: 337–345.

Burress, Elaine P. (1985). Technical Reports: A Comparison Study of Cataloging with AACR2 and COSATI. *Special Libr.* **76 (Summer)**: 187–192.

Canadian MARC Office (1988). *Canadian MARC Communication Format.* Ottawa: Canadian MARC Office.

CANMARC (1988). *See* the preceding entry.

Carpenter, Michael (1981). *Corporate Authorship: Its Role in Library Cataloging.* Westport, Connecticut: Greenwood Press.

Carpenter, Michael and Elaine Svenonius, eds. (1985). *Foundations of Cataloging: A Sourcebook.* Littleton, Colorado: Libraries Unlimited.

Cartographic Materials (1982). *See* Anglo-American Cataloguing Committee for Cartographic Materials. 1981.

Catalog Rules (1908). *See* American Library Association and The Library Association. 1908.

Chapter 6 (1974). *See* American Library Association, Library of Congress, The Library Association and Canadian Library Association. 1974.

Common Communication Format (1984). *See* Simmons, Peter and Alan Hopkinson. 1984.

Commissioners Appointed to Inquire into the Constitution and Government of the British Museum (1850). *Report of the Commissioners Appointed to Inquire into the Constitution and Management [sic] of the British Museum.* London: Her

Majesty's Stationery Office, 1850. Quoted in Strout, Ruth French (1956). The Development of the Catalog and Catalog Codes, *Libr. Q.* **26 (Oct.)**: 254–275.

Condensed Rules (1883). *See* American Library Association. Cooperation Committee. 1883.

Congressional Library (1867). *Rules for Catalogueing in the Congressional Library*. [Manuscript]. Library of Congress, Washington, D.C.

Crawford, Walt (1984). *MARC for Library Use: Understanding the USMARC Formats*. White Plains, New York: Knowledge Industry Publications.

Crestadoro, Andrea (1856). *The Art of Making Catalogues of Libraries, or, A Method to Obtain in a Short Time a Most Perfect, Complete, and Satisfactory Printed Catalogue of the British Museum Library*. London: The Literary, Scientific & Artistic Reference Office.

Cronin, John W. (1967). Remarks on LC Plans for Implementation of New Centralized Acquisitions and Cataloging Program under Title IIC, Higher Education Act. *Libr. Resources Tech. Serv.* **11 (Winter)**: 35–46.

Cutter, Charles A. (1876). *Rules for a Printed Dictionary Catalog*. U.S. Bureau of Education, Special Report on Public Libraries, Part II. Washington, D.C.: Government Printing Office.

Cutter, Charles A. (1889). *Rules for a Dictionary Catalog,* 2nd Ed. with Corrections and Additions. U.S. Bureau of Education, Special Report on Public Libraries, Part II. Washington, D.C.: Government Printing Office.

Cutter, Charles A. (1891). *Rules for a Dictionary Catalog,* 3rd Ed. with Corrections and Additions and an Alphabetical Index. U.S. Bureau of Education, Special Report on Public Libraries, Part II. Washington, D.C.: Government Printing Office.

Cutter, Charles A. (1904). *Rules for a Dictionary Catalog,* 4th Ed., Rewritten. U.S. Bureau of Education, Special Report on Public Libraries, Part II. Washington, D.C.: Government Printing Office; reprint, London: Library Association, 1962.

Daily, Jay E. (1972). Title Entry as Unit Entry. *Libr. Resources Tech. Serv.* **16 (Fall)**: 433–444.

Date, C. J. (1986). *An Introduction to Database Systems*, 4th Ed. Reprinted with Corrections. Reading, Massachusetts: Addison-Wesley Publishing Company.

Denham, Alice and Broom, Wendell (1981). The Role of the Author. *Scholarly Publish.* **12 (April)**: 249–258.

Dickson, Jean (1984). An Analysis of User Errors in Searching an Online Catalog. *Catalog. Classif. Q.* **4 (Spring)**: 19–38.

Dierickx, H. and A. Hopkinson, comps. and eds. (1981). *Reference Manual for Machine-Readable Bibliographic Descriptions*.2nd Rev. Ed. Paris: UNESCO.

Domanovszky, A. (1975). *Functions and Objects of Author and Title Cataloguing*. Muenchen: Verlag Dokumentation.

Dykstra, Mary (1978). The Lion that Squeaked. *Libr. J.* **103 (Sept. 1)**: 1570–1572.

Elias, Cathy Ann and C. James Fair (1983). Name Authority Control in a Communication System. *Special Libr.* **74 (July)**: 289–296.

Encyclopaedia Britannica (1976 Ed.). S.v. "Libraries," by Sir Frank C. Francis.

Enser, P. G. B. (1985). Automatic Classification of Book Material Represented by Back-of-the-Book Index. *J. Doc.* **41 (Sept.)**: 135–155.

Everett, David and David M. Pilachowski (1986). What's in a Name? Looking for People Online—Humanities. *Database* **9 (Oct.)**: 26–34.

Freedman, Maurice J. (1983). *The Functions of the Catalog and the Main Entry as Found in the Works of Panizzi, Jewett, Cutter and Lubetzky*. Ph.D. Dissertation. New Brunswick, New Jersey: Rutgers University.

Friedman, Joan and Alan Jeffreys (1967). Cataloguing and Classification in British University Libraries: A Survey of Practices and Procedures. *J. Doc.* **23 (Sept.)**: 224–246.

Gorman, Michael (1978). Authority Files in a Developed Machine System (with Particular Reference to AACR II). In *What's in a Name: Control of Catalogue Records through Automated Authority Files. Proceedings of the Workshops Held in Ottawa 8–9 December, 1977 and Vancouver 25–26 May, 1978*, ed. and comp. Natsuko Y. Furuya, 129–202. Toronto: University of Toronto Library Automation Systems.

Gorman, Michael (1979). Cataloging and the New Technologies. In *The Nature and Future of the Catalog: Proceedings of the ALA's Information Science and Automation Division's 1975 and 1977 Institutes on the Catalog*, eds. Maurice J. Freedman and S. Michael Malinconico, 127–152. Phoenix: Oryx Press.

Gorman, Michael (1980). AACR2: Main Themes. In *The Making of a Code: The Issues Underlying AACR2: Proceedings of International Conference on AACR2 Held in Tallahassee 11–14 March 1979*, ed. Doris H. Clack, 41–52. Chicago: American Library Association.

Gorman, Michael (1981). The Most Concise AACR2. *Am. Libr.* **12 (Sept.)**: 499.

Gorman, Michael (1983). Reorganization at the University of Illinois—Urbana/Champaign Library: A Case Study. *J. Acad. Libr.* **9 (Sept.)**: 223–225.

Graham, Crystal (1986). Rethinking National Policy for Cataloging Microform Reproductions. *Catalog. Classif. Q.* **6 (Summer)**, 69–83.

Hagler, Ronald (1980). Nonbook Materials: Chapters 7 through 11. In *The Making of a Code: The Issues Underlying AACR2: Proceedings of the International Conference on AACR2 Held in Tallahassee 11–14 March 1979*, ed. Doris H. Clack, 72–87. Chicago: American Library Association.

Hagler, Ronald and Peter Simmons (1982). *The Bibliographic Record and Information Technology*. Chicago: American Library Association.

Hamdy, M. Nabil (1973). *The Concept of Main Entry as Represented in the Anglo-American Cataloging Rules: A Critical Appraisal with Some Suggestions; Author Main Entry vs. Title Main Entry*. Research Studies in Library Science, No. 10. Littleton, Colorado: Libraries Unlimited.

Hensen, Steven L. (1983). *Archives, Personal Papers, and Manuscripts: A Cataloging Manual for Archival Repositories, Historical Societies, and Manuscript Libraries*. Washington, D.C.: Library of Congress.

Hildreth, Charles R. (1982). *Online Public Access Catalogs: The User Interface*. Dublin, Ohio: Online Computer Library Center, Inc.

Holzberlein, Deanne (1982–1983). Computer Software Cataloging: Techniques and Examples. *Catalog. Classif. Q.* **6 (Winter)**: 1–83.

Hunstad, Siv (1986). Problems of Duplicate Records. In *Future of Online Catalogues: Proceedings of a Symposium Held in Essen 30 September–3 October, 1985*, eds. Ahmed H. Helal and Joachim W. Weiss, 169–202. Publications of Essen University Library, 8. Essen: Gesamthochschulbibliothek.

IMCE Report (1970). *See* International Meeting of Cataloguing Experts (1970).

Institut de Recherche et d'Histoire des Textes and the National Library of Scotland (1984). *Fingerprints*. Paris: Institut de Recherche.

Instruktionen (1915). *See* Ministerium der geistlichen, unterrichts- und medizinal-Angelegenheiten (1915).

International Conference on Cataloguing Principles (1963). *Report*. Proceedings of the International Conference on Cataloguing Principles held Paris, 9th–18th October, 1961, eds. A. H. Chaplin and Dorothy Anderson. London: Organizing Committee of the International Conference; Clive Bingley on behalf of IFLA.

International Conference on Cataloguing Principles (1971). *Statement of Principles Adopted at the International Conference on Cataloguing Principles, Paris, October, 1961.* Annotated Ed., with commentary and examples by Eva Verona, assisted by Franz Georg Kaltwasser, P. R. Lewis, and Roger Pierrot. London: IFLA Committee on Cataloguing.

International Federation of Library Associations (1971). *International Standard Bibliographic Description for Single Volume and Multi-Volume Monographic Publications.* London: IFLA Committee on Cataloguing.

International Federation of Library Associations (1974). *ISBD(M), International Standard Bibliographic Description for Monographic Publications.* 1st Standard Ed. London: IFLA Committee on Cataloguing.

International Federation of Library Associations and Institutions (1977a). *ISBD(CM), International Standard Bibliographic Description for Cartographic Materials set up by the IFLA Committee on Cataloguing and the IFLA Sub-section of Geography and Map Libraries.* London: IFLA International Office for UBC.

International Federation of Library Associations and Institutions (1977b). *ISBD(G), General International Standard Bibliographic Description, Annotated Text.* London: IFLA International Office for UBC.

International Federation of Library Associations and Institutions (1977c). *ISBD(NBM), International Standard Bibliographic Description for Non-book Materials.* London: IFLA International Office for UBC.

International Federation of Library Associations and Institutions (1977d). *ISBD(S), International Standard Bibliographic Description for Serials.* London: IFLA International Office for UBC.

International Federation of Library Associations and Institutions (1978). *ISBD(M), International Standard Bibliographic Description for Monographic Publications,* 1st Standard Ed., Rev. London: IFLA Committee on Cataloguing.

International Federation of Library Associations and Institutions (1980). *UNIMARC: Universal MARC Format,* 2nd Ed. Rev. London: IFLA International Office for UBC.

International Meeting of Cataloguing Experts (1970). Report of the International Meeting of Cataloguing Experts, Copenhagen, 1969. *Libri* **20** 105–132.

International Organization for Standardization (1981). *Documentation—Format for Bibliographic Information Interchange on Magnetic Tape: ISO 2709-1981.* Geneva: International Organization for Standardization.

ISBD (1971). *See* International Federation of Library Associations. 1971.

ISBD(CM) (1977). *See* International Federation of Library Associations and Institutions. 1977a.

ISBD(G) (1977). *See* International Federation of Library Associations and Institutions. 1977b.

ISBD(M) (1974). *See* International Federation of Library Associations. 1974.

ISBD(M) (1978). *See* International Federation of Library Associations and Institutions. 1978.

ISBD(NBM) (1977). *See* International Federation of Library Associations and Institutions. 1977c.

ISBD(S) (1977). *See* International Federation of Library Associations and Institutions. 1977d.

ISO 2709-1981. *See* International Organization for Standardization. 1981.

Jamieson, Alexis J., Elizabeth Dolan and Luc Declerck (1986). Keyword Searching vs. Authority Control in an Online Catalog. *J. Acad. Libr.* **12 (Nov.)**: 277–283.

Japan Library Association. Cataloging Committee (1965). *Nippon Cataloging Rules.* Tokyo: Japan Library Association.

Japan Library Association. Cataloging Committee (1977). *Nippon Cataloging Rules.* Preliminary New Ed. Tokyo: Japan Library Association.

Japan Library Association. Cataloging Committee (1987). *Nippon Cataloging Rules.* Tokyo: Japan Library Association.

Japan National Diet Library (1982). *Japanese National Bibliography.* Tokyo: Japan National Diet Library.

Jeffreys, Alan (1967). Alternative Headings. *Catalog. Index* **8 (Oct.)**: 4–5.

Jewett, Charles C. (1852). *On the Construction of Catalogues of Libraries, and Their Publication by Means of Separate Stereotyped Titles with Rules and Examples. Smithsonian Report.* Washington, D.C.: Smithsonian Institution.

JNB (1982). *See* Japan National Diet Library. 1982.

Joachim, Martin D. (1986). Recent Developments in the Bibliographical Control of Microforms. *Microform Rev.* **15 (Spring)**, 74–86.

Joint Steering Committee (1987). Joint Steering Committee for Revision of AACR Makes Final Plans for a Reprint of AACR 2. *Library of Congress Information Bulletin* **46 (Jan. 5)**: 2.

Jolley, Leonard J. (1963). The Function of the Main Entry in the Alphabetical Catalogue: A Study of the Views Put Forward by Lubetzky and Verona. In *International Conference on Cataloguing Principles. Report. Proceedings of the International Conference on Cataloguing Principles held Paris, 9th–18th October, 1961,* eds. A. H. Chaplin and Dorothy Anderson, 159–163. London: Organizing Committee of the Conference.

Jones, Barbara and Arno Kastner (1983). Duplicate Records in the Bibliographic Utilities: A Historical Review of the Printing Versus Edition Problem. *Libr. Resources Tech. Serv.* **27 (April/June)**: 211–220.

Kennedy, Donald (1985). *On Academic Authorship.* Scholarly Communication Reprint 4. Washington, D.C.: American Council of Learned Societies, Office of Scholarly Communication and Technology.

Kilgour, Frederick G. (1979). Design of Online Catalogs. In *The Nature and Future of the Catalog: Proceedings of the ALA's Information Science and Automation Division's 1975 and 1977 Institutes on the Catalog,* eds. Maurice J. Freedman and S. Michael Malinconico, 34–45. Phoenix: Oryx Press.

Knowles, Cherie M. (1979). *The Bibliographic Presentation of Grey Literature. A Report Prepared Under Contract to the Commission of the European Communities (DG XIII).* Leicester: Leicester University, Primary Communications Research Centre.

Lancaster, F. W. (1982). *Libraries and Librarians in an Age of Electronics.* Arlington, Virginia: Information Resources Press.

Lewis, Page (1986). Gorman: Revise Cataloging for the Electronic Union Catalog. Report of a lecture on "Cataloging for the Electronic Union Catalog" delivered by Michael Gorman, 1 April 1986. *Res. Libr. OCLC* **19 (Spring)**: 8–9.

Library of Congress (1899–1940). *Rules on Cards Including Supplementary Rules, Preliminary Rules, Etc.* [Unpublished]. Washington, D.C.; Library of Congress.

Library of Congress (1905). *Supplementary Rules on Cataloging, 1–11*. Washington, D.C.: Library of Congress.

Library of Congress (1986). *Standard Network Interconnection Protocols: Specification of the Protocol Layers for Open Systems Interconnection*. Washington, D.C.: Library of Congress.

Library of Congress. Automated Systems Office (1980). *MARC Formats for Bibliographic Data*. Washington, D.C.: Library of Congress.

Library of Congress. Descriptive Cataloging Division (1949). *Rules for Descriptive Cataloging in the Library of Congress*. Washington, D.C.: U.S. Government Printing Office.

Library of Congress. Network Development and MARC Standards Office (1984). *USMARC Format for Holdings and Locations*, Final Draft. Washington, D.C.: Library of Congress.

Library of Congress. Network Development and MARC Standards Office (1987a). *USMARC Format for Authority Data*. Washington, D.C.: Library of Congress.

Library of Congress. Network Development and MARC Standards Office (1987b). *USMARC Specifications for Record Structure, Character Sets, Tapes*. Washington, D.C.: Library of Congress.

Library of Congress. Network Development and MARC Standards Office (1988). *USMARC Format for Bibliographic Data*. Washington, D.C.: Library of Congress.

Library of Congress. Office for Descriptive Cataloging Policy (1981). *Bibliographic Description of Rare Books: Rules Formulated under AACR2 and ISBD(A) for the Descriptive Cataloging of Rare Books and Other Special Printed Materials*. Washington, D.C.: Library of Congress.

Library of Congress. Office for Descriptive Cataloging Policy (1981-). *Library of Congress Rule Interpretations*. Washington, D.C.: Library of Congress.

Library of Congress. Processing Department (1956). *National Union Catalog: A Cumulative Author List Representing Library of Congress Printed Cards and Titles Reported by Other American Libraries*. Washington, D.C.: Library of Congress.

Library of Congress. Processing Department (1969). [Unpublished Department Memorandum, No. 103.] Washington, D.C.: Library of Congress.

Library of Congress. Processing Department (1970). *Catalog. Serv.* **96 (Nov.)**: 1.

Library of Congress. Processing Services (1980). *National Level Bibliographic Record—Books*. Washington, D.C.: Library of Congress.

Library of Congress. Processing Services (1981). *Authorities, A MARC Format*. Washington, D.C.: Library of Congress.

LCRIs (1981-). *See* Library of Congress. Office for Descriptive Cataloging Policy. 1981-.

Lin, Joseph C. (1985). Rule of Three: A Case of Discrimination against Certain Authors Caused by the Cataloging Rules. *Catalog. Classif. Q.* **5 (Summer)**: 53–65.

Lubetzky, Seymour (1953). *Cataloging Rules and Principles: A Critique of the A.L.A. Rules for Entry and a Proposed Design for Their Revision*. Washington, D.C.: Library of Congress.

Lubetzky, Seymour (1960). *Code of Cataloging Rules: Author and Title Entry: An Unfinished Draft*. Chicago: American Library Association.

Lubetzky, Seymour (1963). The Function of the Main Entry in the Alphabetical Catalogue—One Approach. In *International Conference on Cataloguing Prin-*

ciples. 1963. Report. Proceedings of the International Conference on Cataloguing Principles held Paris, 9th–18th October, 1961, eds. A. H. Chaplin and Dorothy Anderson, 139–143. London: Organizing Committee of the Conference.

Lubetzky, Seymour (1969). *Principles of Cataloging. Final Report. Phase I: Descriptive Cataloging*. Los Angeles: Institute of Library Research, University of California, Los Angeles.

Lubetzky, Seymour (1979). Ideology of Bibliographic Cataloging. In *The Nature and Future of the Catalog: Proceedings of the ALA's Information Science and Automation Division's 1975 and 1977 Institutes on the Catalog*, eds. Maurice J. Freedman and S. Michael Malinconico, 5–19. Phoenix: Oryx Press.

McCallum, Sally H. (1982). Record Linking Technique. *Inf. Technol. Libr.* **1 (Sept.)**: 281–291.

McCallum, Sally H. and James L. Godwin (1981). Statistics on Headings in the MARC File. *J. Libr. Autom.* **14 (Sept.)**: 194–201.

McCoy, Richard W. (1986). The Linked Systems Project: Progress, Promise, Realities. *Libr. J.* **111 (Oct. 1)**: 33–39.

Malinconico, S. Michael (1980). AACR2 and Automation. In *The Making of a Code: The Issues Underlying AACR2: Proceedings of the International Conference on AACR2 Held in Tallahassee 11–14 March 1979*, ed. Doris H. Clack, 25–40. Chicago: American Library Association.

Mandel, Carol A. (1985). Enriching the Library Catalog Record for Subject Access. *Libr. Resources Tech. Serv.* **29 (Jan./March)**: 5–15.

Maruyama, Shojiro (1986). Descriptive Cataloguing and Cataloguing Rules in Japan. *Int. Catalog.* **15 (July/Sept.)**: 28–29.

Merritt, Meredith (1985). Racter the Author? *Libr. J.* **110 (Nov. 1)**: 160.

Milanese, Claudio, Neil E. Richardson and Ellis L. Reinherz (1986). Retraction of Data. *Science* **234 (Nov. 28)**: 1056.

Milhous, Judith and Robert D. Hume (1983). Attribution Problems in English Drama. *Harvard Libr. Bull.* **31 (Winter)**: 5–39.

Miller, Edward (1967). *Prince of Librarians: The Life and Times of Antonio Panizzi of the British Museum*. Athens, Ohio: The Ohio University Press.

Miller, Edward (1979). Antonio Panizzi and the British Museum. *Br. Libr. J.* **5 (Spring)**: 1–17.

Ministerium der geistlichen, unterrichts- und medizinal-Angelegenheiten (1915). *Instruktionen für die alphabetische Kataloge der preussischen Bibliotheken vom 10. Mai 1899. Zweite Ausgabe in der Fassung vom 10. August 1908*. Berlin: Behrend & Co.

Mori, Koichi (1955). Separation of Headings and Description. *Toshokan-kai* **7 (Dec.)**: 195–201.

NCR (1965). *See* Japan Library Association. Cataloging Committee. 1965.

NCR (1977). *See* Japan Library Association. Cataloging Committee. 1977.

NCR (1987). *See* Japan Library Association. Cataloging Committee. 1987.

NUC (1956-). *See* Library of Congress. Processing Department. 1956-.

Oberg, Larry R. (1986). A Model of Cooperation: The VALNet Project. *Libr. J.* **111 (Nov. 15)**: 52.

OCLC (1985). *Bibliographic Input Standards*, 3rd. Ed. Dublin, Ohio: Online Computer Library Center, Inc.

O'Neill, Edward T. and Diane Vizine-Goetz (1989). Bibliographic Relationships: Implications for the Function of the Catalog. In this volume, 167–179.

Osborn, Andrew D. (1941). The Crisis in Cataloging. *Libr. Q.* **11 (Oct.)**: 393–411.

Osborn, Andrew D. (1963). Relation between Cataloguing Principles and Principles Applicable to Other Forms of Bibliographical Work. In *International Conference on Cataloguing Principles. 1963. Report. Proceedings of the International Conference on Cataloguing Principles held Paris, 9th–18th October, 1961*, eds. A. H. Chaplin and Dorothy Anderson, 125–137. London: Organizing Committee of the Conference.

Pao, Miranda Lee (1980). Co-authorship and Productivity. In *Communication Information: Proceedings of the 43rd ASIS Annual Meeting, Anaheim, California, October 5–10, 1980*, eds. Alan R. Benenfeld and Edward John Kazlauskas, 279–281. White Plains, New York: Knowledge Industry Publications.

Panizzi, Anthony (1848). Mr. Panizzi to the Right Hon. the Earl of Ellesmere, 29 January 1828. In Great Britain. Commissioners Appointed to Inquire into the Constitution and Government of the British Museum. *Appendix to the Report of the Commissioners Appointed to Inquire into the Constitution and Management* [sic] *of the British Museum*, 378–395. London: Her Majesty's Stationery Office. Reprinted in Carpenter, Michael and Elaine Svenonius, eds. (1985). *Foundations of Cataloging: A Source Book*, 18–47. Littleton, Colorado: Libraries Unlimited.

Paris Principles (1961). *See* International Conference on Cataloguing Principles. 1963 and 1971.

Pasterczyk, Catherine E. (1985). Russian Transliteration Variations for Searchers. *Database* **8 (Feb.)**: 68–75.

Peabody Institute (1883–1892). *Catalogue of the Library of the Peabody Institute of the City of Baltimore*. Baltimore: Press of Isaac Friedenwald.

Pettee, Julia (1936). The Development of Authorship Entry and the Formation of Authorship Rules as found in the Anglo-American Code. *Libr. Q.* **6 (July)**: 270–290.

Pilachowski, David M. (1986). What's in a Name? Looking for People Online— Current Events. *Database* **9 (April)**: 43–50.

Pilachowski, David M. and David Everett (1985). What's in a Name? Looking for People Online—Social Sciences. *Database* **8 (Aug.)**: 47–65.

Piternick, Anne B. (1985a). ILL Meets Technology. *Can. Libr. J.* **42 (Oct.)**: 267–273.

Piternick, Anne B. (1985b). Traditional Interpretations of "Authorship" and "Responsibility" in the Description of Scientific and Technical Documents. *Catalog. Classif. Q.* **5 (Spring)**: 17–33.

Piternick, Anne B. (1989). Authors Online: A Searcher's Approach to the Online Catalog. In this volume, 29–40.

Pool, Ithiel de Sola (1983). *Technologies of Freedom*, 213. Cambridge: Belknap Press.

Potter, William G. (1980). When Names Collide: Conflict in the Catalog and AACR2. *Libr. Resources Tech. Serv.* **24 (Winter)**: 3–16.

Quint, Barbara (1987). Journal Article Coverage in Online Library Catalogs: The Next Stage for Online Databases? *Online* **11 (Jan.)**: 87–90.

RAK (1977). *See* Bouvier, 1977.

Ranganathan, Shiyali Ramanrita (1971). *Heading and Canons: Comparative Study of Five Catalogue Codes*. London: Blunt, 1955; reprint, High Wycombe: University Microfilms for the College of Librarianship, Wales.

RDC (1949). *See* Library of Congress. Descriptive Cataloging Division. 1949.

Rules (1841). *See* British Museum. 1841.

Rules for Catalogueing (1867). *See* Congressional Library. 1867.

Schabas, Ann H. (1982). Postcoordinate Retrieval: A Comparison of Two Indexing Languages. *J. Am. Soc. Inf. Sci.* **33 (Jan.)**: 32–37.

Schmierer, Helen (1985). Multiple Versions: A Consideration. [Draft]. Washington, D.C.: Library of Congress.

Seal, Alan (1983). Experiments with Full and Short Entry Catalogues: A Study of Library Needs. *Libr. Resources Tech. Serv.* **27 (April/June)**: 144–155.

Shore, Melinda L. (1984). Variation Between Personal Name Headings and Title Page Usage. *Catalog. Classif. Q.* **4 (Summer)**: 1–11.

Simmons, Peter and Alan Hopkinson (1988). *CCF: The Common Communication Format*. General Information Programme and UNISIST. PGI-88/WS/2. Paris: UNESCO.

Smith, David A. (1985). Processing Services 1905. *Libr. Resources Tech. Serv.* **29 (July/Sept.)**: 248–263.

Snow, Bonnie (1986). People in Medicine: Searching Names Online. *Online* **10 (Sept.)**: 122–127.

Soergel, Dagobert (1985). *Organizing Information: Principles of Data Base and Retrieval Systems*. Orlando, Florida: Academic Press.

Stewart, Walter N. and Ned Feder (1987). The Integrity of Scientific Literature. *Nature (London)* **325 (Jan. 15)**: 207–214.

Strout, Ruth French (1956). The Development of the Catalog and Catalog Codes. *Libr. Q.* **26 (Oct.)**: 254–275.

Svenonius, Elaine, Betty Baughman and Mavis Molto (1986). Title Page Sanctity? The Distribution of Access Points in a Sample of English Language Monographs. *Catalog. Classif. Q.* **6 (Spring)**: 3–21.

Tait, James A. (1969). Paper 1: Editor's Introduction and Chapter 1: Entry (Rules 1–33). In *Proceedings of the Seminar Organized by the Cataloguing and Indexing Group of the Library Association at the University of Nottingham 22–25 March 1968*, eds. J. C. Downing and N. F. Sharp, 9–18. London: The Library Association.

Tait, James A. (1969b). *Authors and Titles: An Analytical Study of the Author Concept in Codes of Cataloguing Rules in the English Language, from That of the British Museum in 1841 to the Anglo-American Cataloguing Rules 1967*. Hamden, Connecticut: Archon Books.

Tate, Elizabeth L. (1980). Examining the 'Main' in Main Entry Headings. In *The Making of a Code: The Issues Underlying AACR2: Proceedings of the International Conference on AACR2 Held in Tallahassee 11–14 March 1979*, ed. Doris H. Clack, 109–140. Chicago: American Library Association.

Taylor, Arlene G. (1984). Authority Files in Online Catalogs: An Investigation of Their Value. *Catalog. Classif. Q.* **4 (Spring)**: 1–17.

Tillett, Barbara B. (1987). *Bibliographic Relationships: Toward a Conceptual Structure of Bibliographic Information Used in Cataloging*. Ph.D. Dissertation. Los Angeles: University of California, Los Angeles.

Tseng, Sally C., comp. (1987). *LC Rule Interpretations of AACR2: 1978–1986*, 2nd Cumul. Ed., 1st Update. Metuchen, New Jersey: Scarecrow Press.

UNIMARC (1980). *See* International Federation of Library Associations and Institutions. 1980.

The University of Chicago (1982). *The Chicago Manual of Style for Authors, Editors and Copywriters*, 13th Ed. Chicago: The University of Chicago Press.

U.S. Congress. Office of Technology Assessment (1987). *Intellectual Property Rights in an Age of Electronics and Information*. Malabar, Florida: R. E. Krieger.

USMARC Authorities Format (1981). *See* Library of Congress. Processing Services. 1981.

USMARC Authorities Format (1987). *See* Library of Congress. Network Development and MARC Standards Office. 1987a.

USMARC Bibliographic Formats (1980). *See* Library of Congress. Automated Systems Office. 1980.

USMARC Bibliographic Format (1988). *See* Library of Congress. Network Development and MARC Standards Office. 1988.

USMARC Holdings Format (1984). *See* Library of Congress. Network Development and MARC Standards Office. 1984.

USMARC Specifications for Record Structure (1987). *See* Library of Congress. Network Development and MARC Standards Office. 1987b.

Verona, Eva (1959). Literary Unit Versus Bibliographical Unit. *Libri* **9 (No. 2)**: 79–104.

Verona, Eva (1963). The Function of the Main Entry in the Alphabetical Catalogue—A Second Approach. In *International Conference on Cataloguing Principles. Report. Proceedings of the International Conference on Cataloguing Principles held Paris, 9th–18th October, 1961,* eds. A. H. Chaplin and Dorothy Anderson, 145–157. London: Organizing Committee of the Conference.

Verona, Eva (1975). *Corporate Headings: Their Use in Library Catalogues and National Bibliographies: A Comparative and Critical Study.* London: IFLA Committee on Cataloguing.

Wajenberg, Arnold S. (1989). A Cataloger's View of Authorship. In this volume, 21–27.

Wanninger, Patricia Dwyer (1982). Is the OCLC Database Too Large? A Study of the Effect of Duplicate Records in the OCLC System. *Libr. Resources Tech. Serv.* **26 (Oct./Dec.)**: 353–361.

Weihs, Jean (1984). *Accessible Storage of Nonbook Materials.* Phoenix: Oryx Press.

Wendel, Carl (1949). *Die Griechisch-Römische Buchbeschreibung verglichen mit der des alten Orients.* Hallische Monographien Nr. 3. Halle (Saale): Max Niemeyer Verlag.

White-Hensen, Wendy (1984). *Archival Moving Image Materials: a Cataloging Manual.* Washington, D.C.: Library of Congress. Motion Picture, Broadcasting and Recorded Sound Division.

Wilson, Patrick (1968). *Two Kinds of Power: An Essay on Bibliographical Control.* Berkeley and Los Angeles: University of California Press.

Wilson, Patrick (1983). The Catalog as Access Mechanism: Background and Concepts. *Libr. Resources Tech. Serv.* **27 (Jan./March)**: 4–17.

Wilson, Patrick (1989). The Second Objective. In this volume, 5–16.

Yee, Martha (1989?). *System Design and Cataloging Meet the User: User Interfaces to Online Public Access Catalogs.* Submitted.

Zuckerman, Harriet A. (1968/1969). Patterns of Name Ordering Among Authors of Scientific Papers: A Study of Social Symbolism and its Ambiguity. *Am. J. Sociol.* **74 (Nov.)**: 276–291.

Index